CREATING MEDIA CULTURE

Volume 149, Sage Library of Social Research

RECENT VOLUMES IN
SAGE LIBRARY OF SOCIAL RESEARCH

"CREATING MEDIA CULTURE"

Robert P. Snow

Volume 149
SAGE LIBRARY OF
SOCIAL RESEARCH

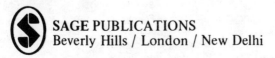 SAGE PUBLICATIONS
Beverly Hills / London / New Delhi

For information address:

SAGE Publications, Inc.
275 South Beverly Drive
Beverly Hills, California 90212

SAGE Publications India Pvt. Ltd.
C-236 Defence Colony
New Delhi 110 024, India

SAGE Publications Ltd
28 Banner Street
London EC1Y 8QE, England

Printed in the United States of America

Library of Congress Cataloging in Publication Data

Main entry under title:

Snow, Robert P
    Creating media culture.

    (Sage library of social research ; v. 149)
    1. Mass media.   I. Title.   II. Series.
P90.S594   1983   302.2'34   83-3125
ISBN 0-8039-1994-8
ISBN 0-8039-1995-6 (pbk.)

FIRST PRINTING

CONTENTS

PREFACE

The phrases "information age" and "information revolution" are popping up almost daily. But aside from reference to the incredible pace of developing information hardware, what exactly does the phrase information age mean? On the one hand, it means we are in the midst of an explosion of information; we are bombarded with information about every conceivable item, event, and idea. Yet this is only a minor part of the story. Much of this information is presented to us through the major media of print, radio, film, and most important, television. These media no longer constitute what was once called the "fourth estate"; today they collectively make up the most influential sector of urbanized society. And yet their influence is barely recognized and not well understood.

We live squarely in the domain of a *media culture,* a culture being constructed and altered continuously through the linguistic and interpretative strategies of media. To understand the power of media in developing culture requires more than simply knowing how much time we spend with media or who controls media's purse strings; it requires understanding the language of media and what perspectives are employed in selecting and interpreting phenomena. And finally, understanding media power requires the knowledge that mass communication is a two-way process between communicator and audience, with the latter holding the key to what happens as a consequence of reliance on mass communication. It is to these points that this book is addressed.

The ideas that follow in these pages have profited most directly from reviews by David Altheide, Dennis Brissett, Beverley Cuthbertson, John M. Johnson, and anonymous comments from Sage reviewers. I also owe an immeasurable intellectual debt to former teachers Don Martindale and the late Gregory Stone. Thanks also to my co-typist Barbara Bellamy.

—*R.P.S.*

CHAPTER 1

MEDIA STRATEGY
Perspectives and Grammar

Mass media is the great love-hate topic of our age. Everyone understands that modern urban society turns on mass-mediated information, and yet we continually decry its omnipresence, pretensions, and outright excesses. Like the lover you can't live with or without, the mass media are integrated into our activity to the point that, like it or not, modern life without some form of mass media is impossible.

Where all this will lead has stimulated considerable speculation, although much of this speculation has focused on media hardware and the sheer volume of exposure to information transmitted in this manner. More pressing is the need for analysis of *how* communication occurs through agents of mass media. This requires examination of the communication strategies used by media professionals and the perspectives these professionals and audiences use to interpret the subject matter.

To accomplish this task, consider rejecting the notion that media act as a neutral conduit in transmitting information—and the metaphor of media acting as a mirror that reflects culture. Rather, consider that through the process of mass communication meaning is created and constructed according to the gammatical structure of media languages and specific perspectives that function as interpretation frameworks. In this manner, the language and perspectives of present-day mass media have produced a *media culture.*

In light of the extensive use and influence of mass media, it is no exaggeration to say that we live presently in a media culture. It means that nearly every institution—including religion, government, criminal justice, health care, education, and even the family—is influenced by the mass communication process. We know that forms of popular culture are largely created and maintained through mass media. For example, video games are the result of a technology and a visual perspective that emerged from television. Many rule changes in professional sports over the past 15 years are a direct result of demands from television for more excitement in scoring potential on the play-ing field. The association of radio and popular music is so taken for granted that many people define a piece of music's popularity by the fact that it is featured on radio. But what many people do not realize is that cultural norms and values of the educational process, religious ritual and belief, political campaigns, an understanding of the criminal justice system, knowledge of health care, and so on are increasingly being formed through our experience with mass media.

This is not a matter of the media serving as a pipeline to pass information from one party to another. Nor is it a matter of media reflecting back to society what society does independent of the media. Frameworks within media affect the overall strategy of what is con-sidered important to audiences and what constitutes the best way to present that material. Over time, media professionals and audience members habitually rely on these media strategies to the extent that such reliance may appear to be an unconscious process. But since the term "unconscious" is nonempirical and nonverifiable, we may substitute the concept "taken for granted," which simply means that people rely on thought patterns on which they do not bother to reflect. For example, people take for granted the fact that news is defined through the frameworks employed by the press and network televi-sion. People interpret their life struggles through various Hollywood film genres and television soap operas, and music subcultures become viable via radio formats.

As the perspectives used by the mass media frame the interaction among media professionals and with the audience, they influence the general collective consciousness of people in a society—the taken-for-granted orientation that people use to guide and make sense of their everyday lives. People in urban mass-mediated societies come to rely on mass media to such an extent that perception and inter-pretation of, and action on, a great many events and issues occur through communication strategies developed and constantly employed by mass media. In this sense, "mass media" is not just a noun or thing to examine as an object in the overall scheme of things. Rather, mass media strategy constitutes a verb or a process of activity that is adopted throughout society as a problem-solving procedure. Stated another way, the process of mass communication cannot be exam-ined apart from the strategies employed by and in mass media organizations.

Until the late 1700s in Western society, religion was the dominant perspective used by the masses to interpret issues and events. Gradually, science replaced the religious perspective so that by the beginning of the nineteenth century nations were increasingly relying on the rational perspective of science to interpret and act on issues and events. But today the dominant framework throughout the institutional structure of Western urban society comes from mass media. This is not just a matter of people within the media industry exerting their personal influence; it is a total strategy and consciousness that pervades society. Taking the example of television's influence on rule changes in professional sports, it is much more than a matter of television executives influencing the National Football League. Since fans, players, team owners, and sports professionals all rely on television in some manner, professional football becomes "made" for television. When the strategy of television stresses the offensive or scoring character of the game, people involved in organizing, playing, and watching the game come to take for granted the idea that offense should be the primary characteristic of the game. Add to this the media culture of politics, religion, economics, and pop culture, and it appears that the collective consciousness of our urban society is emerging through mass media.

At the turn of the century, the French sociologist Emile Durkheim argued that the collective consciousness (frameworks that regulate people's desires and actions) in a society results from the type of social organization or division of labor in that society. For example, in our Western world of work specialization and interdependence, a consciousness of rationality and pragmatism has developed. This consciousness of rationality and pragmatism constitutes a perspective that people use to see and interpret their physical and social environment. While the question of whether the social organization of a society is the cause of this perspective is open to debate. The point is that the perspective exists and that it is critical for how people make sense of their world.

To illustrate, the historian David Howarth recently published (1981) an account of the first Spanish Armada (1588) from the Spanish point of view. In this account Howarth argued that the expedition was conceived and designed by King Philip II of Spain as a religious conquest to put a Catholic on the throne of England. The king and all subordinates believed that God (a Catholic) would guide the mission to an inevitable success, regardless of military strategy. In fact, King Philip made all plans after daily prayer sessions, interpreting these plans as divine guidance. The king had no knowledge of seagoing battle tactics, how his cumbersome ships would negotiate the prevailing winds and sea currents, how many supplies would be needed, how crowded conditions on the ships would affect efficiency, and so on. Since divine guidance lay behind the mission, no one seriously challenged the king's wisdom. In other words, the perspective that guided the mission was formed primarily through religion, specifically Catholicism of feudal Europe. By today's standards King Philip's actions seem absurd, yet at that time they were not.

In contrast, take an example of how media perspectives are used to perceive, interpret, and act on events and issues. In this example, note that what seems to constitute a fact is more a matter of how media encourage believability, which in turn creates the appearance of fact.

In December of 1981, U.S. news media reported an imminent assassination plot against President Reagan and other high U.S. officials. Libya's charismatic and militaristic leader, Moammer Khadafy, was said to have ordered the assassination attempt through a fundamentalist group of Islamic terrorists. The American reaction to Libya was swift, highlighted by President Reagan's call for the immediate departure of all U.S. citizens from Libya. For several weeks news reports on the danger from Libya appeared daily on television, radio, and in the press. Occurring simultaneously with the apparent Libyan provocation were stories on continuing Middle Eastern crises, unrest in several Central American countries, and marital law in Poland. Just two months earlier, America's only dependable friend in the Arab world, Egypt's President Anwar Sadat, was brutally murdered at a military celebration in Cairo. The same Islamic group responsible for the Sadat assassination was said to be responsible for the impending attack on U.S. public officials. As reported by the news media, it seemed clear that America was unwillingly caught in an escalation of prewar events. Was this conclusion warranted, or could these events have been interpreted differently?

The news media claim they only report the facts and "let the chips fall where they may," a phrase used on several occasions by the former dean of broadcast journalism, Walter Cronkite. This attitude, a belief held by many people, holds that facts speak for themselves. The public's conception of the scientific attitude is that through objective investigation facts are uncovered that result in undeniable conclusions. The naiveté of this belief is understandable given the typical reliance on science as the means for obtaining knowledge and solving problems and the simultaneous ignorance of the philosophical base for science.

Yet most professional scientists understand that facts are phenomena that become meaningful only through identification procedures and interpretations framed by theories. Facts do not speak for themselves; they emerge through theoretical frameworks that may be as general and mundane as common-sense knowledge, as far-reaching as quantum mechanics, or as specific as genetics. When someone explains a behavior as the inevitable result of human nature, he or she is applying a set of loose theoretical assumptions about how human behavior is determined. No matter how general or specific a particular fact seems to be, the identification and interpretation of that phenomenon as factual occurs within a theoretical or interpretive framework of some kind. As we shall see, mass media operate with interpretive frameworks (perspectives) of their own, and these frameworks are embedded in quite specific linguistic and social psychological characteristics of mass communication.

Regarding the reported Libyan assassination squad, public officials, journalists, and the public were quite willing to believe that Khadafy was capable of such an act and that it was more than a rumor. Since the president of the United States acted as if the assassination squad was real, the average person was likely to believe that hard evidence existed. But did it? According to *Washington Post* columnist Jack Anderson, the U.S. government obtained information on the assassination plot from an informant who was alleged to have overheard Khadafy planning to have Reagan killed. According to Anderson, the informant demanded $500,000 for his information and was either paid or received other favors. Anderson discovered that members of the suspected "hit squad" were Shiite Moslems and

> that would make them followers of Iran's Ayatollah Khomeine [not Khadafy], so it's conceivable that they might want to assassinate Reagan. But they have an even stronger reason to assassinate Khadafy. It's highly unlikely, therefore, that these people would have anything to do with Khadafy. It looks as if the informant may simply have conned the U.S. Government out of a possible half-a-million bucks [Arizona Republic, December 18, 1982: A3].

The point of the Anderson story is not whether his speculations and information were right or wrong, but that a high degree of uncertainty existed in the original intelligence information obtained and released by the government. There was no hard evidence demonstrating the existence of an assassination plot, whether it was aimed at President Reagan, or whether Khadafy was involved, yet the government, the media, and the public acted as if the evidence existed. Why?

At face value it appears that federal officials authored the "hit squad" story and that the media should not be held responsible for what might have been a hoax. But knowing that government officials leaked information about a reported assassination plot does not explain why the story became "news." Government information leaks are a routine activity and only a fraction of that information ever finds its way to the public. The fact that the story involved a potential assassination is also inadequate to explain the story's importance as many reported assassination plots are uncovered in the course of every president's administration. When asked to respond to the Libyan story, former President Carter stated, "There are always rumors of that sort of thing—I always felt it was better not to broadcast these things" (Time, December 21, 1981: 19).

The fact that Khadafy was reportedly involved might be taken seriously, but would Libya jeopardize its oil sales to the United States and various kinds of U.S. aid? Only when a number of these so-called facts are pieced together along with particular perspectives does the story begin to appear credible. What is important is not the apparent facts, but the perspectives used by media to see, interpret, and even create events. Even though the Libyan story was initially leaked by federal officials, the perspectives used to interpret that event are perspectives used and developed to a fine art by the media.

While reserving the details of media perspectives for the following chapters, one example will help describe this approach. For years, American journalism has operated as a self-proclaimed guardian of the public's welfare. Journalists reserve the right to investigate any matter they feel is in the public's interest. An essential part of this strategy involves "debunking," a term referring to the procedure for uncovering hidden or behind-the-scenes information that may explain an event. Consequently, a news strategy or perspective consists, in part, of the impression that hidden reasons always exist, and journalists do their best to uncover those reasons even when the best evidence is innuendo. For example, the last paragraph in a feature article in *Time* (December 21, 1981: 22) on the alleged Libyan plot reads:

> The American people were indeed alerted last week. They could only hope that they would never grow accustomed to the thought that their elected leaders would have a permanent new peril to face: murder by contract, ordered from abroad.

Examine most any news story and the implicit impression is that something else is going on, and we should wonder what it is. It is this very perspective that has lead to the enormous popularity of the *60 Minutes* television program on CBS. Given the debunking perspective, it should be no surprise that both the media and the public reacted to the government leak on the alleged Libyan assassination squad by assuming there was more fact than fantasy to the story. In turn, since the government was itself acting without hard evidence, public officials may have become caught up in their own propaganda and begun to react to the media coverage of the story. In commenting on this very point, Senator Christopher Dodd (D-Conn.) said,

> Enhanced by tantalizing bits and pieces, what started as a rumor became a full-fledged scare. . . . Soon the White House, FBI, and the Secret Service found themselves forced to react, partly in response to the publicity. Reagan thus was fanning the flames of red-hot speculation when he flatly declared "we have the evidence" [Time, December 21, 1981: 19].

Within a very short time the story had built to the point that it was an established fact in the minds of everyone, even to the point that it was used as the reason for policy decisions toward Libya. Everyone became an investigator looking for information on when and where the terrorist attack would come. People were caught in a media event supported by media perspectives. But this is only a small part of the strategies used by media to gather, present, and promote information to the public. As we examine these strategies keep in mind that the focus of attention is on the peculiar characteristics within media that affect the content presented by media. The argument is that the form of media affects the content, and that both media professionals and audience members adopt these forms or perspectives even to the extent of using them in situations in which media are not directly involved.

A word of caution is in order. It is not being suggested that a media culture is *inevitably* caused by the perspectives employed by media organizations. My concern is with describing the perspectives used in the media industry, considering how content is affected by these perspectives, and suggesting how evidence may be brought to bear on determining various consequences of this condition. No causal model is being proposed; rather, the entire interaction between media and audience should be viewed as voluntary, even though it may involve a high degree of ignorance or lack of critical reflection. In addition, the inner organizational workings of the media industry will be described only insofar as they relate to how the perspectives of mass media result in media influence. I am not engaged in an organizational analysis per se, but rather in an analysis of the communication process through mass media.

McLUHAN'S INFLUENCE

The late Marshall McLuhan startled observers of mass communication in the early 1960s by arguing that a medium itself is more important than the message it transmits. Perhaps more than any other recent analysis of media, this argument brought observers to question the existing explanations of mass communication. McLuhan turned attention from the nature of media messages as propaganda and of their content in general to the nature of the relationship between an audience and the medium. He suggested that media are extensions of the individual. For example, the book is an extension of the eye, clothing an extension of skin, radio an extension of the ear, and television an extension of the central nervous system. At all times people are surrounded with media, and each medium has specific relationship properties for the individual. In addition, he described differences in the logic of each medium. Print media are conducive to a lineal, sequential logic of causal effects and progress, while television and other electronic media have a nonlineal logic, one more circular and with an emphasis on affective expressive moods.

In the McLuhan model, media may also be differentiated by their "hot" and "cool" properties. Hot media, such as radio, are marked by high definition of content and low involvement by the listener. A cool medium, such as television, is characterized by low definition of content and a high degree of involvement by the audience. The ideal situation is to match cool subjects with cool media and hot subjects with hot media.

Presenting a conflicting mix of hot and cool will result in alienating or angering the audience. In fact, McLuhan's fame was achieved when he predicted that John F. Kennedy would win the 1960 presidential election on the strength of the famous TV debate with Richard Nixon. According to McLuhan, Nixon was a hot subject who did not mix with the cool medium of television. A cool Kennedy on the cool medium of TV was elected. In short, McLuhan argued that a medium's inherent characteristics foster a very specific type of relationship between the individual and a medium.

In assessing McLuhan's contribution I am not concerned with a medium's linearity or whether it is hot or cool. People use media for a variety of reasons, and a print medium may be no less emotionally expressive or more lineal than television is affective and nonlineal. The value of McLuhan's work is that he reoriented attention to the relationship between the medium and the individual through the meaning a given medium holds for the individual. For McLuhan, the nature of this relationship was the message; i.e., content is affected by the *form* of the communication relationship. Taking McLuhan's lead, to understand media influence we should examine the properties of media that constitute the framework for communication strategy: in short, media perspectives and grammar.

In an analysis of mass communication strongly influenced by McLuhan, Tony Schwartz (1974) argues that media are most effective when a "responsive chord" is struck between the medium and audience. While Schwartz focuses on television in terms of technical properties—such as picture tube resolution, the brain physiology of viewing a television screen, and the social distance created through camera angles and viewing distance between TV set and viewer—his argument leans toward how these technical properties are molded to fit the communication characteristics people use in everyday interaction. For example, he states:

> If we seek to communicate a situation or event, our problem is not to capture the reality of that situation, but to record or create stimuli that will affect the home listener or viewer in a manner similar to a listener's or viewer's experience in the real situation. What counts is not reality, as a scientist might measure it, but the ability to communicate the situation in a believable, human way [1974: 5].

Making a message believable requires determining why people use media. This means that the mass communicator must understand the motives and beliefs of the audience. With this knowledge, media professionals can construct a message that initially strikes a responsive chord in the audience. It is only after this resonance is achieved that an audience member will interpret and define the message as something meaningful. As such, Schwartz concludes that "accuracy [in a transmission] is often less important in determining the ultimate meaning than the pattern listeners will apply in making sense of something they hear" (1974: 33). Therefore, the task of media is to construct a pattern that will be accepted and used by the audience.

Additional theoretical background for an introduction to media grammar and perspectives involves the dramatic character of interaction as described by Erving Goffman (1959), among others. A drama model of interaction proposes that an individual's behavior should be analyzed from the perspective of theater or drama. Some sociologists argue that life is analogous to theater, while others take the extreme position that life itself is theater. Regardless, the basic principle is that individuals construct performances designed to establish and maintain their identities. Goffman claims that an individual (actor) attempts to manage or manipulate the impressions others develop of the actor's behavior. An example is dressing appropriately for an occasion to show others you are acting properly. A woman professor who keeps a disorderly desk implies that she has a tremendous amount of work in progress with no time to waste on frivolous conversation. A brand name on an article of clothing conveys status. These displays constitute a form designed to elicit very specific responses from others regarding the intentions or desires of the person making the display. However, others also obtain impressions of an actor's performance that go beyond the impressions an actor intends to create. A person may dress up for a formal occasion only to have someone comment that he or she looks like a rented servant. Consequently, people in interaction are constantly involved in negotiating consensus on whose definitions will be accepted (see Appendix A).

Goffman's argument that people attempt to maneuver other people into making responses that benefit themselves is useful in examining the process of mass communication, as this is precisely the strategy taken in the media industry to attract attention and elicit audience response. Communication through a mass medium to an unseen audience of relative strangers requires using forms of communication and content that are instantly recognizable to the audience. All media attempt to reduce the ambiguity of communication to the point that meanings between communicator and audience are shared immediately. For a medium appealing to a mass audience, such as television, this requires the use of a grammar and vocabulary understood by the largest possible number of people. By contrast, media dealing with special interest audiences, such as *Scientific American,* can afford to be more specialized in their perspectives and language. The point is, mass communicators must be highly successful in predicting how audiences will respond.

CHARACTERISTICS OF PERSPECTIVES IN MASS MEDIA

The term "perspective" is a general one describing the framework people use to perceive and make interpretations. In this sense, perspective may be thought of as a quasi-theory or explanatory system. Claiming that facts do not speak for themselves but become meaningful through theoretical frameworks means that perception and interpretation of phenomena occurs through such perspectives as religious dogma, scientific deductive logic, or simply what passes for common sense. For example, entertainment is a perspective on how to view certain kinds of activity. A person who slips and falls on a patch of ice may be viewed though the serious perspective of tragedy or the playful perspective of entertainment. On the other hand, something intended as entertainment may fall flat and be viewed as tragedy. Therefore, for something to be entertaining it must ultimately be viewed through a perspective of entertainment, regardless of the original intent. It follows that in order to increase the chance that something will be entertaining, the initiator of the act must learn the form of entertainment and use it skillfully.

In mass communication the form of the communication must be immediately apparent to an audience as there is not enough time to explain intentions before their attention turns to something else. Because of the need for predictable audience response, mass media use forms that are familiar to the audience and over time add nuances that become routine and unique to the medium. This aids in explaining why theatrical entertainment differs slightly from film, television, or radio entertainment. As the forms of each medium develop they become familiar to both the communicators and audiences and are integrated into a person's knowledge system as perspectives to use in making interpretations. When a situation comedy comes on the television screen, television viewers know instantly that this phenomena is both entertainment and situation comedy as created by television.

While this may seem all too simple, consider what happens when a newspaper reports on a scientific finding that originally appeared in a scientific journal, such as the *New England Journal of Medicine*. A newspaper reporter reads the journal and reworks the scientific report to fit a newspaper or journalistic perspective. The question is, what perspectives are used in newspaper journalism? As discussed in the following chapter on the press, event-centered reporting is the primary perspective used to identify and interpret facts to a newspaper audience. The rules for this perspective require that certain kinds of information are selected to the exclusion of others and a specific grammar is followed in presenting that information. In the above example, the result may be a set of meanings or at least suggestions that were unintended by the medical team. Furthermore, if television news reports the same story, it may use slightly different perspectives, such as "ideal norms." This perspective involves an appeal to society's ideals, such as virtue, hard work, justice, etc. (By upholding these ideals television is able to avoid offending large numbers of viewers.) Thinking ahead, it may be anticipated that ideal norms will result in a rather unrealistic view of everyday life. Nevertheless, this approach has been used extensively in prime-time programming for many years.

Most people would probably agree that understanding the influence of mass media is not a matter of determining whether they are "objective" or biased. All information, from any source, occurs through a perspective of some kind. But saying that all information is biased is a matter of semantics. Honest people report what they consider to be true, but knowledge of their perspectives is still required to understand how they arrived at their conclusion. Yet only recently have students of mass communication considered examining the taken-for-granted or hidden perspectives used in mass media as opposed to the more blatant ideological perspectives, which have received considerable attention. One early attempt at analyzing a hidden perspective in mass communication was William Stephenson's argument that much of the information obtained through mass media is presented in a play or entertainment context. As he stated:

> Play is a relaxed "leave taking" from the serious side of daily routine. . .
> where mass communication involves entertainment it is characteris-

tically a matter of communication-pleasure. It brings no material gain and serves no "work" function, but it does induce elements of self-enhancement [1967: 59].

One among several implications of Stephenson's idea is that people often engage in seeking a here-and-now, self-oriented pleasure in their experience with mass media. As such, this media play is social without being demanding, or socially involving without the pressure to act in particular ways. But Stephenson would not claim that play-communication has no meaning for the participants. Certainly children learn a great deal while at play, and adults engage in play just for the sociability of the activity. But since play is a perspective used widely in mass communication we need to take it seriously for the meanings that people create while in a play context. For example, if news becomes a play activity for some people, what are the implications for the commitment of those people in community affairs?

Since entertainment is the most pervasive form in mass media, a brief look at the more outstanding characteristics of this form will provide some insight into its appeal. One property of entertainment is that it is extraordinary activity, lying outside the limits of daily routine behavior. In staged productions, music concerts, and comedy performances audiences experience a reality that is noticeably different from mundane situations. A joke told by a comic in a Las Vegas showroom receives a different response than when it is retold by an observer to friends in a hotel room. When Neil Diamond or Barbra Streisand sings, it is not the same as your rendition in the shower. Even the traveling carnival has a degree of magic, with its freak shows and hustlers. This is not to say everything extraordinary is entertaining; many people are horrified by a (grisly) auto accident and perhaps disgusted by some "skin" magazines. But when extraordinary activity is perceived as entertainment, the moment is special partially because it is not routine and also because the performers have talent or skills that exceed what is considered normal.

Another entertainment characteristic is the illusion of a "larger-than-life" experience. Slightly different than the extraordinary extension of talent, the illusion of something that is larger than life is a charismatic quality that is difficult to define. In commenting on Hollywood film stars producer Allan Carr once said that Diana Ross, Bette Midler, and Barbra Streisand required very special film projects because of their "larger-than-life quality." According to Carr, an actress such as Jill Clayburgh, who lacks this larger-than-life quality, can successfully act in almost any film. But people with great charisma require special vehicles to match their impact on the screen. Whether Carr is correct in his assessment of these particular film stars is beside the point. Charisma is real, and it is a very important part of the magic of entertainment, particularly when people expect charismatic performances. For this reason, seeing media stars on the street is often quite disappointing.

In entertainment there is also significant potential for vicarious involvement by the audience member. As listeners, viewers, or readers, we often measure the quality of a performance by whether or not we can imagine ourselves in the performing situation. We do not necessarily need to be the person on stage or the character in the book, but we should at least be able to identify with the scene and see ourselves as part of the situation. People will usually not spend good money to see a performer they do not like or a show for which they are not in the mood. Successful personalities are those with whom an audience can in some way identify. In a television documentary on singer Willie Nelson, a man in a concert audience remarked that he liked Willie because he reminded him of his father. After making the film *Honeysuckle Rose,* co-star Slim Pickens said that people see Willie on stage and think "that could be me up there." The same holds true for the likes of Loretta Lynn, Pete Rose, the Fronz, and Johnny Carson. David Victor, producer of the successful medical television dramas *Dr. Kildare* and *Marcus Welby, M.D.,* stated the aim is to:

> get viewers involved in the plight of your central character early on and keep them involved; don't diffuse your focus with too many side plots. Humanize your doctor protagonists as much as possible but avoid making them too tormented or too coy . . . they must be believable characters who enhance each other, and in another sense, enhance the intelligence of their viewers [Goldberg, 1980: 22].

Vicarious behavior is attractive because it is free of the constraints often found in face-to-face interaction. In the vicarious situation people can be whomever they wish with no one to call their bluff. Vicarious entertainment makes it possible to relive *Bonanza*land, be heroic, or just drift through the emotional ambience of a scene. The pure fun of this involvement is often reason alone for buying the theater ticket or turning on the TV.

Along with vicarious involvement in entertainment is the potential for the legitimate expression of emotion. In fact, emotional expression is usually the proof that a person has been entertained, as in laughing hysterically, crying real tears, and feeling pride, love, hate, and even shame. These expressions are evidence that vicarious involvement was achieved and that something extraordinary did take place. Consequently, emotional expression is the most fundamental attribute of the entertainment perspective.

A significant part of the emotional experience in entertainment is drama—the anticipation of what will happen next. While drama is found in most types of entertainment, it is most common in situations involving conflict. The drama of the "whodunit" has always been an appealing characteristic of American entertainment on stage, film, radio, novels, and television. As such, the drama in conflict is a form and perspective in itself and is used by every mass medium even in situations that are not usually thought of an entertainment. For example, news stories in the press or on television often focus on the drama of an incident, ask the question "Who is responsible?" (for some problem in the community), or pit one segment of the community against another on some issue. In many of these situations the conflict is real; the medium simply intensifies the problem by accenting the conflict.

In other situations the news media may create the appearance of conflict for the sake of drama and the audience interest that follows. A prime example was reported by David Altheide in the *Washington Journalism Review* (1981) in his research on the television coverage of the Americans held hostage by Iran in 1980-1981. Based on an extensive content analysis of network news coverage of the Iranian issue, he concluded that basically America was held hostage by network television. By placing the hostage story in the framework of an act of war by Iran, and by ignoring Iran's internal policies and politics and the prior history of U.S.-Iranian relations under the deposed Shah, American television viewers saw only the hostile act of holding hostages without any context other than militarism. Through network news the American viewer was caught up in the drama of what appeared to be a war with Iran.

The Iranian example is not atypical of drama and conflict in the news media. Pick up almost any daily newspaper, or watch almost any network news broadcast, and many of the stories feature the drama of conflict. While journalists may argue that the conflict is real, the questions to ask are, how much intensity is added by the media reporting, is the context of the issue explained fully, is there a suggestion of blame, and is there an accent on dramatic reporting through action film scenes and the urgent, concerned, nonverbal expressions of reporters? In short, do the news media use a form of conflict and drama to shape the story? Certainly this occurred in the Khadafy story described earlier, a story that may have been a hoax. But since one of the prime forms used in the news media is conflict and drama, the media were quick to pick up on the alleged assassination plot and create a major story. The implication for media influence is that when the public accepts drama and conflict in an event as objectively real, it may only be a fictional construction.

Another perspective, a relative newcomer to the major media, is sports. Here we must distinguish between straight reporting of a sports event and the use of a sports framework for interpreting and presenting nonsports events and issues. The sports perspective is a combination of entertainment, drama, and conflict, meeting all the characteristics previously described. Consequently, a sports event qualifies quite nicely as material for the major media, particularly television. Given the versatility of the sports perspective, it should not be surprising that a mass medium could treat an event such as a governmental election as a sporting contest. Using the sports perspective an individual with no interest in an election might be induced to see electioneering activities such as poll results and debates (one on one) as sporting contests and observe election returns on the giant scoreboard with the same perspective used for watching a horse race. If this seems to be stretching the point, notice how often sports terminology and analogy are used in reporting political events, as when political candidates speak of gaining "momentum" and making the "big play." In 1981, the AWACS deal, which sent sophisticated U.S. radar planes to Saudi Arabia, became a major political contest in the news media for President Reagan. Each day broadcast and print journalism gave a tally on the potential congressional vote. After the win, President Reagan was pictured on the cover of *Time* magazine with a triumphant look holding the final role-call voting card, much like a golf scorecard or winning lottery ticket.

In speculating on the implication of the entertainment, conflict/drama, and sports perspectives for media influence, a comment by Walter Cronkite in an interview in 1980 is interesting. He responded to the statement that "television has transformed all our politicians into media creatures," by saying:

I don't know if that's bad. . . . It's unfortunate if it means that you lose some real thinkers who just do not have the ability to communicate. But then they shouldn't be in positions where communication is important. Let them be the back-room boys [Panorama, 1980: 20].

For Cronkite, the ability to communicate means the ability to conform to media perspectives. When television professionals, politicians, and the public begin to think in this manner, we have media influence in action.

Many other perspectives are used in mass media, from the highly specialized "journal" perspective in scientific periodicals to the mass television perspective, which reduces complex issues to simplistic dimensions. The extent to which media professionals and audience members rely uncritically on these forms for perception and interpretation is a prime measure of the extent to which media influence exists. There is no escaping the use of perspectives for creating meaning in the world, as all phenomena are explained through some kind of theoretical framework. But when those perspectives become taken for granted without occasional critical reexamination, the result is that the means (form or perspective) become the end.

GRAMMAR

The most fundamental point about existence and reality is that humans are symbol users; everything we know about our physical and social world is developed through language. Therefore, it stands to reason that the structure, or *grammar,* of a language is critical in explaining how humans interpret their experience. Indeed, experience in a most fundamental sense is a matter of using grammatical rules. These rules actually form a structure for how people think about their worlds. For example, the subject-verb-object structure of the English language orders the world in a sequential procedure of subject acting on object, or cause and effect. Through the English language time progresses from point A to B, birth and death are a lineal progression of stages, and events of all types have future consequences. Other languages, such as those of the Hopi, Chinese, or a primitive Amazon tribe, use different structures and different perspectives on how the world works. While mass media use the common languages of their audiences, they also develop distinct grammatical rules for how they present information to an audience. The grammarian claims these rules are separated among the three categories of syntax, inflection, and special characteristics of vocabulary. For my purpose, the analysis of grammar in mass communication will be broken down into the following: (1) the organization and scheduling of messages (syntax), (2) the rhythm and tempo of presentation strategies (inflection), and (3) special features of verbal vocabulary and nonverbal gestures. The purpose is to discover the unique grammar of the different media and some of the consequences of these grammatical forms.

Functioning as the structure of the mass communication process, grammar enables predictability for both communicator and audience member, giving a medium the appearance of rationality and order. Over time, a particular grammatical structure becomes molded into a format, as exemplified by tabloid newspapers' large headlines and candid photographs, which are associated with the outrageous and seamy side of life. By contrast, a newspaper with five or six single columns and few photos is more conservative and may attempt in-depth analyses of serious subjects. Moving across the radio dial, an avid listener can identify the variety of music formats instantly. And television programs, from soap operas to talk shows, have very distinct grammars easily identified by knowledgeable viewers. Within each medium and for each format (type of program or genre), perspectives, such as entertainment, are linked with a specific grammar resulting in an overall communication logic.

For example, some news is not straight reporting of an event but the result of an entertainment perspective. This perspective uses dramatic staging techniques, a grammar of organizing verbal accounts with film, a particular rhythm and tempo of speech, and a news vocabulary. Audiences have become so familiar with a news format that recognition is based more on its format than on the content. A remarkable example was NBC's Jane Pauley, who achieved instant news credibility with the television news audience despite her lack of training in journalism and very limited experience as a news reader. Since Pauley's gift for appearing vivid and articulate on camera fits the familiar television news format, the public accepted her legitimacy almost automatically. Peter Dahlgren (1980) refers to this as an example of the "nonreflexive" character of television viewing, although it should be added that examples, such as Pauley's rise to journalism fame, demonstrate how the acceptance of form precedes and affects the definition of content.

In remaining chapters I will examine the current grammar in each major mass medium. For example, television grammar encompasses how programs are scheduled throughout the day, week, and year. Each type of program from news to situation comedy has a specific syntax that viewers instantly recognize: Plots of prime-time drama and comedy are so uniform that anyone can predict the sequence of events. Television creates variety through tempo, as in the frantic game show or slow-moving soap opera. Inflection in television is also created through camera work, editing, lighting, and music.

The verbal and nonverbal vocabulary of television grammar is even different than that of other media. Each medium has its own unique grammatical characteristics, which people use to interpret their experience through these media. From the syntax of the press to the rhythm of film, understanding the operation and potential influence of mass media requires an understanding of media grammar. But we must consider that media perspectives and grammar are the result of voluntary decisions made willingly by media professionals and audience members. The entire process is a dramatic activity in which the form of the drama has become a framework for presenting and making sense of that drama. But as drama, this is willful activity, not something chiseled in stone.

Media Use and Influence

The structural properties of mass communication introduced in this chapter constitute a general model for analyzing the process of mass communication and understanding the potential for developing media influence and media culture. It is suggested that mass communication should be analyzed as an interaction between communicator and audience in which both parties use perspectives and grammatical rules to perceive and interpret various phenomena. While the particular motives for using these perspectives and grammatical forms lie with individuals, my concern is with describing the perspectives and formats developed by the mass media industry and finding evidence of and speculating on the extent to which individual action is based on these perspectives and formats.

Following this model it is suggested that both media communicator and audience member use mass media in four distinct ways. *First,* mass media constitute a source of information on subjects of relevance to the interacting parties. This includes the practical information on skills necessary to perform a particular activity and observation of potential role models who perform successfully in those activities. A slow-motion instant replay of a professional golfer at the U.S. Open demonstrates the form of swinging a golf club as well as shows how a professional golfer walks, talks, studies, reacts—in short, plays the game of golf. Here a role model is more than a lesson in specific golfing skill; it is a style of how the activity should be performed in a dramatic sense.

Second, mass media provide information on the assumptions and perspectives that underlie most attempts at learning. Examine any attempt to teach skills or present a model of appropriate behavior and it should become apparent that specific assumptions and a perspective must be accepted before it makes sense to learn those skills. In the golf example we may assume there is some acceptable meaning to using various club-faced shafts to hit a small round sphere around a course lined with obstacles designed to frustrate the errant participant. To answer this question, ask a person why they spend four hours trying to "break a hundred." These tanned, nattily dressed masochists will give reasons ranging from fresh air and companionship to competition and gambling.

On occasion, assumptions are so taken for granted that participants wonder why you even bother to ask. The idea here is that golf and many other activities are American pasttimes that people with time and money engage in because "it is the thing to do." Golf is a means of demonstrating that a person holds to certain middle-class beliefs on what constitutes the "good life." When television spends several hours covering a golf tournament it is reaffirming these implicit assumptions to viewers. While television does not have to articulate these assumptions, it often does so by means of short dramatic promotions and "filler" talk by the commentators. Consequently, a medium not only shows the audience how to perform an activity but also provides the underlying assumptions or philosophy on why someone should want to learn that activity. A search through back issues of *Playboy* magazine reveals that Hugh Hefner did the same thing with his series entitled "The Playboy Philosophy."

Third, mass media are used as legitimate and trusted agents for what is assumed will be credible information. The statement "news is news because a mass medium presents it as news" is a case in point.

Reflect on the way people rely on dictionaries and encyclopedias as legitimizing sources of information. People take for granted that if a word is not in the dictionary, it is not a legitimate word. The same logic is currently being applied to print and broadcast media as a source of news and entertainment. For example, many readers consider *Time* magazine to be the source for whatever is current and important in the world. For many readers "Dear Abby" is not just a source of amusement; she is an authority on what is current in the realm of everyday psychology.

This legitimizing function of media may be graphically presented by thinking of a continuum from the highly specialized media audiences to the mass level. Esoteric media, such as underground film and adult bookstore magazines, legitimize the underlife scene of subcultures such as "gay S&M." Music subcultures are served by FM radio. The pop music scene is found in mainstream radio, and prime-time television is mass Americana. In serving specific audiences, various media become sources of legitimation by virtue of their existence alone. In this sense, the action is where the medium is. Accepting the idea that news is what the evening newscast presents is a tacit acceptance of the idea that television itself is news or where the cameras are located is where news occurs. In part, this is what Marshall McLuhan meant when he said, "the medium is the message." Whether out of convenience, convention, or because other people you respect use it, media are important legitimizing agents in the process of creating and establishing meanings and a sense of reality.

This is not to say that all audiences or media professionals are uncritical or that acceptance of media perspectives is involuntary. Over time, people may simply accept media perspectives and grammar to the point that it all becomes second nature. Consider how watching a football or baseball game at the ballpark has changed since television introduced six different camera angles, slow-motion instant replay, expert (color) analysis, and constant action. Some people in the ballpark now feel a loss when they cannot see an instant replay or hear it described. In response, team owners are adopting the practice of showing the instant replay on a giant television screen. This demonstrates that people are using a television perspective to experience the game at the ballpark. That is media culture.

Finally, there are the vicarious and overt interaction networks within the media industry and between audiences and the medium. As an example of the latter, media professionals often use each other as sources of information and legitimation. When a newspaper editor in Kansas checks the newsworthiness of a national story, a common practice is to consult the *New York Times* News Service, which provides an indication of what the *Times* will print. The delay in investigating Watergate was primarily due to the fact that the *New York Times* and *Time* magazine did not take the initiative. Add to this the vicarious and sometimes personal relationships that audience members develop with media personalities and the constant contact with trust placed in selected media, and it seems clear that media are potentially very influential for both those within the media industry and the audience.

Given the four general uses of mass communication, it seems that the character of American culture and individual action is being developed more and more through media experience. Media personalities are being used as role models to be emulated in both vicarious fantasy and overt interpersonal relationships. In this manner people pattern themselves after media models and then use the continued media portrayals as validation or support for their own actions. For the critically reflective person, mass media may be used selectively for information that will enhance the individual's sense of competence and a feeling of being socially involved. For the uncritical and unreflective media follower, personal concerns and perspectives emerge from strategies used by the media. In a scholarly article, Peter Dahlgren (1980) argues that TV news fosters a relationship in which viewers become dependent on TV. Consequently, the public becomes unreflective about how they fit into the economic and political system and uncritical of its operation. In short, Dahlgren attempts to show how media produce what Karl Marx referred to as a "false consciousness' among the people.

Regardless of whether the consciousness developed through mass media is false, the point in this chapter is that before media influence can occur, the audience must willingly participate and willingly accept the perspectives and content presented through mass media. Media influence occurs when people begin to see and define their environment as the mass media see and define it. But this consequence still depends on what people accept for themselves. On the other hand, television critic Carlie Haas (1978: 36) stated that "the images that surround you in an event are more and more television images, and people minds are working according to television rhythms. . . . The environment is turning into television." And, as Howard Beale, the "mad prophet of the airwaves," in the Hollywood film *Network* admonished his viewers, "You're beginning to think the tube is reality and your lives aren't real."

CHAPTER 2

NEWSPAPERS
The Daily Institution

In 1896 Adolph S. Ochs became publisher of a deteriorating *New York Times* and almost immediately turned it into what many consider the ideal of newspaper journalism. With the motto "all the news that's fit to print," the *Times* set out to report on the significant information affecting the institutional network of American society. Today, news and print journalism is judged largely by the *Times'* standards, although it is commonly recognized that the *Times,* the *Christian Science Monitor,* and a few other great American dailies represent only one extreme segment along a continuum of newspaper publishing. My purpose here is to examine some of the major properties of that continuum with specific attention to the language of newspapers and the interaction patterns between journalists and readers.

Newspapers are, and will continue to be, a major force in American society. Despite the fact that television has become the dominant mass-audience medium since 1950, newspaper circulation (at just over 60 million copies per day) and the number of daily newspapers (about 1750) have remained fairly constant. What do newspapers have that results in this continued loyalty or fascination? To answer this question the sociologist will quickly suggest that newspapers must function in ways significant or useful for readers and the community. While this certainly is true, some of the functions a newspaper fulfills may easily be missed by the casual observer. As a microcosm of a community the newspaper provides information on a variety of topics, from serious international relations to sports and entertainment. In providing this variety of information the newspaper facilitates interaction within every major and most minor institutions in society. But the newspaper is more than a support system for the institutional network of society—it is an institution in and of itself.

Institutionalized Activity

In sociology the term "institution" refers to a standardized procedure for solving a community-wide problem. One problem the newspaper solves is disseminating information necessary to the operation of major institutions such as government and business. In disseminating this information newspapers use a form, a form largely unchanged since Benjamin Day started the first inexpensive commercial newspaper *(New York Sun)* on September 3, 1833. This form, either tabloid (five columns on a 12" × 14" sheet) or full size (six columns, 14" × 22"), has front page headlines, an inside editorial page, feature sections, and ads, all of which are generally in the same location day after day and from one paper to another. Like favorite old jeans or sneakers the newspaper is dependable in its familiarity and in lending stability to our daily lives.

During a newspaper strike in New York City in 1945, Bernard Berelson asked people what they missed by not receiving their regular paper. One thing he discovered was that people relied on the paper for comics, the movie log, ads, fashion, and other rather mundane matters at least as much as they relied on the paper for serious news. For many people the *New York Times* crossword puzzle is a very important, if not the main, reason for buying the paper. Riding the subway without that crossword puzzle to solve can be a traumatic experience for some, while eating breakfast without a newspaper might be unthinkable for others. When my son delivered the *Arizona Republic,* he encountered people who regularly waited at their door at 5:00 a.m. for the morning edition. As most devoted newspaper readers will testify, this regimen is not uncommon. Many people have daily routines that they find difficult to manage without media. Therefore, in addition to the institutionalized, printed form of the newspaper, reading the paper is an institutionalized activity that facilitiates other routines such as eating, riding mass transit, and relaxing.

The newspaper is also an institutionalized community watchdog. Warning us of a business downturn, a crime wave, or government corruption, newspapers have been crusaders since the first broadside was put to ink in colonial America. Horace Greeley called his *New York Tribune* (circa 1830s) "the great moral organ"; Benjamin Day said of his *New York Sun,* "It shines for ALL"; and William Randolph Hearst claimed the aim of his *New York Journal* was to "defend the average person." Check the masthead of almost any newspaper—the tradition of protecting the public through "the right to know" is clearly stated. While people sometimes wonder just who is being protected and at what cost, the tradition of community watchdog is, nevertheless, firmly established in print journalism.

Given the complexities of modern urban society the average citizen often turns to the newspaper for information and leadership in community crisis situations. It was the *New York Times* that printed the Pentagon Papers over President Nixon's objections; it was the *Washington Post* that broke the Watergate story while broadcast journalism looked on. The First Amendment applies only to print media, a protection that is staunchly guarded as is demonstrated almost daily in newspapers and courtrooms across the country. When City Hall fails to uphold the public's interest, people expect the newspaper to uncover the facts and "tell it like it is." Although a well-defined legal system and network of public protection agencies exist, the pubic informally relies on newspapers to safeguard their interests. Yet we hasten to add that this is an institutional ideal and may not be practiced as much as we would like.

In recognizing the community watchdog role of the press, credit must be given to reporters who take seriously the journalistic tradition of investigation. Were it not for a newshound determinism and a cynical attitude toward the facade of organizations and individuals, most stories of corruption, incompetence, and deceit would never be told. Since the beginning of professional journalsim, the backbone of crusading journalism has been and will continue to be reporters with an allegiance to the craft of investigative reporting.

While some publishers and editors from the old school remain, their ranks dwindle in the face of increasing conglomerate control of print media. The late Lord Thompson, Canadian-born newspaper baron whose company owned 57 newspapers in the United States and more elsewhere, said, "I buy newspapers to make money to buy more newspapers to make more money. As far as editorial content, that's the stuff you separate the ads with" (Bagdikian, 1979: 57). Cut from the same cloth, Australian Rupert Murdoch, who recently bought the *New York Post* and owns 88 newspapers in Australia, England, and the United States, said, "You pay three times the [a newspaper's] revenue because it's a monopoly and a license to steal money forever." After he purchased the *Post,* he tried to hire several reporters from the *Village Voice,* who refused, saying they would not work for a sex-and-sensationalism peddler. Murdoch's response was to buy the *Voice* along with *New York* magazine and *New West* (now *California*).

Today, over 60 percent of the total daily press circulation is controlled by chains such as Knight-Ridder, Newhouse, Thompson, Gannett, and Scripps League. Media conglomerates are also diversifying. For example, RCA, which in addition to publishing houses owns companies producing electronic warfare equipment and space exploration guidance systems. CBS was a defense contractor during the Vietnam War with a company involved in high technology government contracts. ABC owns amusement parks, theaters, and recording companies, one of which produces evangelistic recordings and books out of Waco, Texas. Ben Bagdikian, long-time media scholar and antitrust advocate from the *Columbia Journalism Review,* fears the continuing merger trend will destroy the watchdog/investigative role of the press in favor of profits. As he states,

> There is no reason to expect that a person skilled at building a corporate empire is a good judge of what the generality of citizens in a community need and want to know. Today, news is increasingly a monopoly medium in its locality, its entrepreneurs are increasingly absent ones who know little about and have no commitment to the social and political knowledge of a community's citizens. More and more, the news in America is a by-product of some other business, controlled by a small group of distant corporate chieftains. If the integrity of news and the full information of communities are to be protected, more can be expected from autonomous news staffs than from empire builders mainly concerned with other businesses in other places [1979: 60].

One hopes that the newspaper's role as community watchdog will continue in practice and in the minds of the public. If it only exists in the minds of readers, media influence will be an increasingly troublesome matter.

Newspaper Grammar

A very important institutionalized aspect of the newspaper concerns how it functions as a standardized means of communication. The newspaper (as do all other mass media) employs a procedure for locating, organizing, and interpreting its content. To understand the process of newspaper communication attention will first be directed to a description of grammar, followed by an examination of the perspectives used in determining how information is selected and defined.

SYNTAX

To understand newspaper grammar, begin by leafing through any daily edition and notice how the content is usually organized into homogeneous units, such as international and national news, for state and local news, sports, lifestyle information, and finally the classified ads. Commercial ads are placed according to the interests of the people who read a particular section, e.g., airline ads in the heavy news section, automotive ads in the sports section, and so on. The location of standard features (astrology, weather, tips on bridge) follows a similar logic, although some of these features have a neutral or mass appeal and may appear anywhere. Regulars readers know their newspaper's organization so well that they can neatly pull out a section they wish to read with scarcely a glance at the title. Where to find the editorial page, stock report, baseball box scores, favorite feature columnist, or used car ads is accomplished without looking at the index. Even the elaborate Sunday edition may be divided among family members instantly and harmoniously. The syntax of story placement has become so routine that most dailies throughout the country follow the same strategy. How papers differ is seldom due to how they organize content; rather it is based on the emphasis given particular kinds of stories and inflection techniques or style.

Another important syntax feature is the composition of various pages in a newspaper. The front page, editorial page, sports page, and so on all follow a composition that most readers understand implicitly. Front-page headlines draw the reader to the right-hand column (lead story), which along with other major stories is located above the fold on a full-size paper and is continued on the inside near a commercial advertisement. The lead story is usually accompanied by a photo, or "cut" (as it is called in the newspaper business), and a caption, or "cutline." Secondary stories are located below the fold along with at least one smaller photo and the page number index of features inside the paper. Many stories inside the paper are accompanied by photos, and feature columns usually have a photo or caricature of the columnist. News stories are commonly presented in several vertical columns in contrast to the more horizontal look of the editorial page. Major news stories carry a main heading, followed by a second heading (deck), the byline or wire source, a dateline, and subheadings throughout the copy, which serve as summary captions and breaks in the monotony of long gray columns. While front page stores are continued inside, stories that begin on inside pages are usually completed on the same page with more detailed headlines. Stories with dramatic emphasis are enclosed in large borders (rules) and occasionally are colored. Ads for department stores, food, fashion, travel, automotive, and so on appear not only in specific sections but on specific days of the week. Feature columns appear in the same section of every edition, and they are located in approximately the same spot on the page. This format enables one to know immediately the general content of a page even if it is in a foreign language.

Composition also refers to how the content of a story is organized. The traditional rule in writing a news story is to begin with a short summary lead, giving the bare essentials in an almost telegram style. The balance of the article follows an inverted-pyramid organization from major to minor facts and general to specific detail, which enables an editor to chop off end pieces to save space without loss of essential information. The inverted-pyramid formula has been a standard practice in newspapers for over a hundred years and is supported by the rationale that since people seldom read the paper in one sitting, they can obtain the facts quickly, returning to the story as time and desire permit. But this practice is slowly giving way to the belief that setting the scene and the emotional tone of the story is both more informative and interesting.

For example, the traditional lead-in and inverted pyramid approach might begin with:

Cops Shoot Three in Race Riot:
Racial Tension Mounts

Blue River: Late Tuesday night police fired into a mob of angry black youths who stormed city hall. The knife-wielding, rock-throwing youths were "hell bent on destroying anything in their path," said police chief Tom Just. . . .

Instead of this class approach, the story might be rewritten as:

Police Wound Three Black Youths
in Latest Racial Confrontation

Blue River: As summer heat bakes the evening streets, small groups of unemployed black youth roam aimlessly in search of something to do. The sign on the back of a passing bus promises a bright future for anyone who joins the "First Team" of the new

Army Reserve. But kids on this street know only cockroaches, long unemployment lines, and a fear of "white justice." . . .

Despite the fact that readers have the time to read longer articles that follow a descriptive literary style, the rule followed by most newspapers continues to be the traditional "guts" lead and the inverted pyramid of short, choppy, telegram-style paragraphs, creating the impression of facts or hard news presented in an objective manner. Although much news story content is actually background information and dramatically stylized, it is masked with the format of hard, "event-centered" news.

The telegram style of reporting is also a consequence of the rush to complete stories and the demand to save precious newsprint. To avoid deadline pressure, reporters often write a story in sections or takes, piecing it together before sending it on to the copy editor for final editing. Since copy editors are notorious for eliminating all soft spots to save space, reporters learn to write in a concise, staccato manner leaving all self-evident (so they say) material for the reader to fill in.

Herein lies an important aspect of "event-centered" newspaper grammar. Readers are constantly filling in gaps to the point of over-generalization, exaggeration, and presumption. The danger of not providing enough background and interpretive analysis, particularly given the complexities of the modern world, has led some newspapers to expand their news stories from the usual 750 to 800 words to upwards of 2000 words. Examples of this new practice are evident in the Sunday editions of the *New York Times, Los Angeles Times, Philadelphia Inquirer,* and others; this practice has been followed for years by the *Christian Science Monitor.*

INFLECTION

A second feature of grammar that receives a good deal of attention in teaching students to write newspaper copy is how to summarize, emphasize, and maintain a particular flow in a story. Headlines vary according to the impression publishers and editors wish to convey to their readers. In following the text manual on copy editing, Carl Riblet, Jr. (1974) warns students to avoid beginning a headling with a verb, ending with a preposition or modifier, allowing a pronoun to stand alone, and using hanging modifiers. In a humorous essay on writing headings, Michael Frayn (1973) suggests that head-lines often consist of monosyllable words that may be mixed at random without changing the meaning. He reports a study in which 457 people were asked if they understood the following headlines (1973: 192):

Rope Hope Move Flop

Leak Dash Shock

Hate Ban Bid Probe

Although very few of those questioned could explain what the head-lines meant, they nevertheless said they understood them. Since people are accustomed to seeing short groupings of dramatic words in newspaper headlines, they are understood in terms of their form more than content.

Another summary inflection device is the photo or "cut." In practice, photos are selected and used to support at a glance the emotional angle developed by a reporter. However, readers normally look at a photo before reading the copy, and the photo caption or "cutline" usually tells the reader how to interpret the emotional theme of the picture. Whereas sensationalist tabloids use photos and cutlines to tell the story and relegate written copy to minor signifi-cance, more conservative newspapers use photos to supplement written copy for either information or artistic purposes. Regardless of the manner in which photography is used in a newspaper, photo jour-nalism is considered a very powerful device for capturing attention, summarizing, and inflecting mood.

Inflection also involves how newspapers place *emphasis*. In iden-tifying emphasis techniques care must be taken to differentiate be-tween *what* is emphasized as a result of the perspective in contrast to *how* aspects of a story are emphasized. At this point our concern is with the latter.

For example, in emphasizing the dramatic character of an event, a tabloid uses candid photos, inflammatory vocabulary, and punctua-tion, and marks off stories with banner headlines or bold borders. Full-size newspapers use more subtle techniques to accomplish almost the same result. One example is "event-centered" reporting, which directs the reader's attention to particular kinds of information, namely, statistical data, places, names, titles, questions designed to

elicit yes or no answers—in short, what the hard-news journalists call
"facts." A typical example taken from the *Los Angeles Times* states:
"PG&E Hydro Project Tunnels into Problems: Hard-rock job takes
10 lives and has run two years and $300 million over estimates."
While these statistics are important, they are highlighted and
emphasized over other factors in a stark, isolated reality. As opposed
to directing attention to trends, processes, the integration of various
factors, attitudes, or the overall complexity of an issue, the event-
centered approach suggests to the reader that only a particular kind of
information (fact) is necessary to understand what is happening. It
amounts to the construction of a stereotype, which may exaggerate or
even distort the story.

For example, in the Watergate reporting, we constantly heard of
how former President Nixon slipped up, made errors in administering
his office, or privately made damning statements. Seldom did we hear
about the philosophy of the presidency in Nixon's view, the long
antagonism between himself and the press, or the fact that his tactics
were not unknown in previous administrations. As is the case with the
general conception of courts of law, event-centered reporting is based
on the assumption that particular facts decide a case rather than the
subtle construction of a perspective that serves to define the so-called
facts. By emphasizing facts, a newspaper tends to ignore the perspective or theory that interprets those facts.

Newspaper reporters also emphasize the strife, friction, and natural
disagreement that occur in various public agencies, societal institutions, and everyday life. Church versus state, federal versus local
government, owners versus workers, parents versus teenagers, and
similar oppositions make up the content of most newspaper copy. For
example, U.S. foreign relations, especially with the Soviet Union,
China, and the OPEC countries, are portrayed in terms of potential
and real conflict. Rather than discussing how and why all parties compete and support each other's ongoing competition for status and
power within their respective spheres of influence, we constantly get
the picture of international conflict. Consequently, emphasis is also
on the threat or danger that continually lurks around the corner.

Reporters also emphasize their investigative role in obtaining
stories and stimulating action. Since Pulitzer prizes are awarded for
stories that result in action beneficial to the public, reporters constantly emphasize their tireless vigil for the public good. Along with
the emphasis on their investigative role is an emphasis on the fact that

everyone is trying to hide something; therefore, reporters become cynical debunkers, as is illustrated in a *Chicago Tribune* headline: "How Invesco [Chicago-based corporation] Used Tax Loopholes." In a similar fashion, newspapers stress their insider status with reporters claiming to have their ear to the pulse of the nation and the door of the smoke-filled back room. Emphasis is on the notion that something new will be learned in the next edition.

Based on the wealth of information a newspaper possesses, the publisher's editorials are often paternalistic in explaining how things work, what action should be taken, and what benefits the public will receive. As the all-knowing and benevolent patriarch, a newspaper publisher emphasizes his or her duty to the readers. In contrast, feature columnists develop particular slants, as differentiated from news angles, which focus on the apparent significance of events or facts. A slant—such as Art Buchwald's political satire, a sports columnist's angry fan approach, Andy Rooney's trivia, William F. Buckley, Jr.'s, intellectualism, or James Reston's voice of reason—is a special type of inflection injected into the interpretation and analysis of various phenomena.

Finally, the printed word is a special inflection device itself. Words in print have a formality in appearance that lends a large degree of credibility or an official air to the subject. People may mouth the phrase "don't believe everything you read," but in practice they seem to believe "I only know what I read in the newspaper." In this sense, an inflection device that newspapers have established in the minds of the public is the belief that newspaper copy has an official appearing reality. As the saying goes, "If it's on the front page, then it must be news." The point is that something receives emphasis merely by appearing in the newspaper.

A final example of inflection in newspaper grammar involves the *rhythm* or flow in a story. Anyone who has read a good story knows the enjoyment of becoming so involved in a tale that all external stimuli are ignored. Capturing a reader in this manner is largely due to the rhythm established by a writer. While the techniques used to develop rhythm are quite difficult to describe, we are all aware of their existence and importance. As with any enjoyable musical performance, there is an emotional experience associated with a story that flows smoothly and rhythmically.

A recent example of a change in rhythm inflection of many newspapers is tied to the increase in stories devoted to human interest and modern, urban lifestyle. Articles on leisure living, self-help, hobbies, community service, and quality of life have expanded to the point that Sunday editions now devote up to a half-dozen, different sections on these topics. The emphasis in this copy is a "breeziness" in writing style (Bordewich, 1977). This chic, casual, cool, urbane style has become the hallmark of such editions as the *Los Angeles Times'* "Calendar" and "You" sections. All indications point to an increase in this (breeziness) emphasis in an effort to augment what TV culture establishes in much of its programming.

VOCABULARY

Of all mass media, print has the potential for the most sophisticated and varied use of words. Readers have time to ponder unusual words and leisurely relish a well-phrased sentence. However, as with other media, the degree of verbal sophistication depends on the audience. In glancing through a newspaper, one can easily assess the reading comprehension level for a specific section. Editorial page columns, byline features, and a few letters to the editor employ the most sophisticated vocabulary, followed by publisher editorials, economic news, straight news, and a general category of lifestyle features, sports, comics, and so on. For example, a quick scan of opinion columns by James Reston, George Will, and William F. Buckley, Jr., yielded such words as preeminently, atrophy, ominousness, lacerating, pernicious, congruent, orthodoxy, and ferocity, and such phrases as "pursuit of an unsustainable superiority" and "unreciprocated restraint." Although these words should be comprehensible to most editorial page readers, they are far too specialized for straight news or any other copy that follows the rule of matter-of-fact language.

In contrast, the sports page often contains play-on-words humor such as the familiar "Sabers Slash Bruins," "Vikings Club Giants," "Giants Squash Dodgers," "Pirates Steal One from Cubs," and so on, and so forth. Sports story headlines use liberal doses of puns as in "Construction of Muni Stadium Would Be Too Taxing," and "Arizona State Dukes (pitcher's name) Cowboys for Baseball Crown." As we all know, the pun is not restricted to the sports page. Any public official with a name easily used in puns is fair game; for example, Secretary of the Interior James Watts, as in "Watts Knew." Business stories do not escape either: "The World Oil Glut: It's a Gas for Consumers."

In addition, the poetic practice of alliteration is not unknown in newspaper copy (as well as in some textbooks). Former city editor of the *New York Herald Tribune* once described his job as dealing with "women, wampum, and wrongdoing." But with few exceptions journalists are not paid for poetry, good or bad. News copy must be comprehensible to the average reader, and some readers enjoy perusing the paper for those occasional "boners" in headlines and copy. In fact, some publications offer a nominal fee for examples of unintended meanings in the newspaper that either slip by a copy editor or are allowed to appear for the sake of a little humor. Examples include:

Dealers Will Hear Car Talk Friday Noon
—Newark (NJ) News

Quarter of a Million Chinese Live on Water
—Scenectady (NY) Gazette

Donald Blank Fulfills Last Duty to His City, Dies
—Memphis (TN) Commercial Appeal

Man Held in Miami After Shooting Bee
—Jacksonville Times-Union

Autos Killing 110 a Day; Let's Resolve to Do Better
—Boston Globe

Calf Born to Farmer With Two Heads
—Houston Daily Press

One thing that detection of newspaper boners indicates is that newspaper language has a particular grammar, and readers are aware of how that grammar may lead to unintended meanings. A word does not speak for itself; it is interpreted within grammatical structure. Alter the grammar, and the meaning changes.

Perspectives

READER INTERESTS

It is estimated that on the average 60 percent of the space in the typical daily newspaper is devoted to advertising, 20 percent to news, and 20 percent to features. Since commercial advertising brings in 90 percent of the total revenue, it follows that the amount of nonadvertising copy a paper can afford to print depends entirely on the amount of advertising it sells. As with commercial television and radio, ads are a necessary evil or benefit, depending on your viewpoint. But newspaper readers usually do not complain about ads, as they serve the practical function of informing people where they can buy a product and at what price. In contrast to television, newspaper readers usually know what they want to buy; they are looking for the sales. To facilitate this consumer activity, newspapers place ads in sections of the paper that are consistent with reader interests, and they run specific product ads on days of the week that coincide with consumer-purchasing practices. The Wednesday edition provides the food ads, Thursday and Friday are for department stores, Saturday is for house and auto fix-it projects, and Sunday is for real estate, fashion, and home furnishings. With this practice, readers do not feel interrupted by ads as they read the paper; in fact, they often search out ads that are relevant for their needs, and purchase the paper for ads they know will appear. Therefore, the fact that 60 percent of a newspaper's space is devoted to advertising is not a problem for many readers; it is often a primary reason for buying the paper.

In the early 1970s a market survey conducted by the American Newspaper Publishers Association (see Bordewich, 1977: 25) reported that the most widely read stories were: accidents and disasters (by 39 percent of the readers), letters to the editor (35 percent), crime (33 percent), human interest (33 percent), and advice columns (32 percent). Yet at that time the typical paper devoted only 2.4 percent of its space to accidents and disasters, 0.6 percent to letters to the editor, 3.9 percent to crime, 1.2 percent to human interest, and 3.1 percent to advice columns. Findings such as these led publishers to change their strategy from the old view that "we can determine what the people want," to what James E. Sauter, president of Booth Newspapers suggested: "The smartest marketers in America have discovered you can no longer sell what you make but you've got to make what your readers want" (Bordewich, 1977: 25). As a result, the front page of most newspapers began carrying more human interest and crime stories, accidents and disasters received more space, the editorial page prominently emphasized letters to the editor, and advice columns, especially on urban lifestyle, increased. Much of this developed in an attempt to attract the reader under 35, the reader who has grown up with television. In addition, newspapers targeted the 18- to 25-year-old market with more copy on youth-oriented entertainment and fashion.

Newspapers have generally become more specialized, providing what other media cannot or do not provide and adding new material to meet the public's changing interests. For example, since television news is primarily a headline service, newspapers claim to provide depth and detail, although this translates into more attention to interpretation and analysis. As issues apparently have become more complex, and as the desire to know seems to have increased, newspapers have shifted some attention from hard news to soft-news feature columns and analysis articles. At present, news magazines are the only other medium providing news analysis in any detail. This movement also correlates with a demographic change in the population: Today over half of all students who complete high school go on to college and (we assume) become more interested and better prepared to tackle sophisticated news analysis. However, many newspapers also highlight spot news coverage for the individual who has no immediate access to television and wants a quick scan of the news while rushing to work. Yet, as with television, spot news tends to be superficial, overly dramatic, and often trivial.

Newspapers have also increased syndicated feature material, most of which may be classified as entertainment. Astrology, book reviews, bridge, comics, crossword puzzles, "Dear Abby," historical anecdotes, music, stage and screen, things to do, the television and radio guide, and columns on hobbies, health matters, and so on all serve leisure time reading and are commonly found in daily newspapers everywhere. Specialized interests do not end with leisure time or entertainment interests. Large circulation papers have recently developed special sections for suburban and nearby urban locales. A typical example is the *Arizona Republic,* which has special sections for northeast and northwest Phoenix, Scottsdale, Tempe, and Mesa. The *Los Angeles Times* carries a special edition for urban centers as far away as San Diego. These regional minipapers have become popular with readers and profitable in advertising revenue. Since two-thirds of the population now live in metropolitan areas, we can expect daily newspapers to expand their markets and devote more newsprint to the varied aspects of urban living. But precisely what aspects of urban living do publishers consider newsworthy? How, among the plethora of information available, do they select what will be printed? More important, how do journalists interpret the information they select? That is, what perspectives do they use?

JOURNALISM PERSPECTIVES

As defined in the previous chapter, "perspective" refers to a theory that is used to select and define physical and social phenomena. In professional journalism, a dominant perspective since the turn of the century has been objectivity, or reporting the "facts." This framework is based on the general belief in Western society that science is the best method for discovering truth and that truth is discovered through the unbiased identification of facts. But for the scientist, facts are constructions based on a theory, a theory that guides the observer in what to observe and how to interpret what is observed. Nevertheless, belief in objectivity as a form of unbiased observation and in facts as things that have an independent reality still pervades common thinking, and the craft of journalism is no exception.

Given that objectivity in science has primarily been achieved through methods of quantification (counting), journalists over the years have stressed a numerical description of social phenomena and achieved objectivity in terms of event-centered reporting. Events have been perceived and interpreted to readers through a count of things such as time, money, people, acts, and so on. For example, the Iranian hostage crisis during 1980-1981 was constantly referred to by the size of hostile crowds, the number of hostages, and the number of days "America was held hostage" by the Iranians. Economic news is reported in terms of an inflation rate, an interest rate, the Dow Jones index, and the GNP. While numbers are important, they are only significant in the context of particular frameworks that rarely are explained to readers. In fact, these numbers are often misinterpreted or lead to false conclusions. One example is the body count report given almost daily during the Vietnam War. Anyone exposed to the news day after day during the mid-sixties was bound to think that American forces were continually successful. Yet the opposite was true; we were winning the body count and losing the war. Based on experiences such as these some journalists and journalism critics have argued persuasively that an objective formula news approach is not that objective after all. But by and large, event-centered reporting and the perspective of presenting so-called hard facts still dominate contemporary journalism.

In an effort to be objective and report facts that can be supported, journalists also employ what may be called the *official source per-*

spective. Given that a reporter's daily routine occurs during the
normal 9-to-5 working hours and that deadlines must be met, there is
a reliance on official documents and people occupying official positions in public and private organizations. Official documents and
officials are easily accessible and the information provided is
legitimate in appearance. On crime matters reporters contact the
police, on rising utility bills they contact the utility companies, and on
foreign policy they contact the State Department. Although this practice seems logical, the result is that readers often receive only the
"official" or P-R viewpoint. As Neil Shine, city editor of the *Detroit
Free Press* during the late 1960s (a period of racial unrest in Detroit),
told a convention of Associated Press managers in 1970:

> One of the major things we learned in 1967 was that we can no longer
> rely on official reports from official sources when the sources them-
> selves are parties to the conflict. According to every police and
> National Guard source during the Detroit riot, sniper activity was
> rampant, deadly and organized.
>
> The official reports detailed it, and we bought it. In one lead story,
> based on police reports, we had Negro snipers launching an offensive
> from the west side of the city to the borders of Grosse Pointe.
>
> Phrases like "nests of snipers" and "sniper teams" kept popping up in
> the paper. When the police said a death was a sniper death, we reported
> it as such. Official police reports listed at least 15 of the 43 riot deaths
> as caused by snipers.
>
> A six-week investigation by a three-man team of Free Press reporters
> uncovered no evidence of massive sniping. When the smoke of the riot
> had cleared, there was one confirmed sniping incident—a drunk with a
> pistol who was killed by the police.
>
> Reporting conflict has taught us that a riot is not just a succession of
> facts and the tendency to report it uncritically and without asking the
> tougher questions is an abdication of everything a newspaper should
> stand for.
>
> A riot is a civil war being fought in your own back yard and a critical
> role is essential lest the riot itself be used as an excuse for acts that
> would, in another situation, be intolerable.
>
> In normal times the statements of government officialdom may auto-
> matically be news—reportable per se simply for the fact of their
> happening.

But when the established bureaucracy is under attack and the system itself is being challenged, the truth requires that both versions be examined and judged on their merits [Krieghbaum, 1973: 110-111].

Despite these lessons, the demands of deadlines, checking for accuracy, and the perspective of event-centered reporting continue to promote an official-source perspective among journalists. Examine any current newspaper, and examples are bound to emerge.

In the 1960s an alternative perspective to event-centered/objective reporting emerged, principally through the activities of the underground press *(Berkeley Barb, L.A. Free Press,* and the *Village Voice)* and several notable magazine and newspaper journalists (Jimmy Breslin, Hunter S. Thompson, and Tom Wolfe). Actually, *new journalism* is not a new phenomenon as its roots go back to the very beginning of journalism in colonial America. Whether it is called advocacy journalism, as it was during the pre-mass-press days or, more recently, soft news and process-oriented reporting, the result is basically the same. New journalism is a blatant violation of the "objective news" formula. As Hunter S. Thompson states:

> The only thing I ever saw that came close to objective journalism was a closed-circuit TV setup that watched shoplifters in the General Store at Woody Creek, Colorado. . . . With the possible exception of box scores, race results, and stock market tabulations, there is no such thing as objective journalism. The phrase itself is a pompous contradiction in terms [Whetmore, 1979: 54].

In new journalism reporters may emphasize a general trend that seems to engulf a particular event, stress the attitudes of people involved in an event, or describe the interaction of seemingly unrelated factors that give a feel for what is happening in a situation. They may use metaphor or analogy literally to paint a picture of a situation. They may use oblique examples that typify or capture the essence of a story as Tom Wolfe is so fond of doing. In one of his books, *The Right Stuff,* Wolfe describes the behind-the-scenes life of the first astronauts as the life of a bunch of fun-loving, free-wheeling kids who love to play with high-risk toys that take them to the edge of disaster and back. Wolfe found the essence of those first astronauts in Chuck Yeager, who tested the prototype for the space shuttle. These guys had more than training, ability, and brains; they had that emotional ingredient that is "the right stuff." Journalism such as Tom Wolfe's provides readers with a personal view of intimate details and the passion in a situation. Written in a style antithetical to event-centered reporting, new journalism is increasing in popularity as evidenced through the addition of more news analysis, feature stories, and feature columnists in newspapers across the country.

Objectivity via event-centered reporting and new journalism are only two among many perspectives employed in newspapers to select and define phenomena to readers. To discover others, return to the discussion of format grammar. Each inflection technique has a corresponding perspective that guides the editor and reporter. Whereas inflection techniques consist of *how* something is presented, a perspective guides the journalist in determining *what* to report. For example, an important rule is that unusual or bizarre events are newsworthy. You've heard the tired old saying, "If dog bites man it's not news, but if man bites dog . . . !" So pervasive is the criterion of the improbable event that a continuum could be constructed with the commonplace at one end of the unusual at the other. Every newspaper from the conservative *New York Times* to the sensational *National Enquirer* could be placed on that continuum. But the unusual or bizarre has no intrinsic news value without a perspective to provide meaning—and that perspective is entertainment.

The definition of entertainment, as it has emerged over the centuries, involves the notion that anything placed in an entertainment perspective need not be taken seriously. Even tabloid headlines such as "I saw Dad stab Mom" are horrifying but enticing for their morbid curiosity, more so than as a serious news consideration. A headline such as "Cancer-Ravaged Family Loses Another" is tragic yet uncommon enough to be pitied rather than feared. In contrast, a headline stating "U.S. Facing Chaos in Air Traffic Strike" has serious import for many people and contains nothing remotely entertaining. In the first two examples a reader could interpret the message within a serious as opposed to an entertainment framework, but given the unusual character of these vents, readers are more likely to interpret them as bizarre or rare and place them in a perspective that is, at least, similar to entertainment. The same holds true for dramatic events such as fires, auto accidents, miners trapped in mineshafts, shipwrecks, and natural disasters. In these examples the story is always enhanced by photographs depicting the tragedy.

Photojournalism has become an art of portraying the dramatic—often death and destruction. A striking example of a prize-winning

photo was the Saigon National Police Chief shooting an enemy captive in the head on the streets of Saigon during the Vietnam War.
Another photo, one that evoked considerable emotional reaction,
was of a young woman kneeling with outstretched arms beside the
dead body of a student on the Kent State campus in May of 1970.
Cutlines in various papers claimed (Krieghbaum, 1973: 124):

Student Discovers Classmate Lying Dead After Guard Fired on Crowd of Protesters

A Coed Screamed Over the Body of Dead Classmate on the Campus of Kent State University

"He's Dead!" Coed Screams as Classmate Lies Slain ... on campus of Kent State University Monday

The facts were that the woman in the photo was not a classmate of the
dead student but a fourteen-year-old runaway from Florida. While
the photographic symbol of the Kent State shooting may have been
justified, cutline writers in this instance created an image and an
emotional theme to dramatize the event rather than simply reported
facts.

Turning to the more enjoyable side of the entertainment perspective, note the number of feature columns in sports, self-help, advice,
lifestyle, and politics that use humor. Add to these the comics,
anecdote fillers, puns in headlines, political cartoons, Sunday
magazine articles, and so on, and it appears that a large portion of
nonadvertising space in newspapers is devoted, at least indirectly, to
entertainment. Certainly a fair question is, "Where would contemporary journalism be without an entertainment perspective?"

Journalists also employ a *conflict perspective* in framing and interpreting a story. Since competition and conflict are common features
of everyday life, it is somewhat logical that journalists should assume
and perceive competition and conflict in many of the stories they
report, e.g., nation versus nation, business versus government, consumers versus business, citizens versus the bureaucracy, and so on.
Examine headlines on a typical day and note how many imply conflict. Debunking is part of the conflict perspective, an approach
deeply embedded in the craft of journalism. Defined as the practice of
uncovering the hidden or underlying realities, a debunking attitude is

engendered by the assumption that all is not as it appears on the surface. In using a debunking perspective, journalists are prone to imply that people and organizations who are the focus of stories are being less than candid. For example, the Watergate hearing became an arena for debunking the entire political strategy of the Nixon presidential campaign of 1972. When reporters queried President Carter on the attempted rescue of hostages held in Iran, the innuendo was that Carter may have used the rescue mission as part of his reelection strategy. It is no surprise that a savvy public learns to "read between the lines" of many news stories, adopting the same debunking perspective used by the press.

And finally, the time-worn perspective of "scoop" journalism is worth mentioning for two reasons. First, editors constantly demand new information. Whether it is a new item in a criminal case, a fresh approach to a continuing community problem, a new trend, or a scientific discovery, a major criterion for acceptability as news is whether or not the information is or appears to be new. A few headlines may demonstrate the point: "Police Put Bob Crane Case on Shelf: Nothing New" (a case of nothing new being new?), "New Treatment Heals Stubborn Sores," "Homesteaders of the 80's Settle in Inner Cities," "Communication Systems Vulnerable to One Pulse Bomb," and "Can U.S. Survive a Football Strike?" Each headline implies something new even though several of the stories are part of a continuing series and others are attempts to make the mundane look new and interesting. They suggest that creativity in presenting something as appearing new is actually more important than the old notion of exclusive information.

Another point related to the so-called scoop is what may be termed the "insider syndrome." Private or secret information, as suggested by the debunking perspective, is not only commonly believed to exist in most stories of dramatic importance; it is demanded by the public and a rather cynical fraternity of journalists. To have inside information is not only simply a matter of knowing the true story; it carries a sense of intimacy and status in our society. Consequently, there is significant pressure to obtain inside information even when it is difficult or impossible to obtain. The perspective is that inside information exists and that the good reporter is one who has it.

These perspectives, and by no means have I exhausted the list, constitute the framework for what professional journalists and critics call "news angles." Specifically, a news angle refers to an event or a phenomenon around which a reporter can build a story. In the book, *Creating Reality: How TV Distorts Events* (1976), David Altheide states that an "angle facilitates placing unique occurrences in a broader context and, in a sense, rendering meaning by association." An angle, then, is a focus of attention used to construct the meaning of a story. In citing numerous examples, Altheide argues that news angles are often predetermined before reporters to into the field to "get the story." Restated, news angles are based on perspectives common to all journalists.

In summary, the final copy we read from day to day is the result of a particular newspaper grammar and journalistic perspectives. Syntax, inflection, and specialized vocabulary work together with perspectives such as event-centered reporting, new journalism, entertainment, and the like to form the current strategy in printing a newspaper.

Media Influence

Consider what appears to be a mundane aspect of reading a newspaper. In following rather habitual reading patterns, people read the paper at specific times of the day, read sections in a particular order, and often read while engaged in other activities such as eating, riding public transportation, or watching television. As such, an individual can avoid talking to others in situations that may be mildly uncomfortable or potentially irritating. At times, a person may simply look at the paper while thinking about other matters. In this manner, reading the paper is symbolic of doing something useful rather than just wasting time. Sociologically, reading the newspaper is a legitimate activity and consequently a positive attribute in constructing a sense of self—"I am a newspaper reader." Take this a step further to the person who proudly and perhaps haughtily says, "I read the *New York Times.*" In these statements, individuals are fundamentally announcing that newspapers are significant in their lives, serving as references for self-definition and appraisal. As a routine, a legitimate activity, and a self-definition reference, the newspaper is quite likely to be a source of influence. At least the reader is likely to be open to the strategies employed by his or her newspaper.

As stated previously, the familiar strategies employed in newspaper communication involve a knowledge of grammar, which enables journalists and readers to anticipate with ease the composition, inflection, and vocabulary of newspaper stories. Familiarity with this grammar constitutes the rules for interaction between journalists and readers, facilitating selective attention and the construction of meanings through various perspectives used in print journalism. The perspective of event-centered reporting orients journalists and readers to an understanding of social phenomena through specific events, factual summaries of those events, and the objective appearance of official sources of information. In contrast, a variety of alternative approaches under the label of "new journalism" orient the interaction of reporters and readers to understanding various phenomena through constructing scenes, descriptive monologues of significant actions, and the underlying emotional theme of the situation. The entertainment perspective with drama and humor fosters an emphasis on something extraordinary, while the investigation framework (debunking) results in conflict and cynicism as well as an expectation of insider information. Given these characteristics, what are some of the more apparent consequences?

It was suggested in the discussion of event-centered reporting that a superficial understanding of events and issues could easily result from this traditional practice. With only a few facts or implied facts provided in headlines and lead-ins, there exists the distinct danger that reporters and readers will oversimplify complex issues, make unwarranted inferences, and distort what actually may have occurred. For example, examine the following headlines on an earthquake in Iran: The *New York Times* stated matter-of-factly "Toll put at 1,500" and provided a map pinpointing the location of the quake. The *Boston Globe* increased the death figure and said, "15,000-30,000 Killed." The *Minneapolis Tribune* hedged the drama a bit with "Thousands said Dead." And the *San Francisco Chronicle* flatly stated, "Thousands Die." Whereas the *Times* was conservative and gave detailed information, the other papers omitted detail and exaggerated or allowed the reader to exaggerate the death toll. In this example, all but the *Times* omitted important facts and implied others. The person who quickly scans headlines with an uncritical frame of mind is likely to think he or she has an objective understanding of an event when they may not be true at all.

A second consequence of event-centered reporting occurs when the event itself takes on a primacy in understanding a social issue without the understanding of what led to the event or of the context in which the event occurred. This clearly was the case in the Iranian hostage crisis. Both broadcast and print media generally failed to report the factors that led to the Iranian student action of holding U.S. Embassy personnel hostage. Factors generally ignored included the former Shah's rule of terror, religious conflict within Iran, and the desire among these students to overcome a label of being apathetic or neutral and prove to the new leadership they were worthy of continued support in the university. Instead, the media proclaimed that America was being held hostage, and that event alone was all most people knew or cared to know (Altheide, 1982).

A third consequence of event-centered reporting relates to the legitimacy of news content that results from the use of official sources for information. As described earlier, reporters use official sources in part out of convenience and in part because of the official appearance, legitimacy, and accountability of these sources. When the practice of using official sources is placed in context with other dimensions of the factual event-centered approach, the result is a very objective-appearing procedure that adds significantly to the naive notion that newspaper journalism is usually objective and unbiased. Yet official sources are usually a one-sided (PR) viewpoint. As the respected journalist, Joseph Alsop, once stated, "All government handouts lie. Some lie more than others" (Rivers, 1970: 49). For example, in 1981 Israeli aircraft bombed an Iraqi nuclear power plant with the explanation that the plant was a front for a nuclear bomb factory. American headlines read "Begin: Iraq Had Secret A-bomb Plant." Bear in mind, however, that to that date there was no confirmation that Middle Eastern states (except Israel) had nuclear arms capability. But Begin's words lend credibility to such a fact despite the lack of independent evidence.

An additional point on the significance of official sources is that large newspaper chains including Gannett and even The New York Times Co. interlock with many of the top corporations (as listed in *Fortune* magazine). Peter Dreier and Steve Weinberg stated (1979: 51): "300 directors of the nation's 25 largest newspaper companies have thousands of interlocks with institutions these papers cover—or fail to cover."

Finally, influence resulting from event-centered reporting is manifest in a belief that complexity can be reduced to simplicity through brief summaries. Consequently, to feel knowledgeable does not require extensive study; only quick summaries of facts and visual impressions are needed. A few moments with the morning paper and both journalists and readers may feel they have the essential information under hat. Certainly some news items, such as one-time crime stories, accidents, and some human interest happenings, can be adequately presented and summarized through an event-centered approach. The problem occurs when readers and journalists deal with serious and more complex institutional issues in the same manner. Can reliance on quick summaries result in understanding problems such as inflation when all you know are the consumer price index, the prime interest rate, and that the current administration has a plan? At best this allows a person to talk about inflation only in very superficial terms.

New journalism, in all its varied forms, presents alternatives to the traditional event-centered format, although its intent is still to inform the public in the best manner possible. As new journalist Gay Talese (1971: vii) argues, new journalism "is or should be as reliable as the most reliable reportage, although it seeks a larger truth than is possible through an adherence to the rigid organization style of the old form." Many readers enjoy the personalized style and viewpoint of astute reporters such as Talese, and it does seem at a larger truth or more comprehensive picture is possible through good new journalism practices. As Tom Wolfe (1973) argues, these new forms describe issues and events through a scenic construction, they provide considerable background information, they focus on everyday lifestyle social actions ("status life"), they report anecdotal material that seems to typify a subject, and they emphasize the underlying emotional themes.

But as with event-centered reporting, the very advantages proclaimed by new journalists in their approach can have adverse consequences if reporters and readers fail to recognize the potential limitations. The personalized communication of new journalism may be free of the belief that objectivity is more probable through event-centered reporting. However, this freedom is also license for partisanship if the reporter so chooses. The problem is that since new journalism is a more personalized and intimate form of communication, readers and other reporters may come to depend on the ideas of a specific reporter. Over the years this has occurred among the followers of such political analysts as Walter Lippmann, William F. Buckley, Jr., and James Reston. But when the form of the journalism involves an internal narration (described by Tom Wolfe, 1973) in which the reader is vicariously placed in the thoughts of the reporter, the result is far more intimate and potentially more suggestive than traditional objective journalism or political analysis. Through the various forms of new journalism, readers and other reporters may come to define a particular reporter (such as Gay Talese) as a significant other, someone significant for how the reader defines and evaluates him- or herself. Therefore, as communication becomes more personal, social psychological factors become more important, and new journalism's personalized form is potentially very influential.

Differences between so-called objective and new journalism appear to be philosophical, with proponents of objective journalism criticizing the new journalists for being lazy, sloppy, subjective, and concerned more with style than with reporting a story. Consequently, errors committed by the press are sometimes explained as problems inherent in new journalism. For example, in 1981 a Pulitzer Prize was given to Janet Cook of the *Washington Post* for a story on an eight-year-old heroin addict. When it came to light that Cook fabricated the entire story, many looked for something to blame. Norman Isaacs, chairman of the media watchdog National News Council blamed new journalism. In a *Christian Science Monitor* article, Isaacs was quoted as saying:

> It [new journalism] has created a "looseness" in the craft of journalism. You have reporters who've adopted the thesis of Tom Wolfe that a news story can't be explained unless a reporter gives vent to emotion . . . and instinct. Attribution [to a named source] doesn't matter. It's "Don't bother me about the facts. I know this is true. I have a feeling it's true" [Malone, 1981: 5].

Ned Schnurman, executive producer of the PBS TV program *Inside Story,* agreed with Isaacs, "If there has been a failure, it's that there has been a glamorizing of investigative reporting and new journalism and of point-of-view journalism." But Schnurman also added that TV's promotion of journalists to a celebrity status is also a factor: "TV focuses attention on personalities of news reporters and newspapers have followed suit" (Malone, 1981: 5) While Isaacs and Schnurman have a criticism worth considering, it seems unlikely that new journalism is inherently more prone to fabricating stories or exaggerating events than event-centered reporting. However, the increasing star status among reporters may increase the competition, especially among young journalists, for the fame and fortune that follow. It is not new journalism as a journalistic form that lends itself to fictitious or exaggerated reporting, but the quest for fame and fortune.

Yet the trend seems to be in the direction of change in journalism. Note the comments of Howard K. Smith of ABC-TV, who was never considered a radical in journalism:

> Now we simply have to have reporters who are scholars, and who are not cynical but deeply concerned and compassionate. They need training and profound continuing scholarship, and they need a background of wide experience. . . . It is a remarkable thing that in a nation so continuously changing as ours, news writing, in newspapers in particular, is hackneyed, frozen into stereotypes that have not changed for over half a century. We are still taught and we still practice in all our newspapers that the way to present news is to pack the "who, what, when, and where" all in the first paragraph, then let the rest trail off into a dull listing of less essential details. . . . It so happens that we live in a fascinating time, and if journalism doesn't teach journalists to write up to the dramatic level of their times, then it doesn't have any purpose [Lecture at Memphis State University, 1969].

Entertainment has and will continue to be the hallmark of all media that appeal to widely diverse audience interests as it is the common denominator most people share. People do not wish to be entertained all the time, nor even most of the time, but in attempting to appeal to a wide variety of people, entertainment will attract those who normally might not pay attention to a medium. And, since show business sells, a successful strategy has been to increase the amount of space devoted to this perspective. The increase in human interest, lifestyle, sports, and other entertainment features is a direct response to the apparent audience desire for the lighter side of the news. However, of importance for media influence is not the fact that people may simply want more and more entertainment, but that serious news is both replaced and tinged with entertainment.

On the inside of the paper it is easy to find stories on human interest with a humorous twist or the dramatic tragedy of crime, accidents, disasters, and harrowing experiences. What typically occurs in these stories is an exaggerated emphasis on the out-of-the-ordinary event. For example, I obtained first-hand information on an adventure story reported in the *Arizona Republic* on June 23, 1981. The story described a nine-month, ocean-sailing voyage of a local businessman and his family. The report told how he learned the fine points of sailing under adverse conditions, the harrowing experience of lashing all crew members to the deck during gale-force winds, and how they all learned to survive by harvesting the sea's bounty while avoiding sharks. In reality, this would-be sailor was rarely under sail power (relying on his diesel engines), he panicked during a 30-knot fresh breeze at night, and depended on the goodwill of neighboring boats for fish and lobster. The reporter neglected to verify the man's story probably because it was relatively harmless entertainment, although distorted nevertheless.

Stories such as these suggest that journalists and readers are so willing to accpet the bizarre, the comic relief, and the harrowing adventure that exaggeration becomes the rule rather than the exception. Since entertainment by definition is something extraordinary, stories are written to excite or amuse. The media influence in this approach is not only that journalists and readers share the perspective of entertainment, but that exaggeration and distortion become reality. Consequently, to the captivated reader, the world may appear increasingly more crime ridden, more terrifying, and perhaps more insanely humorous.

A more common problem is the use of entertainment to frame more serious institutional matters of community life. Reference here is not to the desirable, humorous anecdotes found daily in public and private life, but to the failure to take seriously, either for reasons of exaggerated drama or humor, the essential issues that affect the value and normative fabric of society. An example would be attention to a political campaign for the sake of its drama rather than to the substance of campaign issues, or poking fun at OPEC nations as a substitute for seriously addressing energy conservation. Certainly a little comic relief is welcome at times, but drama or humor should not mask the challenges that need to be faced, nor should the real human tragedy be exploited for the sake of excitement, mystery, or morbid curiosity.

If entertainment masks, distorts, or changes various issues to a nonserious status, then of what consequence is the conflict and debunking framework? It might appear that in presenting an issue as the natural conflict between different agents in society and constantly suggesting that public appearance needs to be debunked, the press would stimulate greater public awareness and action, which, on occasion, has been true. But there are also indications the opposite is occurring—that is, the public may increasingly rely on media to do the job. Analyzing the work of William Stephenson, Erving Goffman, and others, Dennis Davis and Stanley Baran (1981) argue that as media have become predominant in society, people are less likely to express themselves in action and rely instead on media simulations—simulations that appear flawless and effective compared to our everyday stumblings and apprehensions.

In performing its watchdog role, the press usually demonstrates its skill and prowess in showing the public what to investigate and how it should be done. Yet instead of encouraging public involvement, the press allows readers to sit back as spectators and watch the fight or withdraw with the cynical attitude that little can be accomplished by the average person. Again, the point is not that a conflict/debunking perspective necessarily inhibits public involvement but that in applying this perspective journalists seldom encourage the public to take its rightful place in the action. As a colleague, Beverley Cuthbertson, remarked to me while analyzing the press's role in the aflatoxin and pesticide controversy in Arizona over the past few years, newspapers became an observed arena primarily involving the public in an emotional sense rather than encouraging people to act on their own in solving problems. If the low voter turnout in recent national elections is any indication, the public may be expecting the media to do more than observe and report—to act as well.

The insider syndrome of the investigative framework is one of the most interesting aspects of newspapers to both journalists and readers. Although the "story behind the story," the exposé, the hidden facts, or the new discovery are all part of the debunking perspective, the insider syndrome has a unique characteristic in that it is a primary means for obtaining status within journalistic circles. The dogged determinism required to dig up the facts or uncover the fascinating behind-the-scenes picture has been romanticized by nearly every Hollywood film or TV program ever devoted to newspaper journalism. In these occasionally truthful protrayals, the "good" reporter is defined as someone who takes risks either to life and limb, such as the crime reporter or war correspondent, or who risks losing his or her job if caught using illegal means to obtain the story. As in the code of show business, the news story must be told, and telling it earns the respect and admiration of fellow journalists and readers alike. Indeed, the highest award in journalism, the Pulitzer Prize, is usually given to the daring photographer, the crusading reporter, or the courageous editor and publisher for going beyond the everyday routine to obtain and print the hard-to-get or suppressed story. So important is this status and reward that a few reporters have recently gone too far and fabricated stories and photos. As is the case with the exaggeration in entertainment, the insider zeal can lead to distortion, sometimes of significant consequence. The consequence of this practice is simply that both journalists and readers are, as Daniel Boorstin argues in *The Image* (1964: 5-6), "ruled by extravagant expectations. . . . By harbouring, nourishing, and ever enlarging our extravagant expectations we create the demand for illusions with which we deceive ourselves."

Finally, the investigator role that leads to the insider syndrome may result in an aggravation of all the points made previously plus the potential for raising gossip, rumor, and innuendo to a new level of interaction in community life. Given the superficiality and primacy of events through event-centered reporting; the intimacy of personal viewpoint in new journalism; the mystery, drama, and levity of entertainment; the cynicism of debunking; and a zest for insider information, an encompassing media culture of rather frightening proportions is developing: The newspaper is becoming one giant gossip column. While gossip as media culture may seem rather outrageous, when treated as a hypothetical, the form and content of the press and other media begin to look quite different.

In summarizing the potential consequences of newspaper grammar and perspectives, several points call for additional emphasis. First is the acceptance by journalists and readers of superficiality in news, especially front-page news. Since a few hard facts are often allowed to define the essence of an event without contextual information, the event itself is often emphaiszed in isolation rather than seen as part of a larger process. Although professionals might argue that front-page news is necessarily a superficial summary with detail and analysis found on stories inside the paper, the problem is that people may become satisfied with superficial summaries and fail to be concerned with the detail. In addition, we can fault the nature of the summaries constructed through the event-centered formula as inadequate and sometimes misleading. Therefore, a second aspect of the acceptance of superficiality is an acceptance of the nature of the summary, particularly those summaries that emphasize the entertainment perspective. On this point, journalists and readers appear to be satisfied with the emotional excitement or enjoyment that comes from the exaggerated drama or humor injected into news. The problem associated with this dimension of media influence may not only include a satisfaction with distorted reality, but also an unwillingness to interpret information in a critical manner.

As argued previously, using official sources because it facilitates attribution (naming a source), the official appearance of words in print, and the tradition of the press as a community watchdog all lend the appearance of credibility to newspaper articles. Consequently, journalists and readers may uncritically accept the press as a legitimate agent for determining the nature of problems, the information necessary to deal with problems, and the reasonable solution to problems. A good example of the uncritical attitude among readers and journalists is the acceptance of "government by leak" and of information attributed to unnamed but so-called reliable sources. Particularly since Watergate and "deep throat" (the unnamed source used by Woodward and Bernstein in their exposé of President Nixon), both journalists and readers seem all too willing to believe in the authenticity and reliability of blind news information. Yet acceptance of this practice allows for considerable abuse. Reporters can be manipulated by the official sources who leak information, reporters can dupe each other unknowingly, and readers can be manipulated.

Another point to be emphasized is the potential for seeing more than is warranted by the facts. The accepted role of investigative reporting, debunking, new journalism style, the insider syndrome, and entertainment all interact to produce the potential for exaggeration. Added to these factors is the intense competition, especially among young reporters seeking acceptance and status. The propensity for exaggeration and making a journalistic name by jumping on an apparent big story bandwagon is dramatically detailed by Peter Braestrup (1978) by his massive study of the Tet Offensive (1968) during the Vietnam War. Braestrup describes how the Tet story became exaggerated into a giantic military defeat for U.S. and South Vietnamese forces. Actually, quite the opposite was true; North Vietnam and the Viet Cong never fully recovered from their huge losses in the Tet Offensive, nor did they achieve significant military gain. But the story in the United States was different, and it cost President Johnson an opportunity for reelection.

Finally, it must be emphasized that an audience has complicity in the emerging influence of media. All too often critics of media blame the media and fail to see that communication is a two-way interaction, with the audience as an active participant in the ongoing process (see Appendix A). In each dimension of media influence discussed, the reader must be seen as a willing party by design or the unfortunate loser by default.

CHAPTER 3

NOVELS AND MAGAZINES
Dreams and Subcultures

Novels

If books can be defined as a permanent but mobile record of human interaction, they initially appeared as clay tablets in ancient Babylonia, as bamboo scrolls in ancient China, and as papyrus parchments in Egypt. Each major ancient civilization had some form of written records that could be transported and reproduced with moderate efficiency. But it was not until the fifteenth century that cheap paper and movable type made possible the book as we know it today.

American book publishing has progressed through three or four major periods. In colonial America, individual families published religious works, scholarly political and social treatises, and almanacs, such as Ben Franklin's *Poor Richard's Almanac* (1733-1758), which were prized for artistic and printing craftsmanship as well as content. Given the expense of publishing and distribution, the publisher's audience during this period consisted of the wealthy and intellectual elite.

With the introduction of the dime novel during the mid-1800s and the gradual increase in literacy, publishing expanded to a larger audience. Typical of the emerging *commercial period* were the 120 titles and 30 million copies of Horatio Alger's "poor boy makes good" formula, Herman Melville's sophisticated *Moby Dick* (1851), and Harriet Beecher Stowe's moving *Uncle Tom's Cabin* (1852). At the turn of the century, commercial publishing was enhanced by technological development, which increased the speed of production and resulted in a more standardized format. With the national literacy rate at 90 percent. Book of the Month Club (1926) and the Literary Guild (1927) brought a steady offering of fiction and nonfiction to a large audience at nominal cost. Authors such as Hemingway, Steinbeck, and Mitchell significantly affected public attitudes, established the novel as legitimate entertainment, and expanded what is known as the "trade" market in publishing.

Following World War II, commercial publishing entered *big business*. Aided by the GI Bill, returning veterans flocked to colleges, and the textbook market exploded. The appetite for fiction and nonfiction also seemed insatiable, particularly in response to the new practice of issuing inexpensive paperback editions. Family publishing houses became corporations, which in turn merged or were gobbled up by communication conglomerates. By the 1970s, book publishing was a large-scale and very profitable, although highly risky, industry. Today, 25 percent of the population are considered hard-core book readers, and at least half the adult population read one or more books a year. With 40,000 titles published each year, of which two-thirds are new, gross sales topped 4 billion in 1980. Despite the massive numbers of new books each year, sales of hardcover editions seldom exceed 10,000 copies, and paperback sales are normally under 100,000 (only a few make the million mark)—small figures compared to film and TV audiences and record sales. Book publishing can be profitable but generally on a small scale as only 3 percent of all publishers account for some 70 percent of all sales.

From its beginning as a craft for a select audience, publishing has grown to a diverse industry serving every social strata and facet of American culture. In classifying this diversity, a generally agreed-upon system breaks publishing into the legitimate commercial "trade" of fiction and nonfiction, textbooks, scholarly works, technical and scientific books, children's literature, law books, and medical reports. Of these, I will focus on trade books, particularly the popular novel, as this category may have the most significant effect on the developing media culture of modern urban society.

In very general terms, a novel can be defined as a long fictitious narrative using various techniques to cover unlimited subject matter. But what do novelists write about, how do they do it, and why? Using a little sociological sense we can hypothesize that authors will write for particular audiences and that interests of authors and readers will coincide with the major cultural themes of problems of the times. Using this approach, we can readily see the major differences in novels from the classical Greek period, to the Renaissance, Elizabethan England, nineteenth-century Russia, and the modern industrial West.

In a seminal essay on the nature of novels, Lionel Trilling (1950) characterized the modern novel as a description of the experiences of a single individual who must confront an unfamiliar or ambiguous social environment. Often the plot involves the battle between the ideals of the hero and the corrupted practical reality that must be faced. This characterization suggests that individualism, the complexity and rapid change of modern society, and the viability of various ideologies are as central to the contemporary novel as they are central to modern society itself. Restated, the modern novel often depicts the problems encountered by the struggling individual (often middle class) in striving to make sense of, negotiate, cope with, and achieve success in the modern world. The novelist writes to a literate, somewhat reflective, and critical-thinking individual who is coming to terms with problems many of us share. The symbolism and plots employed by novelists may be oblique (Emily Dickinson once advised, "Tell it slant"), but the central themes are common. Every genre, from gothic romance, mystery, adventure, and science fiction to the new nonfiction, realism, or whatever, fits this sociological analysis. But to describe the success of particular novels we need to be more precise.

Returning to a sociological perspective, a novel comes to fruition through the interrelationships of author, agent, editor/publisher, advertiser, sales personnel, reviewer, and reader. An author develops an idea, the author's agent (most successful authors employ agents who function in the same manner as does an actor's agent) sells the idea to an editor of a publishing house, the author and editor consult over content and deadlines, the editor sells the idea to the publisher (team of decision makers), the author and editor engage in an ongoing negotition over style and content, the editor/publisher arranges for an advertising and sales campaign, reviewers have their say, and the reader responds by purchasing the book and talking about it to others. Since negotiation occurs at each stage of this process, the relationship is never a direct contact between author and literary circle, nor is the final product the result of a pure commitment to an artistic ideal. Writing and publishing novels is a commercial enterprise, tempered by the parameters of public interest, as noted in the previous paragraph.

In describing the interaction process of producing a novel, Ted Morgan (1982) wrote an excellent account of how *Jaws* emerged from a vague idea by author Peter Benchley to an enormous bestseller and film blockbuster. Morgan's description is not only detailed; it is insightful in focusing on the critical interactions that affected the final outcome. He shows that since this was Benchley's first novel, Doubleday was very reluctant to take a chance, and considerable haggling was required to get the project off the ground. The constant editorial review and rejection of Benchley's writing style would have discouraged many. For example, editor Tom Congdon commented to Benchley after the first four-chapter draft: "You just can't graft light humor onto a gory five-death tragedy. . . . I find the narrative unfolding pretty limply and uncertainly . . . there are lots of small confusions . . . the shark scenes, though powerful at first, get repetitive" (Morgan, 1982: 126). Morgan goes on to describe the negotiations over paperback rights, the title (which was changed 237 times before *Jaws* was selected), the problems over a jacket illustration, reviewer remarks (which were not easily obtained, although generally good), and finally, the early sales returns and film negotiations.

In describing the process of publishing a novel, Morgan has provided good data for understanding the definition of a contemporary trade novel. As with any form of communication, the nature of the message must be understood in terms of how the various parties in the interaction affect the message. A novel is not just an idea and yarn spun by a skillful writer; it is a tale that must be sold to (and in the process changed by) all parties in the process. When all is done, the meaning of the novel still depends on the response of peer critics and the consuming public.

Over time, this interaction process has produced a general formula (grammar and perspectives) that everyone involved uses and often takes for granted. At this point, our task is to take such standard formula prescriptions as the "something-about-which-the-public-knows-a-little-but-wants-to-know-more formula, and the external menace formula which makes us want to live out vicariously the cycle of the menace and survival" (Morgan, 1982: 124-125) and break these down into the components of grammar and perspectives.

GRAMMAR

The ultimate aim of an author is to stimulate a reader to become so engrossed in a book that continued reading takes priority over most other activities. To accomplish this an author stimulates a reader to participate vicariously in the story through the plight of major characters. In turn, this requires a flow of events and crises so that readers continually wonder and worry about how the story will end, knowing of course that it will end in some fashion. Returning to the model of media grammar, my concern is with describing the common properties of this process in terms of syntax (organization), inflection techniques, and specialized vocabulary.

The *syntax* of a novel has become fairly standardized and is well understood by hard-core readers. The first few pages must grip the reader and stimulate interest to read on. This usually is accomplished through a dramatic event and the immediate development of a fascinating character; in both cases, an element of suspense or intrigue captivates attention. Following the enticing lead-in, the first few chapters establish a geographical context, the essential attributes of the main characters, the story's time frame, and a mood or emotional tone of the plot. At this point, the author often relaxes the pace and fully develops the story line (major problems in the plot) and elaborates on characterization.

Next, follows a sequence of events in which the main character confronts the problems, building to a climax or resolution. Each chapter is not a complete entity in the sense of reaching closure but is a step or progression (advancing the action) ending with a question that encourages the reader to go on to the next chapter for an answer. For most critics, the mark of a good novel is a logical sequence of chapters, each leading to the next until resolution occurs in what appears to be a natural process (given the interpretive framework established by the author).

Inflection techniques, or the style of the author, constitute a very important criteria for an author's success. It is not enough to have an interesting plot and characters; the author must also develop a rhythmic narrative with a tempo rising and falling in an emotionally satisfying manner, not unlike enjoyable music. The existentialist Jean-Paul Sartre supposedly said that a writer may judge his or her work by the quality of the writing, but a reader will judge it by the emotions it arouses. These emotions are largely achieved through the rhythm and tempo we associate with music. As in music, the consistency of the narrative rhythm throughout a novel aids in maintaining the emotional involvement of the reader. In turn, changes in tempo provide internal variety with action rising to a crescendo followed by a relaxing interlude. Short sentences convey action, while longer sentences elicit reflection and sensuous involvement. Anger is staccato, and periods of calm are drawn out. Through rhythm and tempo an author maintains vitality and freshness, which alternately excite and soothe the reader.

Inflection also occurs through crises created for the main characters. As Ted Morgan stated, readers today are enthralled by the

external menace and the struggle to survive. From the easily understood and common fears to the menace of a seductive ideology, the
reader can vicariously participate in the events of meeting threats and
surviving, particularly as underdogs in the face of overwhelming
odds. Robert Ludlum's adventure mysteries have been enormously
successful primarily because just when the reader thinks a threat has
passed or been overcome, an even more menacing problem is thrown
at the hero full force. This inflection surprises readers and keeps them
slightly off guard in a manner similar to the way jazz music is slightly
off beat, yet stimulating. In contrast, Jane Austen and Joyce Carol
Oates employ intricate designs and progress steadily through movements as does a Mahler symphony.

Finally, an author's use of *vocabulary* is what more clearly
differentiates literature from a spoken word medium. The aim of an
author is to make a novel read like speech, which is accomplished
through syntax and inflection. But writers also desire precision,
clarity, and vivid expression to arouse readers' emotions. In distinguishing between the spoken language of everyday vernacular and
written language, Robert Frost said that written language is more
sophisticated, artificial, and elegant. Similarly, Norman Mailer says,
"The best writing comes obviously out of a precision we do not and
dare not employ when we speak, yet such writing has the ring of
speech" (Burnett and Burnett, 1975: xviii). Such an effort requires
finding just the right words to express a thought, describe a scene, or
construct a convincing and compelling interaction among characters.
Authors often draw on taken-for-granted stereotypes developed over
the years, such as the use of colors to evoke emotion. Red is used for
anger or embarrassment, green conveys tranquility, and suspense
and drama are achieved through shades of gray, stark contrasts of
white or red on black, and the use of sounds and smells. The opening
paragraph from Robert Ludlum's *The Bourne Identity* (1981: 7)
illustrates:

> The trawler plunged into the angry swells of the dark, furious sea like an
> awkward animal trying desperately to break out of an impenetrable
> swamp. The waves rose to goliathan heights, crashing into the hull with
> the power of raw tonnage; the white sprays caught in the night sky cas-
> caded downward over the deck under the force of the night wind.
> Everywhere there were the sounds of inanimate pain, wood straining

against wood, ropes twisting, stretched to the breaking point. The animal was dying.

In another example, this from Chapter One of *The Last Temptation of Christ* (1971: 5) by Nikos Kazantzakis, shows how the use of a sight, sound, and odor vocabulary can be used to quickly shift the reader from one mood to another.

A cool heavenly breeze took possesion of him.

Above, the blossoming skies had opened into a thick tangle of stars; below, on the ground, the stones were steaming, still afire from the great heat of the day. Heaven and earth were peaceful and sweet, filled with the deep silence of ageless nightvoices, more silent than silence itself. It was dark, probably midnight. God's eyes, the sun and the moon, were closed and sleeping, and the young man, his mind carried away by the gentle breeze, meditated happily. But as he thought, What Solitude! What Paradise! Suddenly the wind changed and thickened; it was no longer a heavenly breeze but the reek of heavy greasy breaths as though in some overgrown thicket or damp luxuriant orchard below him a gasping animal, or a village, was struggling in vain to sleep. The air had become dense, restless. The tepid breaths of men, animals and elves rose and mixed with a sharp ordor from sour human sweat, bread freshly removed from the oven, and the laurel oil used by the women to annoint their hair.

In a letter to Guy de Maupassant, Gustave Flaubert advised,

whatever you want to say, there is only one [right] word that will express it, one verb to make it move, one adjective to qualify it. You must week that word, that verb, and that adjective, and never be satisfied with approximations, never resort to tricks, even clever ones, or to verbal pirouettes to escape the difficulty [Burnett, 1975: 20].

On the same point, Thomas Wolfe said that all his life was a search "to find a word for it [life], a language that would tell its shape, its color, the way we have all known and felt and seen it" (Burnett and Burnett, 1975: 20). Whether using action verbs to evoke a reader's vicarious participation or graphic adjectives to connote a mood or emotional expression, an author's skill is largely dependent on vocabulary; without precise and descriptive words, snytax is hollow structure.

PERSPECTIVES

In a widely read book on creative fiction writing, Hallie and Whit Burnett (1975: 180) give the following short piece of advice to aspiring authors on how editors evaluate a manuscript:

> The editor can look for honesty, style, suspense, revealing insights. Will the reader care about the characters, and what happens to them? Is the background colorful and convincing? . . . Does the work as a whole make an impact?

In part, the Burnetts suggest that editors evaluate the interpretive framework of a manuscript in making their decision. The author's honesty, use of suspense, revealing insights (truths), characterization, how background is used, and whether the book as a whole makes an impact are indicative of the perspective through which an author and reader make sense of a plot. If an author appears dishonest a reader will hardly trust in that author's perceptions or conclusions. Suspense constitutes a perspective in that phenomena introduced by an author serve as clues for anticipating future action. Restated, looking for clues is a way of reading. Revealing insights and background information demonstrate what an author thinks is important in unraveling a mystery or analyzing human nature. And the overall impact of a novel says something about the state of knowledge or understanding generated by a novel in a larger sense. But perhaps we need to back up a bit.

One of the two formulas mentioned earlier by Ted Morgan is that people read on subjects about which they know something but want to know more. We have all experienced basic emotions such as love, hate, and fear, and we know intuitively that basic emotions are closely associated with a curiosity and concern about problems in family life, religion, politics, social status, crime, historical reconstruction, and various exotic topics. Not surprisingly, these topics comprise the subject matter of most novels. But it is not enough just to write about these topics: There must be a framework, an angle, or a twist—to give a novel its raison d'être, its justification or motive. Love may be framed as naiveté or the supreme motive for life itself. Hate may be the irrational drive that compels humans to act and ultimately destroy themselves. An author such as Harold Robbins may operate from the perspective that many of us are voyeurs who want to peek at the inevitable corruption of those in the "high" life. His most recent book, *Goodbye Janette,* is advertised by Simon & Schuster as "more daring, more shocking, more deeply erotic than anything Harold Robbins has written before." As reviewed by Bettijane Levine in the *Los Angeles Times* (July 5, 1981), "Every unsavory act you've ever heard about may be described in [his] new novel about the fashion world." It was an immediate bestseller. Other writers, such as Norman Mailer, seem obsessed with the darker and more tragic side of human nature, while John Steinbeck was, in contrast, more optimistic in his masterful characterizations.

We know that a particular genre will have a formula or perspective; mysteries are about understanding and thrillers about winning. Every ideology and theory of human nature is implicit in the works of some author, and this is evidenced in the discussions readers have on authors at book club meetings, cocktail parties, and in reviews by well-known critics. George Orwell criticized the sadism and admiration for dictators he saw in Bernard Shaw's work. Leslie Fiedler, among others, has analyzed the theme of rugged individualism by men and women in the classic American western novel. As a modern western, *One Flew Over the Cuckoo's Nest,* by Ken Kesey, was described by Fiedler as a test of individualism and male comradeship under attack by the castrating white woman (Big Nurse).

Novels have also been categorized into periods, such as the Victorian commitment to moral duty, the mid-twentieth-century commitment among friends and lovers, and more recently a commitment to the elusive self. Perhaps the best conclusion on the use of values as interpretive frameworks in novels comes from Milton Albrecht (1956), who found after extensive research that only those values that are currently under strain in society are the subject matter for popular fiction. Novels are problem-solving exercises, and interpretive frameworks are, to a large extent, the strategies used to solve these problems.

In addition to major frameworks, subtle or miniframeworks creep into most novels almost unnoticed. In *Novel-in-the-Making* (1954), Mary O'Hara advises authors to use appropriate surnames for their characters, and appropriate is a key word, for it refers to the act of stereotyping. Which surname would be appropriate for a contemporary adventure novel—Reginald or Scott? Lillian, Diana, and Eleanor are genteel names, while Sally, Sharon, and Nancy are solid folk. Melissa, Sabrina, and Jennifer are pretty girls, while Nadia is mysterious; Nicole is playful, Edith is stern, and Tessa is stunning. In detective genre, such as Rex Stout's Nero Wolfe, the mastermind could never be named Archie or the second-story man Nero. Villains can hardly be Seth or Jason, and unlikely heroes are Bruno, Marco, or Lex. What this shows is the existence of stereotypes in our society that cannot be violated without consequences.

This example of stereotyping is minor compared to the images of race and ethnic groups, social class images, and women's roles. In *The Return of the Vanishing American* (1968), Leslie Fiedler argues that American myths in popular fiction overwhelmingly are concerned with sex and race. The puritanical and traditional image of women abounds in the harlequin romance novel, which sell over 30 million copies per year, mainly to women. Linda Busby (1975) summarized a number of studies on sex roles in mass media, including children's books, and found conclusively that women were most often depicted in traditional roles rather than as professionals or skilled workers.

Another subtle framework, one that requires a keen mind, is wit, the ability to juxtapose one thought with another to sharpen analysis and accomplish it in a delightful manner. Wit is not just a matter of style; it is a way of seeing and analyzing, such as portraying how ridiculous a behavior pattern may appear when viewed from a different perspective; Will Rogers, Mark Twain, P.G. Woodhouse, James Thurber, and more recently Tom Robbins and Kurt Vonnegut are popular examples.

Similar to wit is the framework of irony—the perspective of twisting something 180 degrees for an unexpected truth. The effective use of irony often involves setting up a reader for the ironic twist at the end of the story. It is a favorite ploy of the relativist and existentialist, who wish to expose the absolute as absurd and virtue as hypocrisy. Sinclair Lewis and Hemingway were masters of irony as is Kurt Vonnegut today. Embedded in irony may also be the perspective of cynicism as exemplified in some of the novels by John Updike and John Cheever.

This overview of interpretive frameworks employed by novelists fails to do justice to the richness of perspectives found in popular literature today, but it demonstrates that cultural themes and strains are a very significant part of the novel. This is due to particular biases and problems with which authors feel compelled to deal, reader interests (or what's "in" at the moment), and the desire among authors to involve the reader vicariously in the plot.

To elaborate on the latter point, many authors elicit reader participation by developing characters that readers can either identify with or understand. Characterization usually involves intimate knowledge of the character's behavioral idiosyncrasies, attitudes, and values—in short, his or her philosophies of life. This knowledge enables a reader to engage in role taking with the character so that subsequent scenes may be predicted with some certainty, or at least understood. As readers, we need to know how characters are likely to behave so we can figure out the puzzle in the plot or become involved in the character's struggle. To develop interest, readers must know who the players are in some fundamental sense, and this requires perspectives.

MEDIA INFLUENCE

For media consciousness, the importance of grammar and perspectives in novels is, at least, threefold. *First,* the novel establishes or reaffirms the efficacy of various theories of human behavior, ideologies, stereotypes, and popular myths. For example, in Anthony Burgess's *A Clockwork Orange,* the theory applied to understanding the main character's plight is behaviorism (stimulus response conditioning). Burgess does not argue the pros and cons of behaviorism; he establishes it as a given theory that readers may accept or reject, depending on their ability and willingness to evaluate critically the theory. Add to the Burgess novel other literature, films, and television programs that also establish behaviorism implicitly or explicitly, and the result is an objectification (appearance of legitimacy) of that theory. The argument is not that behaviorism as a theory is *necessarily* adopted without critical thought by readers, nor that even a majority of media are dominated by the behaviorist model. Rather, the fact that theories are implicit in the plotting and characterization of a story establishes the theory as a perspective that is legitimate to use and discuss and that may influence the reader in a more fundamental sense. Consequently, the potential exists for incorporating various theories, ideologies, stereotypes, and myths into a media-created culture.

A *second* point in media influence developing from novels involves the vicarious participation of readers with the characters in the story and in the plot itself. New journalist Tom Wolfe suggests that people "read novels because they're getting a picture of the emotional life of human beings that they can't get in any way except in the best forms on nonfiction" (Gilder, 1981).

In a casual analysis, vicarious emotional involvement in a novel may appear to be little more than fantasy or escape. It certainly is true that living vicariously through a novel's characters is not the same as dealing with the overt actions of people in a live situation, and it is also true that a reader can always put the book down and avoid the confrontations faced by its characters. On the other hand, vicarious participation is a social exercise that may involve the same behaviors required in overt interaction—role taking, anticipation of future action and responses from others, and commitment to identities. The main difference between vicarious participation and overt interaction is that one is a conversation in the mind and the other results in consequences that may be unavoidable. The Walter Middy syndrome of living in a fantasy world may be highly unrealistic, and it is a temporary withdrawal from the world of overt interaction, but it may also be a means for working out and rehearsing problems for future action. Very simply, vicarious participation may be a safe training ground. If nothing else, it is often fun and a pleasant reprieve from the toils of serious day-to-day interaction.

Expanding a bit on the rehearsal notion of vicarious involvement in novels, consider the empathy that authors evoke from readers for the characters in a story. Empathy is considered by most behavioral scientists to be an essential requirement in analyzing and understanding human behavior. Prediction of behavior is based on knowing how a person thinks. In turn, this knowledge may lead to critical self-analysis. Fundamentally, who you are is the result of how you think and want others to respond to you. Therefore, critical self-awareness and self-analysis occur in the process of evaluating yourself with respect to the responses others make toward you, and this requires an empathy into the motives or desires of others. Authors of popular fiction provide the information necessary to become empathetic with characters and, consequently, provide the basis for critical self-awareness and self-analysis. In a study of viewers' responses to an entertainment television series, Beverley Cuthbertson and I (1979) discovered that audience members do engage in self-counseling. If self-reflection and counseling can occur while watching a television program, they may also occur while reading an engrossing novel.

In a series of editorials on literature, Norman Cousins (1981a: 7) made several comments worth noting. In reference to authors, he said: "A novel is a processing embyro that . . . nourishes and replenishes. Thus it becomes a process for growth and change for the novelist himself." In turn, "The writer enables people to discover new truths and new possibilities within themselves" and to fashion new connections to human experience" (Cousins, 1981a:7). In the case of novels and other media, it seems clear that a positive aspect of media influence is the potential for self-reflection and counseling. However, this optimism must be tempered with the realization that some perspectives used to construct fictional characters are more desirable than others, and some readers engage in voyeurism rather than developing empathy for a story's characters.

Lastly, media influence through popular fiction involves the sociology of knowledge. Defined as the social conditions (milieu) that affect the development of knowledge, the sociology of knowledge is a serious endeavor to understand why particular knowledge statements develop in specific locales and at specific times. In part, knowledge is the result of an evolution of ideas and technology, but we also have numerous examples of great leaps that cannot be explained simply by the natural evolution or progression of science. We also know of ideas and theories that are anomalies given the acceptable scientific knowledge for a particular period in history. How, for example, does one account for the development of psychoanalysis in the late nineteenth century in Europe, for the apparent irrational but popular appeal of Aryanism during World War II Germany, for the popularity of est, Transactional Analysis, Transcendental Meditation, and a number of other therapeutic techniques in contemporary American society?

One answer lies in the social conditions in which these various thought systems emerged—the interrelationships of people and ideas. During the 1930s, the German theorist Karl Mannheim developed an elaborate structural model for explaining the development and acceptance of ideas. Central to his theory is the importance of ideology, particularly utopian ideology, which interacts with the more practical side of veryday life. The importance of ideology is that it functions as both a motive for action and as an explanation for how things are at a given moment. For psychoanalysis we can see the part played by guilt associated with imperialism and rugged individualist ideology before and after the turn of the century. In post-World War I Germany there was a desire to overcome the mortification of the Versailles Treaty and the economic collapse of the German middle class. In recent American society there has been a preoccupation with discovering the "true" self, consciousness raising, and the legitimacy of emotions. In each of these examples, an underlying ideology is constructed to bolster and justify action.

Since literature (both nonfiction and fiction) is the primary source of ideological applications, it stands to reason that what constitutes acceptable ideas or knowledge is both established and reaffirmed through literature. Certainly this is tautological, but that is precisely the point. Knowledge emerges from a particular source and then that source is used to justify the legitimacy of that knowledge. When the source is university and scholarly publications, few people challenge the statements. As people become more imbued with media culture, media serve as a source that becomes increasingly acceptable (legitimate). James Michner's historical novels (e.g., *Hawaii, Centennial, The Covenant*) stand as history, Sinclair Lewis was a sociologist—one of the best—and many authors are considered good psychologists. The point is not that novels have no right to contribute to our wealth of knowledge, but that for better or rose they do contribute, and people accept their contributions.

Even mystery novels make contributions to knowledge, especially in the sacred and hidden realms of society. Mystery writer Ken Follett (1981: 67) made the following observations in the review of Martin Cruz Smith's best-selling mystery *Gorky Park* (a murder mystery set in Moscow).[1]

It is the way Smith plays with the differences and similarities between East and West that gives the book its distinction. Now, if you sat down to write a straight novel "about" life in the Soviet Union you would be in grave danger of producing something didactic and boring that nobody would read, because a novel must be first and foremost "about" a person. Smith places in center-stage a human being struggling with a concrete problem, and then he is able, as if incidentally, to light up all aspects of life under the dictatorship of the proletariat . . . those aspects of life that are intriguingly different in the USSR: just how Communist Party control works; what it is like to get a divorce in Moscow; whether an innocent man accused of a crime has any real chance of getting socialist justice; how an honest Joe can make a buck.

A nonfiction book like Hedrick Smith's *The Russians* gives us a lot of information but we need the sympathetic imagination of a novelist to tell us what it feels like to be a human being in the Soviet Union. Sadly, popular novelists have so far done little to enlighten us, preferring out of intellectual laziness, to take their picture of Russia and the Russians straight out of George Orwell's *1984*.

Martin Cruz Smith is certainly not lazy. *Gorky Park* is good entertainment and has intelligent and illuminating things to say about a subject of importance. I should like to think that this is what popular literature is all about.

While we can only hope Smith's descriptions of Soviet life are accurate, the point still is that *Gorky Park* makes a contribution to what we call "knowledge."

Magazines

The quicker you act, the bigger your prize can be—$750,000 to be awarded! Win your $250,000 dream house, $100,000 in cash, an Oldsmobile Cutlass Supreme, vacations, clocks, cameras, luggage, and much, much more.

No doubt everyone has seen the Publisher's Clearing House magazine promotion at one time or another. Over 100 magazines are offered, including *Collectors' News, Analog, Farmstead, Humpty Dumpty, Horse of Course, The Mother Earth News, Neddle and Thread, Savvy, Pickup Van & 4WD,* and *Next.* How can there be so many different magazines and who reads them? From its genteel origin for a literary audience, magazine publishing has grown and proliferated into a giant industry catering to the highly specialized interests of affluent Americans. Today, with nearly 10,000 periodicals in circulation, there is virtually no interest that is not served by a magazine or journal. What accounts for this amazing spectacle is one of the most interesting aspects of the entire range of mass communication subjects. Since magazines have evolved through a series of stages from highly specialized communication to a mass phenomenon and back to specialization, they represent a model of what we may expect to occur with all media, including television.

In the 1850s *Harper's Monthly* and *Atlantic Monthly* began publishing short stories, poems, and scholarly essays on scientific and social issues. These magazines have stood the test of time because they continue to appeal to an audience whose interests have not changed appreciably. Both *Harper's* and *Atlantic* still publish short stories, poems, and scholarly essays for faithful readers who rely on them for intellectual and artistic stimulation. Consequently, these magazines are used to support and symbolize an identity for their readers, a highly definitive sense of who they are or want to be. Therein lies the most important characteristic of magazines today— they serve the interests of subcultures ranging from the esoteric to popular and general culture, and provide information and validation for the identities associated with the subcultures.

Perhaps more than any other mass medium, magazines have chronicled cultural change through the description of cultural and subcultural characteristics which emerged, flourished, and in some cases waned. In colonial America, *American Magazine* and *General Magazine and Historical Chronicle* (the latter formed by the ubiquitous Ben Franklin), appeared in 1741. Although both failed during the first year, they were indicators of what was to come. A number of small literary magazines, such as *Graham's Magazine,* the *Port Folio,* and the *Messenger,* enjoyed moderate success during the first half of the nineteenth century. However, as with book publishing, the real boom in magazines did not occur until after the Civil War.

Between 1865 and 1885 the number of periodicals increased nearly fivefold to 3300. *The Nation,* a prototype for *Time* and *Newsweek,* began in 1865. Magazines for women (*Ladies' Home Journal* and *Good Housekeeping*) began attracting a fairly large readership in the 1880s. During this same period, popular fiction and eclectic nonfiction were featured in *Colliers, Cosmopolitan,* and the *Saturday Evening Post.* By the early 1890s the mass magazine made its appearance with *McClure's,* selling for 15¢ a copy, and a competitor, *Munsey's,* which sold for a dime. At the turn of the century these mass audience magazines turned to muckraking through exposés of urban problems, corruption in big business and government, and deviant street behavior.

While advertising revenue was not a significant factor until after the muckraking period ended (1912), by 1920 this revenue exceeded $100 million, soaring to $200 million just before the Depression. The year 1922 saw the founding of *Reader's Digest,* committed to collecting the best articles from other publications and presenting them in condensed form. *Time* began in 1923 and the *New Yorker* in 1925. By the mid 1920s magazines expanded their market through newsstand sales, adding the grocery store outlet in the 1930s. Despite the Depression, *Life* and *Look* simultaneously made a successful debut in the mid-1930s. Selling for 10¢ a copy and employing dramatic photo journalism to describe American culture, *Life* and *Look* may be seen as prototypes of modern television.

Coinciding with increased prosperity and leisure time, magazine circulation and advertising revenue rose dramatically between 1950 and 1970. But as 1970 drew near, mass magazines began to lose their advertising base to television and specialized magazines. In the early sixties, both *Life* and *Look* reached an estimated 70 million readers, an estimate based on the belief that each copy changes hands ten times. With circulation figures at 7 million multiplied tenfold, *Life* and *Look* charged advertisers over $60,000 per full-page color ad, and many products carried tags stating "As Advertised in *Life*."

However, by 1971 the cost per thousand ad rate was $7.71 for *Life* compared to $3.60 for television (Welles, 1971). Since *Life* and *Look* depended on advertising revenue for 70 percent of their operating budget, they began to lose money sharply in the late 1960s. *Look* ceased publication in 1971, and *Life* followed a year later, despite the circulation of approximately 5 million. The rebirth of *Life, Look,* and the *Saturday Evening Post* in the late 1970s as special topic publications targeted for small audiences clearly demonstrated that the age of mass magazines was over. Although a few magazines today have rather large circulations (*TV Guide*), they are considered special-interest rather than mass culture publications.

While mass magazines were failing, those devoted to special interests were gaining strength. During the 1960s 160 magazines failed and 753 were founded. Special interest magazines are not a new phenomenon, as demonstrated by the success of women's (1880s), political opinion (early 1900s), crime stories (1920s), and sports (1930s) magazines. But in the 1950s magazines oriented to these special interests proliferated and expanded in circulation, a trend that continues to this day. Overnight success was experienced by magazines dealing with new urban lifestyles, changing sex norms, the expansion of spectator and participant sports, information on every conceivable hobby, advice for the career woman and investor, outlooks for the future, and the ever-present peek at the lives of celebrities. Even activities such as motorcycling have a separate magazine for every type of bike on the market. Today over 90 percent of all consumer magazines serve rather specialized interests, many of which have circulations under 500,000.

In addition to the consumer magazines or "slicks," *Writer's Market* categorizes periodicals into trade journals, such as the *Meat*

Packer's Digest, sponsored publications by organizations (e.g., the American Legion), and over 100 publications for farming and rural life, such as the *Goat Breeder's Gazette.* This analysis will focus on the slick, specialized magazine, as this category continues to have the most impact in the emerging media culture.

GRAMMAR

A recent survey sponsored by Publisher's Clearing House estimates that one-fifth of the adult population accounts for three-fifths of all magazines sold. Two-thirds of this group are women, 50 percent are between the ages of 18 and 34, and half of the heavy purchase group is college educated. While this market analysis does not represent all readers, it is the target group for subscription and newsstand sales. With these demographics it is not surprising that a majority of newsstand magazines have a youthful, middle-class style, with articles and ads oriented to women but also appealing to many men. The *syntax* or organization of most consumer magazines is also strikingly uniform. Even scholarly periodicals such as the *Atlantic* and *Saturday Review,* opinion magazines such as *Mother Jones* and *National Review,* and quality features such as *Smithsonian* follow a format similar to that used by *Sports Illustrated, Ms.,* and *Ski.*

Beginning with a magazine's cover note how most use a large, vivid portrait or graphic to capture attention. Usually related to the lead story, this photo or graphic is an emotional appeal and an indication of the content contained inside. The familiar cover of *Cosmopolitan* always pictures a sexy vixen showing a good deal of bosom and the classic burlesque pout. *Esquire* uses a lead story action shot, often in a tongue-in-cheek manner. The *Atlantic* uses a fine art graphic such as a caricature or a sketch of something pertinent to the lead story. For years, *Time* has used official-looking portraits, and *Playboy* has the ever-present rabbit ears somewhere in the picture. While most every magazine uses a pictoral display of some kind, each has a very distinctive style that conveys a unique identity to the reader.

Examining the inside of the typical consumer magazine, one is immediately struck by the placement of ads. All easily accessible pages, such as the covers, center sections (*Playboy* excepted), and pages adjacent to or inside feature articles, are advertisements. Since over 99 percent of all newsstand magazines depend on advertising (notable exceptions include *Consumer Report* and *Mad*), ads must be featured prominently. But notice how these ads are stylized in a manner consistent with the identity and style of the magazine itself.

Ads in the *Atlantic* and *Saturday Review* are always classy; *Good Housekeeping* food ads excite the taste buds, and *Playboy* ads are urbane and occasionally spiced with double entendre. While magazine advertising uses perspectives designed to take advantage of the publication's cultural content and identity of its readers, it is also an aspect of syntax in that it provides a break in the action of reading without being disruptive. Incidentally, ads also serve to break up or surround main articles, a practice that aids in clipping articles for files and future reference.

In content organization, magazines are designed to be read from front to back. Although this format is so self-evident as to appear superfluous, consider the fact that most people leaf through a magazine by thumbing it from back to front. Following this practice, an individual will stop at points of interest, such as photos. As a result, even though the traditional linear, sequential practice of placing lead articles at the front and classified ads at the back (as in newspapers) is uniformly followed, a photo will often stop the leafer or thumber at the beginning of an article. More important in the syntax of articles is the practice of using the newspaper format of bold headlines, deck headings, subtitles, and boxed inserts for shorthand summaries. The avid reader will also notice that many magazines have reduced the length of articles and abandoned or curtailed the practice of continuing articles on back pages. Page format itself has changed from the narrow four columns with small print to the use of two or three columns separated by bold borders, photos, graphics, and cartoons. Regular "department" features, such as editorials, contributor biographies, letters to the editor, book and film reviews, and tips on what's new, are placed unobtrusively at the front or on back pages to avoid interference with major articles. The fact that few magazines deviate from these syntax strategies provides a standardization and predictability for the reader.

The most conspicuous *inflection technique* found in the majority of consumer magazines is the emphasis on emotional expression through the vivid use of artwork and photography. While boxed inserts, summary and accent statements raised in bold type, and the narrative pace of articles are important devices for developing rhythm and pace, it is the use of color photography and graphic art that gives magazines their uniqueness in print media. Printed on hard-gloss paper, magazines afford the fine grain of photography optimal potential, as any reader will testify. In addition, many magazines have brought back illustrations as practiced during the nineteenth century, the most notable being the *Atlantic, Harper's, Psychology Today,* and *Omni.* Examine issues of these magazines and it is immediately apparent how artwork effectively aids in accenting the emotional tone and content of articles, in a manner consistent with the magazine's social class and subculture identification.

More common is the practice of placing pictures everywhere. Often an article will begin alongside a full page or even a page-and-three-quarter photo capturing the emotional essence of the article. Any article dealing with personalities, adventure, food, or travel will be fortified with numerous pictures of varying sizes inserted almost randomly throughout the copy. Even the table of contents will feature small photos to stimulate reader interest. Some magazines, such as *People, Us,* and all sports and fashion magazines, provide the reader more looking than reading—much like a television set. Even *Time, Newsweek,* and *Saturday Review* have recently increased photographic display. *Life* and *Look* were not just forerunners of television; they set a format style that is very prominent in the magazine industry today.

Color itself is used effectively as an inflection technique. Summary inserts are colored in pastel hues to set them off from black-and-white copy. Photographs use color boldly for action shots, portraits, and advertisements. Even print type is often set in color. Recently such futurist magazines as *Omni, Science '81,* and *Discover* have employed computerized television photography and the radically new variations in x-ray technology (tomography and anigiography; see *Discover,* May 1981, for a good example) to give color photography a whole new scope. Magazines such as these may be purchased for the excitement generated through color alone.

Finally, an inflection technique almost everyone enjoys is the cartoon. Political cartoons made their appearance in magazines well before the turn of the century, although from a present-day perspective the humor of these old cartoons is difficult to discern. However, as magazines became more entertainment oriented, humor cartoonists became major figures in their own right, as demonstrated by such well-known names as Gahan Wilson in *Playboy;* Opie, Ziegler, and Joe Mirachi in the *New Yorker;* E.C. Vey in the *National Lampoon;* and Jules Feiffer everywhere. In fact, mention the *New Yorker* and what immediately comes to mind are all those wonderful cartoons that seem to appear every other page. In the case of the *New Yorker,* the cartoon is not only an inflection device used to spice up the pages;

it is a major reason for buying the magazine. Some magazines even feature cartoon characters in serial comic form, such as "Little Annie Fannie" in *Playboy*, Don Martin's bizarre antics in *Mad*, and new-wave comics in the *National Lampoon*. As we have learned over the years, cartoons and comics can produce biting satire as well as enjoyable entertaiment.

In identifying the unique vocabulary characteristics of magazine grammar, we may basically apply what is found in trade book publishing. Since magazines are written for special interest groups, the vocabulary must be consistent with the reader level of these groups. Therefore, in addition to action verbs, descriptive adjectives, and the occasional mystery word that necessitates a trip to the dictionary, glossy magazines use liberal doses of specialized jargon. In fact, the reader untutored in the world of motorcycling will find it necessary to bone up on "biker" jargon in order to understand the descriptive terminology used in most of the copy. Similar examples are found in *Tennis, Ski, Audio, Analog, Gourmet,* and every other subculture periodical from the consumer magazine to professional journals. Readers of these periodicals desire a sense of belonging and are reluctant to accept a vocabulary watered down for outsiders.

PERSPECTIVES

Novels and consumer magazines are primarily concerned with constructing situations that involve readers emotionally. An author stimulates readers to identify with characters and act out the drama developed for those characters. Advertisers want consumers to feel through a heightened sensory involvement what it is like to own and use a product. Magazine editors are concerned with developing a package that integrates the variety of factors necessary for satisfactory experience in a particular social areana. Consequently, editorials, feature articles, photo essays, advertisements, spot news, and even the classified section must have a consistency that is meaningful to readers.

At the level of general society the sociological boundaries are broad and flexible, allowing considerable variation in defining what constitutes a society or community. In its prime, *Life* magazine employed only a few commonly shared values and norms to frame most of the magazine's content. For *Life*, the norms were action and drama, and the values were realism tempered with optimism, progress, and the strength of American society. Moving from the general end of the continuum to highly esoteric subcultures, we witness increasingly greater specificity in the criteria that define the meanings of those subcultures. Obviously, the subculture of motorcycling has a more specific sociological boundary than does the general cultural style of modern city life, and the hobby of building model airplanes is more specific than is the variety of bikes involved in the motorcycle subculture.

As the continuum criteria changes from general to specific, emotional satisfaction also depends on an increasingly more limited set of activities. As a result, magazines must identify the activities essential to a particular cultural arena describe or portray the emotional responses that are appropriate for those activities. The task may appear simpler than it is, as magazine communicators must be accurate or run the rsik of losing credibility with readers. For this reason, the perspectives employed in specialized magazines are crucial.

The perspectives of magazine media are among the most interesting of all mass media, as they have clear philosophies ranging from general ideologies and value systems common to many people to the rather esoteric meaning systems followed by a few. To identify these perspectives look for pictoral and verbal statements concerning what is valued in the particular cultural realm and the norms that guide a person in achieving the goals that encompass those values. A shorthand method for this procedure is to identify the beliefs and behaviors that encourage reader commitment. Specifically, how does a person become a member of a subculture such as skiing, what is necessary to sustain this membership or identification, and what rational and emotional criteria constitute proof that a person is indeed experiencing the appropriate cognitive and emotional states for that subculture?

To begin, readers must feel they are involved in an interaction with other members of the cultural arena that the magazine represents. This requires a personalized or first-person form of writing. While first-person writing may be considered an aspect of grammar rather than a perspective framework, it is discussed here as this grammatical form establishes a framework of seeing through the eyes of people who are close to and understand the action. Some may consider the personal viewpoint too subjective, but it is critical for readers to know they are obtaining information and perspectives from knowledgeable "insiders." Consequently, credibility is established, in part, through personal familiarity. Magazine writers speak directly to the reader in a personal manner and from a position of expertise and shared emotional commitment. The last point is very important as writers must not only understand the subcultural activity; they must also be emotionally committed at least to the same extent as the reader.

Working through a first-person or personalized form, magazine communicators develop and maintain the values and norms peculiar to a cultural realm in every facet of the magazine. Beginning with the most general end of the continuum, we may take *Reader's Digest* as the only magazine today that approaches a mass audience. The *Digest* lacks some of the characteristics of mass appeal, such as pictoral drama at a common level, but it establishes values and describes experiences common to most Americans. Since its beginning in 1922, the *Digest* has promoted America as a great nation, selected articles that foster optimism, the spirit of altruism, and human dignity, and used humor to temper the problems of everyday life. To most readers, this magazine has become an institution that symbolizes middle America in its most ideal state, supporting this general ideal with the norms of hard work, hope, and a smile. Using this perspective, the fact that the *Digest* is at times politically conservative is of minor concern to its more than 18 million readers.

Other magazines may appear to qualify as general cultural phenomena or near mass magazines by virtue of their circulation. But this is an error. For a magazine to have mass appeal it must cut across most sociological variables, such as social class, age, gender, occupation, and education. Some magazines, such as *TV Guide, Family Circle,* and *Playboy* cut across these variables with one feature of the magazine but not with others. If *TV Guide* (20 million) is defined only in terms of its function as a schedule of television programs, it is a mass magazine. However, most articles in *TV Guide* are oriented to a critical analysis of television rather than being entertainment for its own sake. *Family Circle,* sold at the grocery store check-out stand at a very low price, caters mainly to women looking for inexpensive homemaking ideas. This makes *Family Circle* a highly successful specialized magazine catering to middle-class housewives. *Playboy* is directed to an upper-middle-class, urban male audience, although its sex appeal in pictorial features is enjoyed by a much larger audience. *Time* and *Newsweek* are candidates for mass appeal by virtue of their subject matter, but their style and political slant limits circulation primarily to the professional and business communities. *People* and *Us* are mass-oriented entertainment and celebrity magazines for the hard-core television viewer. Functioning as slick voyeurism, these magazines also have the potential for a mass audience, but since their treatment of subjects is fairly superifical and since they are ancillary to the superficial medium of television, they attract a sporadic readership.

At the general culture end of our continuum, we find middle American ideals, such as those framing *Reader's Digest;* a general interest as exists in *TV Guide, Playboy,* and *People;* and general class, age, and gender characteristics as found in *Family Circle.* Of this group, the magazines that satisfy both general interest and a more specific subcultural group are *TV Guide* and *Playboy. Playboy* is more interesting for my purposes as it is more specialized than *TV Guide* and still enjoys a fairly high circulation.

At its peak, *Playboy* had a circulation in excess of 9 million, but due to competition, mainly in sexual display, the present figure is just under 5 million. The main reason for *Playboy's* instant success in 1953 was the existence of an affluent middle-class ready for a publication presenting sophisticated sex and an urbane lifestyle. At that time, the only magazine that was at all similar was *Esquire,* although *Esquire* never articulated a rationale for sophisticated sex as occurred in *Playboy.* Hugh Hefner, creator of *Playboy,* carefully developed a philosophy and commitment among his core readers to a fast-paced, liberated, urban style of life for men (Brissett and Snow, 1970; Gerson and Lund, 1971). Hefner articulated his philosophy in a poignant series entitled "The *Playboy* Philosophy," which later continued under the heading "The *Playboy* Advisor." Despite the initial success, Hefner did not attempt to be all things to all people. He stayed with a philosophy that justified how to experience and enjoy being sexually liberated and cosmopolitan as applied to both men and women. As a subculture, *Playboy* is a club and action scene for men and women and a reference group for a lifestyle that many desire and a select few enjoy.

Other magazines serving large-scale subcultures include those that deal with regional lifestyles, the fashion world, women's interests, the single life, and sports. Notable examples are *Sunset,* for Western living; *Metropolitan Home,* for the art of affluent urban living; the *New Yorker,* for the intellectual urbᵢnite; *Vogue,* for avant-garde women's fashion; *Good Housekeeping,* ₆ middle-of-the-road approach to the woman's world; *Esquire* and *Cosmopolitan,* for the adult sophisticate; *U.S. News & World Report,* for the business and politically oriented individual; *Sports Illustrated,* for the middle-class sports enthusiast, and a host of others. This category may be defined by a demographic profile of social class, age, and gender characteristics, but its main feature is a common interest in a lifestyle that incorporates a number of similar interests and activities within one arena. For example, *Sunset* is a service to the family that spends considerable time in household projects, outdoor living, and travel within a moderate budget. It's a how-to-live-a-comfortable-and-stylish-family-life-without-going-broke magazine. *Vogue* serves the active and vicariously fashion conscious adult woman of middle to moderate wealth. It provides information on what is "in" or "out" and the trends in both directions, and it promotes the latest in popular culture. *U.S. News & World Report* follows a newspaper format of tersely informative inserts relevant to the conservative middle-class, business-oriented adult. In each of these and other examples there exists a common bond and identity. This bond may be an everyday reality for the reader or something to which readers aspire.

Magazines serving these broad-based common interests have an implied or explicit editorial slant, emotional tone, and artistic style. For example, *U.S. News & World Report* periodically runs articles on the forgotten, hard-working, nonstriking, middle class, who are fed up with inflation, lawlessness, and welfare cheats. The artwork of *U.S. News & World Report* is a sober, functional, black-and-white format with occasional color highlights and few photographs. After reading one issue of this magazine there is no doubt as to editorial slant and emotional tone, which its two million readers prefer.

In contrast to the conservative framework of *U.S. News & World Report* is the exciting fashion world of *Vogue.* In no uncertain terms *Vogue* presents the world of high fashion without apology or trepidation. *Vogue* culture is a dare-to-be-different, alluring, impractical, yet classy look of striking, sultry, sometimes aloof but always primed for action women. In *Vogue* the ads tell it all, although editorial comment and departments such as "Point of View" and "*Vogue* View" are authoritative projections giving readers the confidence that statements in this magazine are slightly ahead of their time. *Vogue* readers are not concerned with how to dress for practical occasions; they

want to know and feel what it is like to be part of the haute culture as
the advertisement for Saks Fifth Avenue featuring an evening gown
describes:

> The ultimate luxury. The sense of ornamentation. The spendour of
> Oscar de la Renta. His style is grand, unparalled, as he traces spins and
> webs of lace with beading. Here, a wrap blouse of sheer off-white lace,
> to slide over a camisole discreetly bare. The skirt—a great, rustling
> sweep of embroidered lilac. For sizes 6 to 12, $1850. His wondrous
> faux-jeweled belt. One size, $300. In the Oscar de la Renta Bouti-
> que . . . where we are all the things you are.

The philosophy of *Vogue* is beauty and verve at any price; the fact
that few can afford it does not detract from the fact that many want it.
Being an avant-garde statement, *Vogue* also unabashedly presents
pop culture fads in a manner that legitimates them for the upper middle class. In the past decade, fashion layouts have featured implicit
themes of S&M, punk, new wave, as well as the healthy, "muscles are
the curves that count" and "everything in moderation" lifestyle (see
Appendix B for discussion of advertising).

Returning to *Sunset,* we find the ideals of the high-quality, active,
sensible family life described in detail. Everything from gardening to
diet, summer projects for bored children, travel tips, and so on is
organized into sections with cross-referencing for easy accessi-
bility. Close examination of this thick magazine shows that it is more
than a how-to-do-it manual for the modern homemaker; it is a justification for the family lifestyle for which many Americans have
been searching since the end of World War II. In this sense, it is a
statement of what the modern family represents in its best form. *Sunset* is bright, optimistic, and wholesome without comment on political
or religious ideology. To obtain a good feel for the perspectives in
Sunset, try reading a copy while watching any television situation
comedy or network newscast; the contrast is striking.

All magazines dealing with subcultural themes on a fairly broad
scale are framed with definite perspectives that inform and validate
the corresponding identity concerns of their readers. When someone
reads *Vogue* or *Sports Illustrated,* he or she does it with a purpose
and is rarely disappointed. As such, these magazines function as
reference works for the norms and values of people who share these
popular interests. In addition, these magazines function as symbols
to others, just as the prominent display of books informs others about

the owner's interests and tastes. Magazines casually lying on the table or carried under the arm tell visitors and onlookers something definitive about the host, opening avenues of conversation and perhaps friendship. And when these magazines are more specialized, the interaction potential is even more intense.

As previously stated, highly specialized magazines make up the vast majority of publications in the consumer market. All hobbies, popular culture activities, social movements, and sociological categories by age, gender, occupation, and intellectual interest are served by one or more magazines. *Modern Photography, High Fidelity, Field and Stream, Audubon, Rolling Stone, Ms., Mother Jones, Young Miss, Learning, Business Week, Psychology Today,* and *Science '81* are just a few of the more common examples. Searching further yields legitimate publications for homosexuals *(Gay Rights)* and mercenaries *(Soldier of Fortune)* and newsletters for soap opera addicts, contest aficionados, model train builders, knife collectors, and any other interest shared by more than a few thousand people. The perspectives of these magazines are concerned with defining the total experience of membership in the subculture including the informative "how to" participate, what is of value in the experience, and how to know when that experience has been achieved. Unlike the more flexible and often vicarious or episodic involvement of readers in the broad subcultural realms just described, the reader of the highly specialized magazine is more likely to be an intensely involved and highly committed individual with an identity in the making or fully at stake.

Glance through almost any specialized magazine and it is immediately apparent that most articles are informative, such as how to improve on skills, the latest in technology, the most current issue-oriented rhetoric (social movement publications), and pictoral displays of people in action. At first it may appear these stories and photos are straight information and glossy dramatization. Closer scrutiny indicates the articles and photos explain to readers how to act like insiders, how to gain the respect of others already firmly entrenched, how to avoid being gauche, how to enjoy, and the emotional sensations that should be felt when one is achieving success. In learning to act like an insider, photographs continually show people with acceptable attire, which is true for both a tennis player and a political dissident reading *Mother Jones.* Periodic humor articles indicate appropriate etiquette and style. Articles on those individuals who have mastered the skills implicitly explain what it takes to be respected by others. Most important, editors and feature writers give significant effort to the therapy of how to enjoy the activity. In fact, instruction articles often emphasize the fun and the emotional high of the activity on a par with developing technical skill. Popular examples includes Vic Braden's tennis instruction in *Tennis* and Stu Campbell's ski tips in *Ski*. Similar examples are found in almost every specialized magazine, from *Cycle World* to *Working Woman,* as editorials, advice columns, photo features, ads, and so on, involving readers in the total experience of the subculture. Consequently, reading can be an emotionally bonding experience as well as the means to obtain the information necessary to converse and act intelligently and appropriately with others.

Other aspects of the perspectives of specialized magazines deserve brief mention, such as the entertainment perspective, the new journalism or process-oriented style of feature articles, and the problem-solving approach, which frames most of the copy in these specific subculture publications. But the primary framework is the establishment and maintenance of the identity of belonging to the group, which in turn has an important implication for media influence.

MEDIA INFLUENCE

To determine the influence of magazines, consider that reading a magazine occurs in two different awareness contexts: It is either a highly involved activity with subjects relevant for the reader's identity concerns, or it is a very low-involvement activity used to kill time. In the latter case, people read to fill a time period or to appear occupied when they are stuck with nothing to do, for example, sitting in a health care waiting room or hair salon, and many other situations that require waiting for something more important to happen. In these situations a person is often thinking of other things while reading or looking, and, in addition, the choice of reading material is often less than desirable. It is unlikely that magazines will captivate the reader's attention when they are just filling time or waiting for a more important event.

On the other hand, some reading situations afford the opportunity to select with care what will be read. In these situations people read for the purpose of obtaining information and emotional satisfaction considered vital to their self-concept or sense of well-being. Given these contextual features, magazine influence is either quite minimal or it serves as a validation for cultural frameworks already desired or firmly ensconced in the reader. Since reading magazines is either a selective attention to subjects on which individuals have formed pre-determined concerns or is a haphazard activity without commitment, there is little cause for major concern over the impact of this medium. How then do magazines contribute to a media culture?

If magazines represent a cultural realm that is significant to a reader's self-concept, interaction with that medium will generate meanings that apply to the cultural realm in question. For example, if skiing is a significant subculture and identity for an individual, skiing magazines may affect how that reader defines the experience of skiing, although this effect will depend on the reader's trust in the credibility of those magazines. The influence of magazines, as with any other medium, is not a matter of the amount of exposure but of commitment. A reader committed to a skiing magazine can be influenced far more by a short-duration contact than can an uncommitted individual who may spend hours looking at the magazine but lacks a commitment to that activity as something significant for his or her identity. Incidentally, this same argument can be used to temper the potential effect of pornography or other subversive material. The selectively attentive reader must be committed to the activity the magazine represents and to the magazine and its perspectives before any intended influence can occur. However, individuals may always reinterpret any message for their own purposes.

When commitment to a magazine occurs, the meanings that emerge through the interaction will in all probability be significant for the reader's definition of the subcultural experience in question and the reader's definition of self. A reader may define skiing as a highly daring activity requiring great skill and see him- or herself as a daring, exciting, and skilled individual. Or a person may define skiing as a civilized, high-status activity increasing the probability of meeting affluent and attractive individuals and see him- or herself as a chic individual with style and good taste. The influence of a magazine is particularly acute for the person who jumps into a new subculture without previous experience or knowledge. Recognizing this fact, specialized magazines devote considerable space to the novice by describing basic skills and the emotional benefits of the activity. But regardless of whether the reader is a committed novice or experienced expert, interaction with a magazine can affect the interpretation of the subculture experience.

However, unlike the novel, the media-conscious individual involved in a specific subculture is not likely to restrict involvement to the vicarious level. In most cases, the reason for purchasing a specialized magazine is to learn how to become actively involved. Once active involvement occurs, the individual is in a position to make critical comparisons between the overt experience and what is gained from the magazine. This is not to say that a definition of the situation gained from a magazine will not influence the interpretations of the overt experience, but prolonged overt activity should eventually make the individual a much more critical reader. This point cannot be overemphasized. Since media become influential by seeing through the framework of media and taking media descriptions as fact, only active involvement in the outside world can afford the ability to analyze critically what media do. In the case of specialized magazines, readers are in a good position to make the critical comparison necessary to avoid the dangers of media influence. As will be argued in the chapter on television, this is precisely the reason why cable TV, with its potential for specialization, offers hope.

In analyzing any category of magazines, it may be hypothesized that the more removed a reader is from active participation in the cultural activity described by the magazine, the more likely the reader is to rely on the magazine's interpretations. As a quasi-test of this hypothesis, ask yourself how often you have relied on a magazine's interpretation of a subculture about which you had no knowledge or previous experience. In the late 1970s, when trying to obtain information on "lowriders," a car culture among Chicanos in the Southwest, I followed the obvious course and bought a few magazines addressed specifically to this group. The question is, do you stop at this point, feeling the information obtained is sufficient, or do you dig further for critical comparison? All too often many people stop with the magazine coverage. Although in many instances a magazine will provide accurate and adequate information, the point is that we rely, perhaps entirely, on the magazine as a legitimate, authoritative, and sufficient source. Media influence begins with a reliance on media and may be followed by an uncritical attitude toward media activity.

Applying our hypothesis to such magazines as *Times, Playboy, Vogue, Sunset,* or *Us, Heavy Metal,* and *National Lampoon,* we must consider the extent to which we rely on the descriptions they provide as our main source of information. Does *Playboy* really represent the typical sex and lifestyle code of the affluent cosmopolitan adult? Is *Vogue* typical of the avant-garde fashion followed by chic women? Will *Us* really provide the inside dope on lives of celebrities? Does *Times* present the best understanding of current American political and cultural concerns? Or do we accept these descriptions as accurate representations and stop there? Again, our first concern is not whether magazines do in fact present a false or misleading view but that we may become dependent on and uncritical of the medium, accepting it at face value. As people come to rely on magazines as references and even reference groups, the danger of uncritical attitude and action becomes even more serious.

Expanding on the last point, attention should be given to several additional matters of sociological interest in media culture, namely, the status accorded some magazines and voyeurism that occupies the attention of many people. Perhaps more than any other mass medium (excluding a particular class of novels), magazines serve as status symbols for social class interests. How often have people put the latest copy of the *New Yorker, Atlantic, Daedalus,* or some other prestige publication on top of the magazine pile just before guests arrive for dinner? How often have you heard the question, "Did you see in *Time* that . . . " or "In the latest issue of *Atlantic* . . . " While these status plays are understandably self-serving, they also maintain an influence level for magazines—sometimes with justification.

Whether magazines deserve their reputation or not, the point is that audiences establish and legitimate reputations for these magazines. Since this is an indicator of audience power, it also suggests that responsibility for media influence lies, to a large extent, with the audience. Indeed, the argument throughout this book is that potential dangers from media are primarily overcome by action from the audience. Regarding the conferral of status on magazines, readers interact among each other to establish a magazine as a reference group with status or prestige, which in turn grants status to the reader by association. The irony of this process is that media-conscious individuals become the architects of their own plight. While this process may end happily in the case of bestowing status on such quality periodicals as the *Atlantic,* concern should arise over the elevated prestige of inferior publications. At this point the question is, what criteria will be used to confer status?

A more serious indication of audience vulnerability to media concerns the fascination with voyeurism that is a result mainly of the confession magazine. Given the popularity of these magazines over the years, it is apparent that people love to read about the private and often sordid features of people in public life. In part, this fascination results from a hero worship, a phenomenon probably as old as human life itself. In addition, curiosity may be piqued by an urge to see whether these heroes have problems similar to our own and an impulse to clip their wings when they outgrow their usefulness. (Note: We keep major heroes at a distance in order to maintain our belief in the efficacy of ideals, but when these heroes become problematic, some people have a propensity to go for the jugular and see them mortified in public.) The *National Enquirer* has been sued numerous times for this practice, the most recent being the successful suit (1981) by actress Carol Burnett. In addition, some people become fad celebrities (Brooke Shields in 1981), and a nosy public searches to find out all there is to know about this person. Magazines rise to the occasion and provide the most candid information anyone would care to know.

Several implications for media culture result from this voyeuristic attitude. First, some people are all too willing to believe in extremes, good or bad, and confession magazines have been providing these extremes for years. In part, this stems from the fact that both heroes and villains are people who are extreme in many respects. In themselves, extreme characteristics of heroes or celebrities are nothing new in the chronicle of history. The problem arises in the demand for bigger and more exaggerated extremes, which is a natural consequence of the entertainment perspective—"Can you top this?" The process becomes a vicious circle with extremes piled on extremes until gross distortions and unreasonable expectations are applied to the celebrity, a common complaint among TV and film stars.

Following logically, a second point is that in the process of creating extremes, we use up, burn out, or otherwise destroy real people, a consequence that is also exacerbated by the morbid curiosity for sordid detail. In turn, what this may do to the concept of privacy is a third aspect of a voyeuristic media culture.

A fourth point concerns the result of people developing vicarious relationships with media personalities or identifying with them as role models. As discussed in other chapters, this identification may lead to unrealistic expectations for audience members, particularly when it becomes apparent that cannot obtain their ideal or personally measure up to the role model as established in the media. This, in turn, may result in feelings of inferiority or even depression.

Finally, it should be recognized that in the process of creating media personalities, magazines serve as a support medium for the television and film industry. As personalities emerge in the electronic entertainment media, magazines become vehicles to publicize these personalities for the purpose of increasing audience size in television and the movie theater. In this manner, magazines manipulate voyeuristic readers for a commercial purpose and aid in expanding the entire phenomenon. Although voyeurism may involve a degree of fun and excitement, a price is paid for this fun and profit in the toll it takes on celebrities and the audience.

Despite the negative features of a voyeuristic media culture, the positive benefits of communicating through magazines seem to outweigh the negative effects. This seems particularly true in the case of specialized subculture magazines, where well-defined identities are at stake, inducing readers to be more critical of magazine form and content. The chapter on radio that follows continues the discussion of specialized media and shows how mass communication may extend to an interpersonal and even intimate level.

Note

1. Excerpts from Ken Follett's review of *Gorky Park*, "A Moscow Mystery," which appeared in *Saturday Review*, April 1981, pp. 66-67, are reprinted by permmission.© 1981 by Saturday Review Magazine Co.

CHAPTER 4

RADIO
The Companion Medium

With more radios in America than television sets and telephones combined, this is the most ubiquitous and the most taken for granted of all mass media. People rarely reflect on how often they listen, how many activities they carry on to the accompaniment of radio, how significant radio is for some of their subcultural involvements, or simply how much they rely on radio for contact with the outside world. Newspapers are praised for defending freedom and attacked for ideological bias. Film is applauded for artistic achievements and disdained for its unrealistic fantasy. Television is acclaimed for its educational value and vilified for its violence. But the best thing people say about radio is that it's always there and the worst thing is that it sometimes is too noisy. Why is it that radio is rarely given critical attention even by people who study mass communication? Scan the pages of most survey tests on mass media, and you will notice that radio usually receives the least amount of space and analysis. But consider the reaction if radio suddenly vanished.

As with other major media, radio began as a toy or hobby for a few electronic eccentrics at the turn of the century. It was not until 1920 that a station (KDKA—Westinghouse, Inc.) began regularly scheduled broadcasts. During the affluent twenties, radio grew rapidly through the competitive efforts of RCA, which formed a dual coast-to-coast system (the NBC Red and Blue networks); CBS, founded by William Paley out of profits from his cigar empire; and the Mutual Network, which pioneered entertainment serials including *The Lone Ranger.* Throughout the thirties these three companies developed the mass entertainment formats of situation comedy *(Amos 'n' Andy),* drama through such favorites as Orson Welles's *Mercury Theatre,* deejay remotes from famous ballrooms, detective thrillers (*Ellery Queen* and *The Fat Man*), day-time soap operas (*Our Gal Sunday* and *The Romance of Helen Trent*), quiz shows, talk shows, news, sportscasts, and religious programs. In fact, radio, during its "golden" mass age of the thirties and forties, served as the prototype for television entertainment. In was a creative, free-wheeling period governed only by the licensing regulations of the Federal Communications Commission (FCC), established in 1934.

Today, all that remains of these giant radio systems are several news networks that serve a loose system of affiliated stations. Radio has changed significantly from the mass entertainment age of the depression and war years, but it is still a vital and significant part of American culture and an essential medium in the daily lives of a great many people. Despite the entertainment power of television, radio has not suffered the collapse predicted by so many. With an average of five sets per home and over 8600 stations on the air, radio is more popular and profitable today than at any time in its history. With inexpensive battery-operated transistors, radio goes everywhere. It turns on and off automatically, listeners develop loyalities to stations and broadcasters, and it is used routinely to accompany many activities. Periods in a person's life, such as adolescence, can be recalled through reference to a station's call letters or the name of a disc jockey. We wake up to the clock radio, enjoy its compansionship while driving to work, use it as background for a variety of activities from housework to tinkering with the car, and we fall asleep to its mellow sound. If radio suddenly disappeared, most people would quickly discover how significant, perhaps even essential, radio is in their daily lives.

In the early 1960s Harold Mendelsohn (1964) completed what is considered by some media analysts to be the most important study of how listeners use radio. He found that radio provides listeners with much more than practical information and general entertainment. People use radio as a tension release, an accompaniment for various moods, and as a companion. These points are significant particularly in light of the fact that many people listen to radio when they are alone. As a companion, radio keeps people in touch with the outside world and brings that world into the listener's realm of activity. As a housewife reported in Mendelsohn's study: "To me when the radio is off, the house is empty. There is no life without the radio being on. As soon as I get up at six-thirty, the first thing I do is turn it on" (1964: 91).

In this capacity, radio provides some of the same satisfactions that people obtain from normal face-to-face conversation. In providing some assurance that you are still part of an on-going world, radio is a means for being alone without feeling alone. Unlike most television programs, which are taped and rerun, or a newspaper, which is history, radio is a "live" companion and an activity that involves a listener in a present-oriented social endeavor. It is this personal or, more accurately, interpersonal dimension that gives radio its special appeal. While music can be a background companion, listeners also know that a broadcaster can augment that music with a personal touch. Advertisements tell prospective listeners that stations and announcers create moods and other experiences just for them, and, since radio is communication directed at a specific audience in a specific locality, listeners can personalize the experience in a manner similar to face-to-face encounters. While Mendelsohn emphasized that radio gratifies certain listener needs, it seems legitimate to consider the extent to which the process of communication through radio is similar to interpersonal interaction.

Mendelsohn hinted at the interpersonal dimension of radio when he remarked that radio serves as a "social lubricant." In making this observation he claimed that radio binds people together through common shared experiences and provides subjects to talk about with others. While he restricts radio to the category of a catalyst for face-to-face interaction, evidence will be presented that demonstrates that listeners actually interact with broadcasters in a fashion very much like interpersonal conversation. Radio may facilitate social activity outside the immediate listening experience, but broadcasters and listeners also create the image of communicating with each other. This point will be examined in some detail throughout the chapter.

Another point that orients our analysis of radio is that it is a specialized medium delivering specialized subjects to specific listener interests. Specialized radio has become so successful that it is not uncommon for a large city to offer over thirty stations catering to interests from popular music to education and news. Even the large middle-of-the-road (MOR) stations maintain a degree of homogeneity in music with either country, soft rock, or standards.

Since radio functions much like highly specialized magazines, listeners with these interests come to depend on particular stations for the content of their subcultures. As a result, a radio station becomes symbolic of a particular identity for the listener. In contrast to television, in which viewers form attachments to particular programs, radio listeners are more likely to identify with a particular station, as exemplified by bumper stickers announcing the driver as a KDKB listener and T-shirts emblazoned with WXRT. For these listeners a radio station is much more than a channel communication or a source of information—it is a dimension of self. Stations even add this factor to their cash-call contests such as, "What is your favorite country?—KNIX."

Assuming that a definition of radio as a personal companion and a subculture medium is correct, the first phase of our analysis will be to describe the communication strategies employed by stations and broadcasters. The next step is to examine the meanings listeners make of their listening experience. Finally, we shall compare the strategies used by stations and broadcasters to listener experience with attention to some of the implications on how radio is part of the media culture of our age.

Radio Format: Perspectives and Grammar

Communication strategy in radio, as with other media, may largely be described under the heading of *format.* Format is simply a shorthand term that describes the perspectives and grammar used in presenting programmed material. As described previously, perspective is a way of "seeing" or defining various phenomena, such as the entertainment perspective used in television to present everything from news to sports. Radio also uses entertainment, but it is designed to appeal to a more narrow range of interests, such as folk music subculture. Every subculture has a set of norms and values that orient its members and provide a framework for evaluating life within the subculture. For example, rock fans value youth and have a rebellious yet playful attitude toward most traditional institutional practices. Rock subculture includes a style of dress, a brashness in personal demeanor, and high volume on the stereo; rock fans are robust in their listening and dancing behavior. These values and norms become the general orienting perspective for a station in every phase of its strategy. When stations advertise through slogans such as "It's what FM ought to be," "The no-disco kick-ass rock of K— — —," or "The rhythm of Phoenix KQFusion," the explicit message is that your music subculture is served by this station.

The grammar of syntax, inflection, and vocabulary in radio is part of the strategy used in making a subculture come alive to its members. It is commonly understood that each radio subculture has a specific grammar. It takes an experienced listener no more than a few seconds to identify that grammar and the particular subculture when dialing across frequencies. Certainly knowing the difference between classical and country music is evidence for instant recognition, but in cases where musical selections are used in more than one format or where music is absent, such as on all-news stations, listeners rely on subtle aspects of grammar to decide quickly whether the station they have dialed is all news, or just a news segment on a rock, beautiful music, or country station. Listeners also know instantly whether they have tuned-in a hard rock or a bubblegum station, an uptown or more traditional country station, or a gospel compared to a modern evangelist religion station. The grammatical differences among some subculture formats may be subtle to the untutored ear, but experienced listeners instantly recognize the differences.

The scheduling or *syntax* part of radio grammar is based on following listeners' activity through their typical daily routines. We take it as common sense that most people follow particular behavior patterns that are appropriate for particular times of the day and days of the week. Waking in the morning, driving to work, doing household chores, relaxing in the afternoon, or informal evening activity may be facilitated by specific information available from radio. From the simple reporting of time and temperature and news briefs to household tips, lost pets, and closing stock market reports, listeners obtain information that is generally relevant for what they are doing at a particular time of day. With this organization radio aids in bracketing or breaking the day into meaningful periods. A listener in Phoenix once commented, "When Haywood's show [early morning—KOY] is over, I know the work-day has begun." Similarly, another person stated, "When 'All Things Considered' [National Public Radio] comes on I feel the job part of my day is over." In this fashion, radio not only brackets specific routines but serves as a signal for changing from one routine to another. Just as twelve noon signals the lunch hour, a radio station provides signals for a wide variety of routine behavior. In turn, personal interests vary during each day of the week from mellow Sundays to TGIF and seasonally from winter holidays to summer vacation.

In addition to the bracketing of routines, a primary characteristic of radio grammar is the familiar organization of music selections according to prescribed subculture formulas. In fact, the organization of music selections is what radio professional specifically refer to as format. In 1961, Bill Drake, a bright young broadcaster in Los Angeles, designed a simple and very successful formula for rock music that took the guesswork out of music selection. The formula consists of time segments, such as a quarter or half-hour period, in which a specific pattern of popular tunes is logged and played. A segment may begin with a current hit, followed by a recent hit, a golden oldie, a newcomer, and so on. Often these selections are color-coded as red, blue, yellow, and so on so the disc jockey can't go wrong. At many stations the format is so precise that each record is logged by a program or music director on a log sheet and timed along with commercials and announcements.

While this rigid, formalistic procedure eliminates much of the deejay's creativity, it ensures a definite "sound" for the station. Basically, this procedure is a formalization of informal practices used by broadcasters for many years, such as the tradition of following an up-tempo selection with a ballad and a lyric rendition with an instrumental. What program and music directors discovered was that listeners wanted a degree of predictability (when and how often the hits would be played), and also a particular *rhythm* (inflection) of musical selections, which in turn aid in maintaining the style of a particular music subculture.

On the last point, music subcultures have particular rhythms that vary from frantic beat to an easy swing. Even beautiful music, or Muzak, all-news, and MOR radio are programmed according to specific formulas that correspond to listener's lifestyles. The matching of music format to listener lifestyle is so common in radio that most professionals believe that rating points are gained or lost primarily on the basis of these formulas. As one program director remarked, "It's the format [syntax and inflection formula] that gets me the points, not the disc jockey."

In addition, variations in music rhythm match the tempo changes in listener routines from the rush of early morning activity to the midday slowdown, the evening race to get home, the relaxing early evening, and the mixed bag of late-night listeners.

Broadcasters' delivery is consistent with the tempo and rhythm of music as exemplified by the length of time they are allowed to talk between records, the pace of delivery, the apparent volume of their voices, and a high or low pitch. Top-40 stations typically reduce the amount of talk between records to a minimum of giving station ID, time, temperature, and the deejay's name while one record ends and the next begins. An MOR station allows broadcasters more time to establish their personalities, while beautiful music and adult rock stations play three or more selections before any words are spoken. Knowing these unstated grammatical norms, listeners easily identify the rock jock's familiar rapid-fire, high-pitched, compact style of talk, the beautiful music announcer's somnambulent, pear-shaped tones; the adult rock and folk station announcer's normal room conversation manner; and the soul deejay's hip style. When the king of rock radio in Los Angeles (KHJ) changed to a country format in 1980, *Los Angeles Times* radio critic James Brown commented that the deejays were still using the "accelerated, overly mdulated banter of Top 40 chatter.' He advised them that for a country format, "They'll get a lot more accomplished by slowing down . . . way down."

Finally, there are specific aspects of radio talk *(vocabulary)* that set radio apart from other media. Broadcasters in all major markets demonstrate great facility in clear crisp enunciation and speech devoid of embarrassing pauses or slow-witted phrasing. In fact, listeners have come to expect and demand an articulation and polish in radio talk that far exceeds what is expected in normal face-to-face conversation (Goffman, 1981). Listeners also expect a broadcaster's vocabulary and jargon to be cosistent with the subculture the station represents. Broadcasters must talk to their listeners in words that are not only understood but also remind the listener that this is indeed the world of rock, jazz, classics, country, or mainstream Americana.

Combining these facets of radio grammar results in radio having a high degree of clarity that is seldom confusing to the audience. Music is distinctive, speech is clear, the content is aimed at the cognitive and emotional desires of a specific audience, and material is presented at a tempo that is consistent with a typical listener's routine. In short, radio grammar is designed to produce a fairly low degree of ambiguity for the intended audience.

HOW BROADCASTERS COMMUNICATE

To communicate with listeners, disc jockeys or "communicators" (as they prefer to be called) must follow the prescribed format designed by the radio station. Disc jockeys generally rely on the fact that listeners will find the program acceptable if they follow the station's format. However, attracting listeners by following the format is not sufficient for most radio communicators. Since they talk to an unseen audience, there is a desire to discover whether listeners relate to them personally or are listening simply matter-of-factly to the station. (In everyday life there are few situations in which a person wants to be an impersonal voice or nonperson.) In fact, the term "communicator" implies something distinctive about the abilities and special talents of an individual over and above the more formalistic criteria of station format. Simply put, disc jockeys want to become radio personalities; to accomplish this they engage in role making and altercasting (see Appendix A).

Role making is an activity in which an individual develops and acts out a particular behavioral strategy designed to elicit particular responses from others. But to make a role, an actor (individual) must cast the other (the person to whom one speaks) in a reciprocal role— i.e., he or she casts an alter role for the other. For example, a disc jockey may wish to be known as a satirical wit among listeners. To achieve this the broadcaster casts the listener in the reciprocal role of entertainment spectator and attempts to elicit a favorable response from the listener.

There is nothing complicated or mysterious about this process as everyone engages in both role making and altercasting in their daily life. We establish roles (identities) with friends, family, and co-workers and elicit responses from these people that will support our identity intentions and claims. From single activities around the home to making a point with the boss, role making and altercasting are part of the normal, everyday interaction process.

But how does a radio broadcaster know whether his or her role-making activity with the unseen listener is successful? One source of evidence is found in the previous discussion of listener routines. Since the organization or scheduling of program content is designed to be consistent with listener routines, a communicator can anticipate the type of role or identity that is relevant for the listener at that moment. Literally, the communicator projects images of typical listeners and their activities, such as driving to work, doing housework, or relaxing on the patio.

This projection enables the broadcaster to create a role that will be relevant to the listener's concerns. The constructed role may follow strict conformity to the listener's expectations or be a creative endeavor, making a slight variation to what the listener might normally expect. An example of the latter point is the deejay who becomes a comedian or repertoire actor in addition to announcing records and reporting news. In this case the radio communicator has constructed a role and cast the listener in a particular relationship, one that the broadcaster anticipates is acceptable within broad entertainment parameters for an audience.

In addition to a general knowledge of listener routines, a broadcaster has contact with listeners through the telephone and letters, as well as public settings. Through these interactions a broadcaster may form specific images of the type of people who listen and how they evaluate the broadcast performance. This facilitates the broadcaster's ability to develop a more personal and even intimate relationship with the listener. In describing this process, most broadcasters claim they attempt to speak "one on one" to the listener. Specifically, they project an image of a listener or group of people and talk directly to that visualized image. When a significant other is not present in a situation we may construct an image that enables a vicarious acting-out of a conversation even to the point of creating the responses the imagined other might give. This is precisely what occurs in radio communication; by speaking one on one to an imagined listener, a broadcaster is able to personalize the communication beyond the limits of the station format.

The functions of radio discussed by Mendelsohn provide additional evidence of how broadcasters develop strategies and evaluate their role-making performances. In addition to knowing typical listener routines, broadcasters understand the desire among many listeners to enhance moods and obtain a sense of companionship. For example, radio professionals are aware that listener moods will change as they go through various routines during the day and week. Getting to and from work, midday work schedules, and evening relaxation involve an emotional experience as well as cognitive-rational activity. Broadcasters facilitate typical changes in listener moods mainly through techniques such as variations in the tone of their voice, the length of pauses, inflection, and selected comments. Many broadcasters believe that it is not precisely what one says but how it is communicated that enhances a mood or feeling. One disc jockey remarked, "I try to understand how a listener might feel and then deal with that." This empathy, followed by various affective expressions, enables a broadcaster to create and meet a listener's emotional desires as they change throughout the day and from day to day.

A period of the broadcast day in which listener mood takes precedence over utilitarian concerns is evening and late night. Via the request line broadcasters become quite sensitive to the desires of the lonely, the romantic, and the nighthawks. In my research on radio broadcasters, some of whom specialized in late-night programs, disc jockeys claimed vehemently that communication during late-night hours requires a greater sensitivity to the emotional or affective desires of listeners. During the late-night hours deejays imagined listeners on dates, at parties, or doing a variety of solitary work tasks, and callers during these hours confirmed the accuracy of those images.

Listener comments such as "play the blues," "make it mellow," or "get me out of this funk" were typical. One broadcaster stated, "It's a real kick to think you're playing a part in making love or chasing the blues." A graveyard shift broadcaster was more egotistical in stating: "I orchestrate and swing moods for my people. But I won't take requests when I feel it's going right. You see, I have an intuitive sense of the right flow for night action. It's what I do best." In a similar sense, a night talk show host said, "I sense the mood of the caller and try to flow with their mood. When someone talks loud and fast so do I. If their voice is soft and slow I become very calm." Some of these broadcasters were so successful at playing to the moods of night owls that they became entrenched or typecast as nighttime broadcasters. One familiar example is Franklin Hobbs, whose low, sandy voice drew a national audience during the night hours from clear-channel WCCO in Minneapolis for many years.

Consistent with the role of mood facilitation is the role of companion. Developing a friendship or companion relation with listeners is for most broadcasters the best strategy for eliciting loyalty and commitment from listeners, and developing commitment through companionship is no different through a mass medium than it is in face-to-face situations. Usually, commitment and loyalty are given in response to a feeling of security and trust established in a relationship. Since broadcasters understand that a continued expression of friendliness is what many listeners desire, it becomes part of their delivery. From my research, some broadcasters claimed that they actually practiced smiling through their voices but were quick to add that listeners could easily hear when the attempt was "put on" or phoney. Stations even adopt friendship as a focal point of their public relations campaigns. In Phoenix, Bill Haywood (morning personality of KOY) was pictured with five different friendly facial expressions in a recent billboard campaign. In a 1980 interview the station manager of KABC in Los Angeles stated, "Trust, warmth, honesty, communi-

cation. They all have to be there. Our personalities become friends to
the listeners, somebody they feel they can turn to." While achieving
companionship with listeners is still a matter of acceptance by the listener, the point is that promoting friendship is an important concern in
radio strategy.

Research data also indicate that radio broadcasters have a special
sensitivity to loneliness, which in part is due to their working conditions. Many of these individuals work in the solitude of a soundproof
booth with little opportunity to see or hear other people, a circumstance that is particularly acute or the late-night disc jockey, who
may work up to six hours alone. Common sense suggests that in
experiencing isolation during these periods, broadcasters develop
empathy for the plight of the lonely listener. Almost everyone has
experienced lonely periods when they have obtained a degree of comfort through radio. Common examples are the social isolation of driving long distance, especially at night; coming home to an empty house
or apartment; and the emotional isolation after a lost love or weekend
without friends. As mentioned previously, radio can normalize these
situations or at least reduce the anxiety.

For some listeners in these situations the companionship of radio is
not just chatter and musical rhythms; it is the personal touch provided
by a surrogate friend—the radio broadcaster. In interviewing several
late-night deejays, I had the opportunity to talk with listeners who
phoned the station. When asked why they listened and called during
the early morning hours, several candidly admitted they were simply
lonely. Responses such as these indicate that a kindred spirit exists
between some broadcasters and listeners, both empathically understanding the other's situation.

To promote friendship with listeners, broadcasters claim to use
three role-making strategies: an expression of sincerity, a spontaneous and relaxed delivery, and an avoidance of talking down to the
listener. Most broadcasters state that sincerity is not easy to express
to listeners on rigid format stations that require the hard sell or rock or
urban country. Others offer the rationalization that you either have
sincerity or you do not. However, many radio communicators, especially those on MOR stations, admit to working hard at conveying
sincerity through such techniques as the use of personal pronouns,
references to ideals of honesty and fairness, concern for listener
safety on the road, and the ever-popular "hope you're having a good
day." Regardless of their ability to express sincerity, the point is that

it is considered an important quality for successful radio communication.

Spontaneity and a relaxed voice quality are the speech characteristics that enable the broadcaster to appear as the typical nextdoor neighbor. As one deejay remarked, "The biggest compliment you could pay me is to say I sound off-the-cuff." While a relaxed voice quality is not found in formats such as rock or disco, even broadcasters at these stations will occasionally attempt to create the impression of spontaneity, usually through prepared ad libs. Ex-disc jockey Dan O'Day developed a lucrative business by putting out a monthly newsletter, "O'Liners," which supplied humorous stories, anecdotes, and one-liners to disc jockeys throughout the country. Yet it takes a special ability to make prepared material sound spontaneous. As Fred (Dr. Voice) Lewis, a veteran of over twenty years in radio, stated in a recent interview, "Good voices are nice, but what I'm trying to convince my students is that naturalness and believability are the really important ingredients in speech."

Finally, friendship strategy involves the conscious attempt to avoid talking down to the listener. On the practical side, broadcasters believe they cannot sell products to listeners who feel that a condescending attitude is being expressed. The same logic holds for establishing a friendship and companion role; friends simply do not establish superiority over one another. While listeners demand a superior level in speech characteristics from radio broadcasters, they will not tolerate being "lorded-over" or conceit from these same broadcasters.

In being attuned to listener routines, attempting to communicate one on one, enhancing listener moods, and in striving for a companionship with listeners, broadcasters seek to go beyond the boundaries of format and achieve a sense of personal interaction with listeners. When they sense this has been achieved, they feel they have earned the right to think of themselves as communicators and perhaps as radio personalities.

To be considered a radio personality is the highest status anyone can achieve in commercial radio, and with it comes stardom, a lucrative salary, talent fees, and prime-time broadcast slots. Radio personalities from Arthur Godfrey to Wolfman Jack, Cousin Brucie, Larry King, and many others obtained their success in at least two ways: they became supreme entertainers, and they created a sense of intimacy with their listeners. As entertainers, disc jockeys such as

Murry the K (often called the Fifth Beatle) or Wolfman Jack can enhance a particular type of music, elevate the fame of performers, and develop a subculture to the point that it is impossible to separate the performer, broadcaster, and music; each is interdependent with the other.

Listeners are as loyal to these broadcasters as they are to musical performers. Loyal followers of Bill Haywood's morning show (KOY) are so addicted to him that they feel a sense of loss if they miss his show. Talk show host Larry King commands a nation-wide audience who would rather miss some sleep than miss his show. These personalities may even become cultural heroes, as was the case among rock fans with Wolfman Jack. At one time broadcasters Al Collins and Symphony Sid were as important to jazz fans as were the musicians featured on their programs. There is little doubt that a few radio personalities have and will continue to achieve the status attributed to Hollywood film stars and recording artists.

A significant feature of success in entertainment is the sense of intimacy that fans feel toward a performer. While songs are significant for their lyrics, a fan may feel the performer is singing directly to them and about their joys and sorrows. From Frank Sinatra to Elvis Presley, there is a closeness that fans believe exists between themselves and their idols. Although a person must have the talent and skills to perform, an essential part of talent is charisma. In part, charisma translates into the ability to captivate and influence people through emotional rather than rational appeal. This definition also describes the bond between intimate friends. It follows then that a sense of intimacy is an important factor in measuring the relationship between performers and spectators.

As evidence to support this claim, consider how anyone explains why they like a particular performer. Along with admiring or respecting a performer's talent, the spectator will usually mention a feeling of closeness or identification they have with that performer (this is especially acute with singers). How else does one explain the reaction of fans to Elvis, John Lennon, Willie Nelson, Odetta, and the like? Therefore, it seems reasonable to suggest that charisma and the attending intimacy are necessary ingredients to becoming a radio personality such as Arthur Godfrey in his radio days, Murry the K during the Beatlemania days, Wolfman Jack during the sixties, or Larry King as the master of the talk show. Radio broadcasters understand the necessity for intimacy, and successful personalities are constantly aware of the need to project and achieve it with their listeners. As one of the more successful radio personalities in Phoenix said, "I want you to feel I'm there in the room or car talking with, not at, you, and that you know that I care . . . and that you can trust me. And that's why radio is a personal medium."

LISTENING EXPERIENCE

The task at this point is to examine the experience of listening to radio and determine the extent to which the meanings listeners attach to their experiences coincide with broadcasting strategy.

A major feature of listening to the radio is that it is an activity that is integrated with many other activities. Today people rarely sit and listen intently as they did during the 1930s and 1940s, when *Fibber McGee* and *The Shadow* were mass entertainment hits. In contrast to those days when the large Philco or RCA was the focus of livingroom entertainment, the small transistor is now a commonplace device taken everywhere and used in connection with almost every activity imaginable. Recalling Mendelsohn's findings, radio goes beyond the simple entertainment desires of listeners to become a means for dealing with problems ranging from getting the day started to feeling part of ongoing society. In this sense it is misleading to think of radio simply as background or as a conduit for information. Rather, radio is a highly significant, and to some people even an essential, factor in the process of everyday life.

As mentioned previously, radio follows a typical listener's daily routine so that it is used to mark off or bracket those routines. For some people radio aids in initiating, getting through, and ending something as mundane as driving to work. Just as an early-morning routine is not (for some people) the same without the newspaper, others depend on their favorite radio programs to begin the day. In this sense sociologists say that radio is an institutionalized activity (serving as a standardized means for dealing with a problem), one that may be very mundane. For the person who listens to radio while performing other tasks, radio has become more than incidental to the activity at hand; it may be part of what makes that activity appear normal. In short, since some listeners use radio to bracket routine activity and to facilitate its completion, radio becomes an integral part of the activity itself. For example, some people find it very disconcerting to drive a car without listening to a radio, be in a house or apartment alone without a radio turned on, or go anywhere without carrying a portable blasting their favorite music. In these situations radio enables people to manage (or at least feel they are managing) the situation with greater ease than if the radio were absent.

As suggested by Mendelsohn, other interesting and perhaps more important reasons why people listen to the radio are those that run tangential to serving practical concerns in daily life, e.g., maintinging or altering emotions. It is commonly believed that feelings are both the desired result of certain activities and proof that a particular activity was successful or a state of mind "true"—"trust your feelings." To this end, most people seek to create conditions that give rise to feelings. Put sociologically, we engage in "emotion work" (Hochschild, 1979).

However, since many people find it difficult, if not impossible, intentionally to talk themselves into a desired emotional state, they often seek out facilitators such as music (here radio and mood enhancement through music are almost synonymous). From relieving tension through relaxing music to enhancing romance, adding life to a party, or negotiating rush-hour traffic, listeners may rely on radio to initiate and support desired feelings. In fact, a major reason for radio's continued popularity is that particular stations maintain a fairly consistent sound on which listeners may depend. In a recent survey (conducted by the author) of 208 urban listeners from their late teens to middle age, 96 percent said radio enabled them to relax or reduce tension, and 74 percent claimed they used radio to obtain or enhance particular moods. Radio stations are aware of the importance of mood to the extent that billboard and station identification announcements carry such tags as, "the station for feelin' mellow," "the quiet sound of KQYT," or "ecstacy on KXTC."

Some of the moods listeners desire are short-term feelings that are appropriate for specific situations. Since many of these feeling states are experienced through routine behavior, an individual rarely needs to work consciously at them; simply engaging in the activity is sufficient to feel right. (On this point I have already discussed the fact that mood shifts corresponding to changes in routine throughout a typical day are programmed into radio format.)

However, on occasion an individual may feel depressed or uptight enough so that it is necessary to make a mild or even drastic and immediate change in feelings in order to get on with a new activity. In addition, an individual may want to add some assurance that other people in the situation will develop feelings conducive to a proposed activity. In such cases the radio and its continued, dependable music is a useful aid. Starting the day and surviving freeway traffic when you have the blahs may require changing from your usual station to another in search of a mood to shake those blahs. Having people in for dinner may require the even tempo of "elevator" music to induce relaxation and a mellow mood. On Sunday mornings a person may need classical music to bring out a sense of civility after a raucous Saturday night. In these and similar situations people understand that appropriate feelings are evidence that things are going right. Consequently, radio is used by only listeners to facilitate short-term emotion work. While few people want a steady diet of elevator music, on occasion it may be exactly the right feeling.

In addition to facilitating transient moods, radio can play a major role in providing emotional support for listeners who identify a station with a particular subculture. Rock, classical, jazz, soul, country, and ethnic stations serve such specialized interests that many listeners ascribe to the station a leadership status in a particular subculture. In Los Angles, KHJ was the leader in Top 40 for over ten years with "boss jocks" Robert W. Morgan and the Real Don Steele. To paraphrase the observations of one newspaper columnist in Los Angeles: "If you were an L.A. teenager or young adult from 1965 to the late 1970s, chances are KHJ was your station—whether it was to cruise around in your customized wagon, lounging at the beach, or simply walking around town with that $4 transistor anchored to your ear."

Similar stories are found in all major radio markets to the extent that during the Top 40 heyday listeners did not identify themselves simply as rock fans, they were "KB" listeners in Buffalo, KRIZ in Phoenix, and "DGY" in Minneapolis. For listeners in a subculture a station's call letters arouse a viseral reaction, a feeling of being part of something special that provides uniqueness for that person's identity. In modern urban society people often belong to several subcultures simultaneously and move in and out of a number of subcultures throughout their life. Examples include intense involvement in hobbies, such as four-wheeling, groups such as The Miss Piggy Fan Club, fads such as the urban cowboy scene, gangs such as outlaw bikers, and loose aggregates of jazz buffs, bluegrass lovers, punk rockers, and new waves. In each example, part of how a person defines him- or herself is in terms of the form (structure) and content (subject matter) of the subculture.

The importance of radio as a subculture is that listeners feel a station and/or a particular broadcaster represents or symbolizes both the form and content of their subculture. Stations advertise their subcultural identification—"KMCR is Jazz" or "Your Favorite Country—KTUF." Radio personalities have ID tags such as "Crazy Dave Otto," and ID's for listeners—"I was Morganized." When a radio personality becomes a leader in a subculture, listeners may depend on him or her for advice about music and follow them in a role-modeling fashion in speech style and jargon, humor, and even dress. This subcultural familiarity and the familiarity with the format of presenting the subculture can be taken almost anywhere through the portability of the radio, and listeners know that stations in one part of the country are similar to those in another. Consequently, a person is never very far from home when a radio is available.

The link to a subculture and sense of belonging that radio provides many listeners is an example of what Mendelsohn had in mind in stating that radio serves a companionship function. For many listeners radio is a companion only to the extent that it provides a sense of contact. However, some listeners actually develop an imagined interpersonal relationship with particular broadcasters. In such cases the listeners may define the broadcaster as a significant other, i.e., a person whose behavior is significant for how the listener acts and feels about him- or herself.

This form of companionship may even reach a stage of intimacy in the mind of the listener. In the listener survey we have been discussing, 71 percent felt that at times broadcasters attempt to relate on a personal level, 63 percent thought of some broadcasters as companions, and 59 percent went so far as to claim that some broadcasters had a sense of their (listener) personal needs. From these data there is little doubt that a majority of listeners use radio for companionship in a fashion similar to face-to-face relationships with friends and relatives.

This helps explain why some audience members of various media use media personalities as role models. As a role model, a broadcaster may become a highly influential person, and the opportunity for commercial manipulation or imitation of undesirable deejay behavior traits worries some critics. But role models may serve a positive function in that the person who looks to his or her heroic model feels socially bonded rather than isolated or alienated.

One of the best examples of radio as a companion is the talk show. Talk shows with listener phone-in are not new, but their popularity rose dramatically in the 1970s and continues into the 1980s. Some talk shows have become so successful that with clear-channel broadcasting and syndication they are able to command a nationwide audience. Formats vary from sports to selected topics with experts answering listener questions. Some listeners even classify themselves as talk show "junkies," listening almost exclusively to this type of program. The main appeal for these listeners seems to be the opportunity to be part of the conversation, either directly or vicariously. Conversations may be on intimate topics, although most are the typical lunchroom, coffee break topics of politics, inflation, raising children, and health. In summarizing the general appeal of talk radio, one listener remarked, "These programs are a modern version of sitting around the pot-bellied stove at the general store." However, while the general appeal of the talk show is conversation, many listeners are quick to point out that the radio host is a very significant factor.

In a study of talk shows conducted in 1976, Jeffrey Bierig (1979) found that people who phone talk show hosts are generally lonely (75 percent of the regular callers were single, divorced, or widowed), desire interpersonal contact more so than controversy, belong to few organizations, and perhaps surprisingly, are higher than average in educational background. In another study that focused on the nature of the talk on talk shows, Avery, Ellis, and Glover found that callers tended to call particular (favorite) hosts in search of emotional support as they would in calling a friend.

> The talk hosts, or "communicasters" as they are frequently called, come into the home as companions who are willing to listen to personal problems, share ideas about social and political issues, remind listeners that their beliefs and values are shared by others [Avery and Ellis, 1979: 114].

Since these studies were completed, talk radio has expanded to the point that most large markets have one or more stations devoted entirely to talk, particularly the self-help variety. In Los Angeles, psychologist Toni Grant gave up her clinical practice to become a full-time talk host on KABC. As she commented: "It's sort of like the E.F. Hutton commercial. You're talking intensely with one person about some intimate, important thing and others suddenly stop vacuuming and listen in."

Similar ventures are reported in San Francisco, Salt Lake City, Detroit, New York, and Atlanta. In New York, Bernard "Uncle Bernie" Meltzer hosts "What's Your Problem," giving financial and other advice to hard-luck callers. In Cincinnati, Jerry Galvin serves up a scam or "put-on" every Sunday night, such as proposing a law requiring every American to write two book reports a year—type-written and double-spaced. Some callers advance the scam while others are conned, adding to the hilarity. And in a non-talk-back talk show there is the very popular "Prairie Home Companion Hour," hosted by Garrison Keillor from the fictious Lake Wobegon, Min-nesota. Keillor actually recreated the general store for radio.

Ed Dunbar, program director for Atlanta's WRNG says, "Talk radio is a fabulous forum for people who feel somewhat impotent. People can pick up the phone and talk to the entire city." Ellen Strauss of WMCA in New York claims that radio "achieves its highest state with talk. It becomes two-way radio." Ms. Strauss's statement indicates that talk radio's popularity may be due to the fact that some listeners feel they gain a sense of intimacy through this par-ticipation. As talk show host Michael Dixon on KOY in Phoenix stated,

> With a talk show being the best doesn't mean just being quick with a retort. It means drawing out opinions, caring if someone is in trouble, and getting both the caller and the listener involved. People listen not because they should, but because they want to.

COMPARING RADIO STRATEGY AND LISTENER EXPERIENCE

In comparing the strategies of radio stations and broadcasters with reasons for listening there is a striking compatibility. When radio serves the subculture interests of listeners, complaints are rare. Lis-teners accept radio because it meets their specialized desires whether for rational, utilitarian concerns or emotional satisfaction. Similar to specialized print media, people usually do not listen to stations out-side the boundary of their lifestyles, except for curiosity, occasional mood changes, and when someone else controls the dial. Even when a person is forced to listen, the experience may be tolerated rather than perceived as a threat, as sometimes occurs with the limited alter-natives on television and newspapers. Even parents who find their teenager's rock station irritating may tolerate it as a passing phase. Consequently, radio usually makes a well-calculated attempt to meet the desires of listeners within a monetarily profitable framework.

However, if the profit orientation expands to the point at which stations attempt to enlarge their audience to near mass proportions, they run the risk of destroying the compatibility that initially led to their success. Since radio has achieved success by catering to sub-cultural interests, it may easily lose its appeal by diluting its approach. Indeed, this has recently occurred in large urban markets where formerly esoteric FM stations decided to become all things to all people or jumped from one format to another in search of the magic number one rating. The old formula of "play it safe," meaning hit the middle or top of the bell-shaped curve, is risky business, especially when the radio audience may not be characterized by a normal statistical distribution. As long as radio caters to specific rather than general interests, its success is, in part, assured.

But radio communication is more than a compatibility of interests as found in a music subculture or a sports talk show; at times it is a personal interaction between listener and broadcaster. While many people listen routinely at specific times of the day to particular broadcasters, this action is more than a ritual; it is a stable relationship with a consistent form and content. This consistency is achieved through the same procedures found in everyday, face-to-face interaction. Both broadcaster and listener form images of each other, imagine each other in a social setting, and speak or listen to each other in terms of those images. Once this role-taking process is routinized, both parties can predict the concerns of the other and how the other will act with a fair degree of accuracy. Listeners can depend on the fact that a broadcaster's emotional demeanor will remain consistent each day. They can anticipate without fear of disappointment that unique features of a broadcaster's program, humorous vignettes, anecdotes, quips, or serious features, will occur. Broadcasters can also predict with accuracy the profile of a typical listener and the social context in which listening occurs.

In other words, both broadcaster and listener can depend on the form and content of the relationship in much the same manner as occurs between friends. Therefore, compatibility between broadcaster and listener may occur on a personal level, providing a sense of stability to life. Surprisingly, this occurs in a communication context that appears at first glance to be fraught with ambiguity. In a setting in which neither party has visual contact with each other, and in which only one party, the listener, can form a somewhat specific image of the other, radio interaction can take on many of the characteristics of a compatible friendship, even to a level of intimacy.

MEDIA INFLUENCE

A major characteristic of radio communication is that its grammar and perspectives (subculture values and norms) have become so routinized that people take the language of radio for granted. Listeners depend on the fact that radio will provide utilitarian information, facilitate the accomplishment of various tasks, support various moods, and generally bracket the day in a consistent manner. In itself, this is an influence that has rather positive benefits for smoothly expediting everyday life and providing a sense of stability through predictability. A person can always turn on the radio and find the world pretty much as it was or is expected to be in a practical, although slightly superficial, manner.

In a more specific sense, radio links people within a subculture together, providing a feeling of belonging and a means for identity validation. In this fashion, radio functions as a significant other or reference group. Defined as a perspective anchored in a social network, reference groups serve to set forth and sanction values and norms for an individual. Radio can serve as an intermediary between a listener and a reference group, it may serve as a surrogate in place of a reference group, or it may serve as the reference group itself. In the latter case, a station becomes a source for identity validation, and listeners proudly proclaim their identification through T-shirts and bumper stickers. Certaily this is a goal of stations, as loyal listeners make prime advertising targets. As a reference group, stations and broadcasters also become a source of interpretation and legitimation on a variety of listener-interest topics. Examples include the definition of what constitutes good music, appropriate grammar and jargon within a subculture, acceptable humor, evaluations on subjects from the state of street repair to community morals, and proper citizenship.

The music a program director selects may be drawn from the hit-list in *Billboard* magazine or *Cashbox,* but how songs are ordered for air play carries the program director's personal mark. Therefore, the listener who relies on that station may accept the program director's selection and define it as what is good and "in" at the moment. What broadcaster's talk about and the manner in which they speak (hip, sassy, cynical, reverent, fast, slow, and so on) can be suggestive of how listeners should interpret various subjects. When Larry King selects a topic or personality for discussion or interview, he may legitimate the topic and elevate the significance of the interviewee in the minds of listeners. Consequently, broadcasters may become significant as opinion leaders as well as role models. As with any medium, when radio functions as a reference group, its influence with listeners is potentially significant, and listeners may become rather uncritical in their evaluations.

If radio can function as a reference group, it follows that broadcasters can facilitate a highly personal relationship with listeners. At the extreme of interpersonal interaction, a broadcaster may become an intimate friend in the mind of a listener. Since this all occurs "live," radio is at present the most personal of all major media. As one broadcaster summarized,

> Radio is a personal medium and that's its magic. A smiling voice is nearly always on the dial and I know listeners want that; if I didn't, I wouldn't be doing this.

From the listeners point of view came the following comment: "I feel he is talking right to me, that I am part of his special club." The commitment and loyalty associated with this intimacy results in a high sense of satisfaction for broadcasters as it would for anyone involved in a close interpersonal relationship. A talk show host, Roger Carroll, remarked in an interview recorded for the *Phoenix Gazette* (Doup, 1978: E-1):

> I have to be a lot of things to a lot of people, a minister, a psychiatrist, a leader, and a parent. They'll say some very personal things on the radio before all these people. There are things people wouldn't say to their minister. . . . The bottom line is to be a friend. . . . There are far too many lonely people and we serve a purpose by talking to them. I see myself as a social worker in mass communication.

From comments such as these there is little reason to doubt that radio communication can provide some of the same benefits found in face-to-face relations. In itself, this is a major point in the media culture of contemporary urban society.

In contrast to the highly personal character of radio communication is the potential for broadcasters to become casual and blasé. For example, some stations and broadcasters tend to present a "don't worry" attitude. Since listeners generally approach radio through a positive framework and stations wish to keep listeners happy, a don't worry attitude may develop. For example, a station may give a few editorials on conserving energy and then spend a lot of time talking about events to attend, places to shop, "see you at the arts festival this weekend," and so on, as if to say there really were no problem with energy after all. By creating the impression of abundance and unlimited fun, listeners may be encouraged to stand pat and go on blithely ignoring issues and controversies that are critical in the long run.

People in this frame of mind who also have a high exposure to other entertainment media constitute a real threat to those people who are actively engaged in promoting political and social involvement for the purpose of change. On this matter, radio is no different or not better than other major media that employ the entertainment perspectives. Consequently, media influence through radio may result in a slightly conservative or apathetic attitude. On the other hand, a sense of stability can be gained from a position of apathy or conservativism.

The contrast between intimacy and the casual blasé attitude raises a question on the potency of radio. Radio is considered by some a less potent medium than television, film, or print because it lacks visual impact. Yet ask people who grew up with radio and they will defend the potency of this medium through its ability to excite the imagination. Those of us old enough to remember radio's golden age recall with fondness the images stimulated by the likes of *Inner Sanctum, The Shadow, Fibber McGee's* closet, *You Are There,* or baseball games and boxing matches (for their excitement and impact these may never be replaced by television). In the absence of direct visual cues, a listener creates images and elaborates on those described by announcers. This process results in a key ingredient in generating excitement—anticipation. In fact, the emotional satisfaction of anticipation often exceeds the real thing. Perhaps it is anticipation that leads some advertising experts (see Schwartz, 1974) to claim that radio has a higher retention capability and consequent influence than either television or print.

We cannot discount radio's potential to influence listeners, yet few people criticize radio for harmful effects. The major reason is not that radio avoids controversial topics, as song lyrics, talk show subjects, issue-oriented forum discussions, and even news, clearly constitute controversial material. The answer lies in the fact that listeners use radio as a link to a social world that is relevant for their concerns. The form and content of radio are perceived by the public as oriented to specific groups. Consequently, the standards applied to a mass medium, such as television, simply do not apply to most radio stations. In addition, many listeners use other media, rather than radio, for the purpose of stimulating controversy. Even studies of talk shows discovered that most callers were not interested in argument but in making conversation with a real person. That radio is not a means for vicarious escape, sensationalism, or controversy in no way detracts from radio's potential power. Rather, the important point is that a media culture from radio is found mainly in the meanings listeners develop for their listening experience. Whether listeners develop a blasé attitude or a high degree of emotional excitement is a matter of how they use radio. Therefore, the influence emerging through radio is also based more on how the audience influences radio format and content than on how radio influences the audience.

Finally, we may conclude that an influence associated with radio language does little to promote cultural standardization. With the exception of magazines, radio is the most demassified of the major media. To a significant extent, the variety of subcultures and regional differences in American society are maintained through radio. It is still possible to find small-town radio stations broadcasting hints to the homemaker, education on health and safety, high school sports, a montage of corny but enjoyable music, and the halting speech of the amateur announcer who reminds us there is still room for pleasant unsophistication outside the slick and rapid pace of urban life. Stations such as KBWN in ShowLow, Arizona, "The Voice of the White Mountains," demonstrate that media can still serve local interests in a grass-roots fashion. Still, upwardly or outwardly mobile youth may view their small-town radio station as representative of a bush league they wish to escape. Whatever the definition, a radio station is a reference point and a microcosm of culture that many of us use as either a perspective to adopt or as a means of bracketing or defining some reality.

By and large, radio listeners do not fall into an uncritical attitude toward radio nor do they seem overly blasé in their response to radio form and content. Since specialized media, such as magazines and radio, cater to specific identity concerns of the audience, the audience tends to impose its subcultural language on the media, and woe be the station or magazine that does not heed its audience's desire: As yet, this is not the case with television.

CHAPTER 5

TELEVISION
The Cultural Mainstream

A few years ago, a noted media critic stated, "TV has become a reality for many people because it is more tolerable than any other. Real reality is too impossibly complex to deal with . . . television we can bear" (Littlejohn, 1975: 79). If this statement is correct, we have a serious problem on our hands. As the decade of the eighties began, Americans were spending more time watching television than ever before (nearly 7 hours a day per household in 1982). No doubt many factors account for the amount of time spent watching TV—increased leisure time, boredom, the desire for a little diversion, the security offered by routine viewing habits, and the attractiveness and stimulation of particular subjects. But these reasons are only superficial indicators of the real problem.

To understand the labyrinth of contemporary television culture we need to discover the meanings people attach to their television viewing experiences and to compare those meanings with the communication strategies used in television. For some people television is simply an escape no more serious than an occasional daydream. For others, television may constitute background noise used to fill a room with sounds approximating social activity, or it may serve as a guide for interpreting much of what goes on in the outside world. But for extremely media conscious viewers, television represents a realm that is substituted for a nontelevised reality. We need to examine how these people watch television, not just in terms of the subjects that interest them but through the language and perspectives they use to perceive their television experience. To answer these and other questions requires suspending judgment on what we normally take for granted about television.

To begin, what does it mean to define television as a medium of mass culture? Television is a true mass medium in that it presents the commonly held values and norms in American society. Prime-time programs appeal to a middle-class family with middlebrow artistic taste and middle-of-the-road politics and religion. The ideals of hard work, rationality, sensibility, fair play, and good humor abound in such all-time favorite hits as *Gunsmoke, Bonanza, Marcus Welby, M.D., The Mary Tyler Moore Show,* and, of course, Johnny Carson's *Tonight Show.* Over the past thirty years, television stars such as Andy Griffith, James Arness (Matt Dillon), Lorne Greene (Pa Cartwright), Johnny Carson, Mary Tyler Moore, Walter Cronkite, and recently Alan Alda and the Fonz have represented the honesty, strength, goodness, fair-mindedness, and vulnerability of ideal American character.

Through these images television follows a status-quo strategy of upholding America's traditions, and it is precisely this strategy that enables television to attract a mass audience. The mass audience is not achieved through an appeal to the lowest common denominator; rather, it is achieved by framing programs in ideals that result in the least amount of objection from the audience. Even the slapstick, crude humor of the top-rated *Beverly Hillbillies* and *Laverne & Shirley* did not stray from honesty, kindness, industry, and so on as central problem-solving measures. Compare the *Beverly Hillbillies* to *The Waltons,* and the only major difference is grammatical style, not the interpretive prespectives.

To understand the specific character of television's mass audience strategy we turn again to an examination of grammar (syntax, inflection, and vocabulary) and perspectives. This analysis is followed by a description of the television influence and various implications including cultural change resulting from television and the influence of television on other media.

Television Grammar

Most people are quite familiar with the grammar of television, yet viewing has become so routinized that many viewers seldom think about the specific methods television uses to present news, entertainment, or sports. Beyond some obvious technical factors, such as camera shots, dissolves, slow-motion replays, and the like, viewers assume that seeing something on TV is much the same as seeing in everyday life. These viewers fail to understand that television employs a unique language that has a particular logic all its own. Seeing something on television is not the same as just looking through a camera lens; it involves a multiplicity of factors that orient and shape interpretations of phenomena. The meanings that emerge from television experience may be much different than meanings arrived at through other media. Marshall McLuhan noted the difference between a world experienced through television as opposed to print media, and while critics took McLuhan to task for such unscientific concepts as "cool" and "hot" media, he was on the right track.

Media organizations construct language and logic variations just as people do in creating colloquial dialects, such as "jive" talk, Cajun, or Tidewater Virginian. Each language and dialect has a structure that must be understood as a precondition to arrive at meanings through that language. Therefore, the first concern in understanding television is to examine its unique language.

SYNTAX

As defined earlier, the syntax of media grammar involves the organization of subject matter. In part, the syntax strategy of television follows two separate cycles of viewer behavior: consumer habits and daily work and recreation routines. Since TV programs are packages for commercials, the strategy is to stimulate people to watch commercials, especially during those peak buying periods throughout the year.

Buying habits of Americans follow seasonal cycles with a peak period beginning in the fall and ending before the New Year's holiday. After a midwinter slump, consumption of major items increases again in the spring and drops off late in May. Television programming follows this seasonal consumption cycle with new programs unveiled in the early fall followed by a second season of new programs or miniseries beginning in February. Summer is a period of reruns and experimentation for future schedules. The obvious logic is that since viewers will watch new programs, especially when their routines are homebound, they constitute a captive audience for heavy advertising exposure.

The other viewer cycle follows typical daily and weekly behavior routines. As creatures of habit (habits that are not easily altered), viewing behavior is highly predictable. Network programmers know when a family is likely to watch TV together, when an audience will consist mainly of preadolescents, and so on. For example, since Sunday evening is a fairly relaxed period and all family members are usually home, programs are geared to the entire family. Weekend afternoons are reserved for sports and recreation programs appealing mainly to adult males. Kids wishing to do nothing on Saturday morning watch cartoons. During the most intense and active part of the work week, prime-time drama and comedy provide relaxation for everyone.

Viewer interest also varies throughout the day. Weekday morning programs are oriented to news, education, and human interest; lively game shows are scheduled during the domestic chores period; relaxed soaps are for the midday siesta; old reruns and clown shows entertain kids after school; news either precedes or follows dinner, which blends into prime-time entertainment; and, finally, night owls are satisfied with talk shows and an old series or movies. Thus the syntax of television scheduling follows the routine rhythms of viewers, whether on a seasonal, weekly, or daily cycle.

Within these cycles, networks and local stations are constantly attempting to get the lion's share of the audience. Strategies such as "block" or "power" programming are used to put together a package that will hold viewers through a three- to four-hour time period. Since news precedes prime time, it is critical to develop a large and loyal news audience. Consequently, it may be hypothesized that salaries paid to anchorpersons are based more on their ability to attract an audience than on professional news skills, although the two are not necessarily mutually exclusive.

Following the news, each network usually begins a weeknight, prime-time block with a comedy or a light drama. The sequence may be one of beginning with something light and preferably a proven hit, followed by a new program, and ending with a heavy dramatic hit. Since hour-long programs and movies begin on the hour, half-hour programs are placed back-to-back, with sitcoms usually in a four-pack, two-hour block. On any given week night one network will schedule four sitcoms and a drama while the other two schedule three dramas or one light drama and a movie.

This scheduling syntax has been moderately successful, but with cassette recorders and cable, viewers are becoming far more selective in determining what and when they will watch. It will be interesting to see the impact that increased viewer selectivity will have on the ratings business and program scheduling; there are some who predict that selectivity and flexibility in viewing habits already place the networks in the category of dinosaurs.

Syntax also involves the organization of content in particular programs. These syntax rules, most of which we take for granted, are important as prior conditions to interpreting program content. For example, except for a slight deviation in soap operas, each program has a beginning, a middle, and an end in that order. This may seem superfluous, although the French film maker, Jean Luc Goddard, once defined his avant-garde films as having a beginning, middle, and end but not necessarily in that order. The fact that television programs begin clearly with a problem of some kind to be solved and end in resolution results in a high degree of predictability. Viewers have the satisfaction of knowing a program will have a distinct beginning with no missing parts and that it will conclude with no loose ends.

Rarely does a television program work backwards through a plot, as is the case with some movies, and rarely is there any question as to the chronology of scenes. Consequently, the linear sequential order of a television program follows a cause-and-effect logic understood by all viewers. The subtleties of this syntax, as aided by inflection techniques (for example, music and the pace of action), cue viewers to anticipate what will occur next—an action or love scene, a commercial, or the climax. For entertainment programs it is not even necessary to watch the clock to determine how much time has elapsed in a program: Television syntax has been internalized as a clock.

It is also important to note that a television script ensures that interaction will unfold in an orderly sequence, with each person politely taking their turn and viewers seeing and hearing all the relevant dialogue. This is not the case in everyday life. We often must ask people to repeat themselves, and we often are obscured from the critical responses people make toward our actions. In television, questions get immediate and clear answers, dialogue is never confusing, awkward pauses do not occur unless they are appropriate, and the star usually has the last word. Even the innovative *Hill Street Blues,* which allows viewers to witness several subplots simultaneously, has a clear chronology through a day in the life of this precinct. And the final scene in *Hill Street* often shows the stalwart Captain Furillo and sophisticated Joyce Davenport providing the episode's denouement.

One of the most interesting examples of syntax applies to television news, particularly the evening network newscast. For several decades viewers have become accustomed to a precise ordering of visual and auditory events. The broadcast opens with a full-length view of the anchorperson at a desk in a newsroom setting. Slowly the camera zooms to a close-up of the anchorperson, who gives the introduction to the lead story. For each news story the syntax consists of an introduction by the anchor, a report from a correspondent usually on location, and accompaning film or graphics. Graphics on economic statistics are presented at the program's midpoint, and the program closes with a light story, a medium camera shot of the anchorperson, and a dissolve into the logo backed by a familiar electronic theme.

The importance of this syntax is not ony its familiarity, but also the significance it imparts to the anchorperson who opens and closes the broadcast and introduces each story. Through this practice the anchor is seen as someone who lends personal credibility to the stories, ultimately establishing what is considered "newsworthy." Through this grammatical technique, news is not just an information report—it is Dan Rather's, Tom Brokaw's, and Frank Reynold's report to the nation on what is news that day. Even field correspondents are given credibility by the anchorperson's introduction to their stories.

An additional point about news syntax concerns an observation recently raised by several journalists (John Roche, Ron Rosenbaum, and George Will) that television news emphasizes moments in time, particularly emotional moments, rather than stressing historical sequence. The idea is that given the importance of news film or tape, emphasis is placed on involving the viewer in the emotion of the moment rather than interpreting events as part of a chronological sequence with historical significance. While the emphasis on emotional moment is an inflection device, the impact has implications for the syntax of news over the long run. The notion that some news is old and not worth reporting stems in part from the position that if the event is connected to some prior event and now lacks emotional punch, it is irrelevant. Over time viewers may lose a sense of history as they orient primarily to what's happening now, just as they do when viewing an entertainment program.

Although there is a danger in overgeneralizing this point, it is worth considering for the sake of examining how any news event is interpreted. In short, news for the moment is contextualized within emotional appeals of immediate relevance and decontextualized from an interpretive sequence of events that may soften or eliminate the immediate emotional appeal. In this case a rational lineal syntax of news events is abandoned in favor of a nonrational syntax.

INFLECTION

With both visual and auditory sensory involvement available to television, syntax is embellished through a variety of inflection techniques, which for my purpose is divided into accent or emphasis techniques and features of rhythm and tempo. Beginning with accent techniques, the title track of an entertainment video production is a one-minute ministatement of what to expect in the form and content of the entire program. Music themes, title graphics, optical effects, and the montage of character images establish the mood of the program, indicate the rhythm and tempo that the program will follow, and serve as a program's identity symbol. The instant a title graphic is flashed on the screen a musical theme underscores the program's identity; hear the theme and the title graphic can be visualized or vice versa. Like an advertising jingle, many viewers recall the distinctive music themes of favorite programs long after their cancellation. More than bits of trivia, these devices remind viewers of a host of feelings associated with the program. Sandy Dvore, a specialist in TV titles states:

> A good main title can produce that little bit of good feeling that it's your time of the week, and that there is some consistency in life from week to week. You know where you belong for those couple of hours. It's like a comfortable shirt [Director, 1980: 39].

Nostalgia is always "in" because recall of old emotional identity feelings is often quite satisfying. How many viewers will forget the title scene for *Gunsmoke, Bonanaza, All in the Family,* and for old-timers, Milton Berle's *Texaco Hour* or *Have Gun Will Travel*? This nostalgia exercise demonstrates the power of title tracks to represent the entire style and emotional emphasis of a program. As Sandy Dvore adds, "It [title track] has to have the successful continuity of a one hour show in one-minute form." A few outstanding examples in recent memory include *M*A*S*H, Happy Days, Star Trek,* and *60 Minutes.*

Accent techniques are probably the least noticed features of television grammar. It is common knowledge that costuming and physical traits of characters instantly establish them as heroes, villains, or fools, but taken for granted are camera distances, angles, lighting, set design, sound effects, and editing.

Camera distance and angle effect affect the physical location of viewers with respect to the action. We do not simply see the action—we see it from a vantage point determined by a director. For example, the distance between a viewer and actor and the length of the shot affect a sense of social distance just as they do in real life. The closer a person is to another and the longer a person has a close-up view, the more intimate the relationship.

Soap operas are notorious for long, drawn-out close-up shots affording the viewer a good view of many body language cues. In contrast, the situation comedy uses more group shots, enabling viewers to see the comedy reactions to straight lines. In the dramatic program, action shots begin with an establishing long shot and zoom in to capture the intensity of emotional reactions. In newscasts, note how most reporters are shown from the waist or chest up, standing with perfect erect posture in front of the story's setting. The anchorperson sits erect with head slightly bent forward suggesting a serious demeanor. Rarely do news journalists blink, perspire, or use their hands nervously on camera, and the light is always just right.

Regardless of the type of program genre, camera angles are used to indicate the status and power of characters to each other and between actors and viewers. A camera angle directed upward to place the actor above the viewer's eye level establishes submission, and the star is always favorably situated when action commences and concludes. And let's not forget the romantic kiss, which usually ends with the woman's face toward the camera for a close-up of her expression and nonverbal participation.

Lighting is critical not just for the exacting requirements of color photography, but for establishing characterization and mood. Lights directed from below eye-level of the actors produce a sinister effect, whereas back lighting, soft fill, and key lights suggest honesty, virtue, and strength. The extraordinary character of television and the intensity of a scene are due to the right combination of light, camera shots, and set design.

Set design is important for at least two reasons, the first of which aids in establishing the stereotype of characters. Bachelor pads, blue-collar family homes, and a professional's office all have furnishings that accent the character's lifestyle. Archie Bunker's chair became almost as famous as the character himself. Second, the types of interpersonal relationships that exist on a formal to informal continuum are aided by the type of furnishings in a scene and how characters are placed with respect to those furnishings. For example, to establish intimacy and to facilitate the mood of informality, sets should have soft comfortable furniture. But a tense scene between lovers often takes place in an office or with the characters standing in order to blur out the surrounding props. Whether it takes place on a sofa, at a kitchen table, or in a barren hallway, the character of a conversation is partially established by set design.

Of all inflection techniques, *sound effects* and sound quality are probably the least noticed of all inflection devices. Given our familiarity with the medium of film, we are accustomed to high-quality sound and expect the same from television—a reason most television shows are produced under studio conditions. Background noise must be absent unless appropriate, actors are given the right amount of base or treble to enhance their voices, popping p's and hissing "s" sounds are muted out, and sound tracks are "sweetened" with everything from audience laughter to the sound of chewing foods. Technicians use elaborate machines consisting of tape loops of realistic sound effects, which are integrated to produce thousands of different combinations. Almost every television program has sound effects added to the final product. Laughs are even scripted according to a rating scale so that each line in a sitcom receives the appropriate type and amount of laughter from quiet chuckles to thundering guffaws. Gone are the days of when canned laughter sounded like a rattling trash can; today laughter is from real folks but embellished so viewers feel safe in laughing and know the type of laughter that is appropriate.

Finally, *music* is the element that eliminates any remaining ambiguity in identifying types of characters and the type of emotions to expect in a scene. Evil villains are french horns, violins and flutes are fair maidens, piccolos are kids, bassoons are old men, and trumpets are heroes. This may be a bit exaggerated but not unfamiliar. Programs are also given identifiable theme music, some of which have become popular hits like the themes from *Star Trek, Welcome Back Kotter, Hill Street Blues,* and of course *Sesame Street.* To establish and maintain familiarity these themes are integrated with dialogue and scenes throughout the program. Music subculture styles are also matched to the appropriate programs. *The Dukes of Hazzard* is scored with modified bluegrass, *Dallas* has a full orchestra, and *The Jeffersons* uses an uptown gospel ditty.

Among television technicians, *editing* of film and tape is considered the most important skill in putting together the final product. All the techniques used to accent and establish emphasis may be ruined through poor editing. As an accent technique, the edit places emphasis on particular scenes to the exclusion of others, something that is especially important in news. When voice-over dialogue in a newscast is supported by carefully edited film or tape, the emphasis in the story generally emerges from the film rather than from verbal narration. Unfortunately, viewers may not understand that news is edited in the same manner as situation comedy or soap operas. As discussed in event-centered newspaper reporting, placing emphasis on the dramatic aspects of a story may deemphasize other, more significant aspects. Viewers may see conflict in an event where very little actually exists. There are many aspects of news story that may be emphasized to the point that viewers are misled, and some of these will be covered later in the chapter.

At this point, the concern is with establishing that editing is a common feature of television grammar used to tell a story. Without editing, television would be experienced much differently than it is at present. To underscore the importance of editing, particularly in news production, a short anecdote may be of value.

Some years ago I had the opportunity to be a judge in the annual Radio and Television News Directors Awards contest. Discussing the merits of various news and documentary entries with a panel of judges from the television industry, I was constantly struck by the fact that the major criteria they used to judge news quality consisted of production technique rather than news content. A colleague, David Altheide, had exactly the same experience, described in an article published in 1978.

Editing is not only an accent technique; it is also vital for developing the all-important rhythm and tempo in television programs. In fact, all inflection accent techniques in television grammar are important for developing the flow and pace of a program. Television genre such as talk shows, sitcoms, drama, and news have a particular tempo similar to different types of music. Soap operas are slow, sitcoms upbeat, and game shows frantic. While each of these programs is written and directed to achieve a particular pace, it is only through editing that an exact tempo is achieved. Scenes are blended together through dissolves, jump cuts, or those cute devices called "wipes"—the closing circle, rectangle, or diamong that erases one scene while adding another. The editor synchronizes the edit with dialogue and smooths it over with music to maintain the pace. In this fashion, we see the fast chase scenes so prevalent on *Starsky and Hutch* and *The Rockford Files,* the love triangles on *General Hospital,* and uninterrupted laughter on all those wonderful sitcoms recently so popular.

Action programs present a challenge for editors and directors. How does one maintain the up-tempo beat of action for an hour-long program? It is accomplished by reducing the amount of time for dialogue and expanding the apparent action with fill shots of people driving from one point to another, speeding police cars with sirens blaring, jets taking off and landing, people running up and down stairways, and the all-time favorite, dueling cars on a narrow mountain road. Substracting the time for such scenes leaves approximately fifteen minutes or less of actual dialogue in an hour-long program. This formula was taken to the extreme by Steven Spielberg in the made-for-television film, *Duel,* in which the hero, Dennis Weaver, battled an 18-wheel tanker on mountain roads in his Plymouth Valiant (how appropriate).

Inflection in television grammar is also found in the rhythm of the daily program schedule, the internal rhythm of specific programs, and variations in rhythm preference by categories of listeners. As evidence for the rhythm of the daily schedule, notice that most stations broadcast news, game shows, soaps, and children's programs at nearly the same time each day. In addition, each program has the internal pattern of beginning with the prelude or "grabber," followed by an easy rhythm for developing the story, a build to a climax, and an ending on a moderate beat. Perhaps this internal rhythm is analogous to the change in musical rhythms from 2/4, to 4/4, 3/4, and 6/8, ending with 4/4. This pattern will vary by the type of program, with detective shows using greater variety in rhythms than soap operas or talk shows.

The main point here is that television scheduling and specific programs have rhythms that viewers implicitly understand. When those rhythm norms are violated, such as a detective show that follows waltz time for an entire hour (e.g., NBC's low-rated *Remington Steele*), viewers become uncomfortable. The most common example of this violation is the movie or play that works well in the theater but has far too little rhythmic variation for the hard-core TV viewer. Various age and social class groups of viewers have differing rhythm preferences, with older adults favoring relaxed rhythms, kids seeking a bouncy beat, and teenagers demanding high energy. This variation in preferences is one reason why it is sometimes so difficult to get children and teenagers to sit for an hour-long educational documentary or classic play. It also may explain why adults become edgy watching youth-oriented sitcoms.

The final component of television grammar consists of the *vocabulary* characteristics in television talk. Since the appeal is to a mass audience, it is no surprise that television requires a vocabulary that will be understood by the largest possible audience. However, word selection is not based on a lowest common denominator comprehension level. Television vocabulary must fit within a range acceptable to the middle class, since middle-class norms and values best represent the idealization of American society. In other words, vocabulary must be easily understood but not insulting to the class taste of middle America.

On the other hand, vocabulary must not be too sophisticated, as any attempt to use so-called big words will be criticized as being a conceited status ploy. Soportscaster Howard Cosell's deliberate use of apparently sophisticated descriptive terms is occasionally the object of ridicule, although he has turned this into an entertainment strategy. In examining the vocabulary of most television programs it is apparent that little variation exists in the sophistication level of words whether it is a newscast, sports event, or prime-time entertainment program.

In describing the linguistic characteristics of radio talk, Erving Goffman (1981) noted that listeners expect to hear talk that appears spontaneous and fresh. It seems reasonable to assume that this criterion may apply to television as well. Freshness or spontaneity is achieved in television by emulating typical, everyday, polite conversation in middle-class society. In this situation, the attempt among interacting parties is to be clear, friendly, and equal, rather than obtuse, formal, and superior. Words in everyday conversation and on television must flow easily, convey instant meaning, and never put a viewer down. In addition, a general rule of thumb in selecting vocabulary for television is to avoid detracting from the visual impact on the screen. Viewers must see the action and be able to make an instant interpretation without stumbling over the dialogue. Therefore, TV vocabulary is descriptive and active without being noticed by viewers.

An interesting exercise in TV vocabulary is constructing titles for TV movies. Since there is no word of mouth advertising, a title in the program schedule must lure the viewer. An executive for NBC says:

> We look for words of movement, words of action. . . . We like to have the word "love" in the title if at all possible. If we can get an action word

and "love" in the same title *(A Cry for Love)*, it's perfect [Stein, 1981: 35].

Deanne Barkley of Osmond TV commented that titles are so important she has purchased pictures on the strength of the title alone (a victim of TV's influence?). Paul Klein, a leading program specialist in television, has even more dramatic principles, claiming that "a title must have sex, love, but especially human abuse. Human abuse works far better than sex. Sex can scare off people over 50. But roll it with abuse and you get everyone." He also adds that "mystery" is a key word as it indicates something unexpected will happen. On the other hand, an ABC executive claims that sex is well ahead of violence, and he looks for more rape in titles. CBS countered by betting on terror (Stein, 1981).

But television also uses a great deal of vernacular expression, jargon, and dialect, especially in the entertainment fare of prime time. While this seems to represent a deviation from middle-class standards, the deviation, if at all, is slight. Television makes an effort to achieve some accuracy in portraying subcultures, regional characteristics, and contemporary slang, but it orients this strategy toward the middle-class observer rather than toward the people within the subcultures or geographic regions portrayed in the stories. Consequently, vernacular or slang may be used liberally as long as the terms are consistent with what is tolerated in normal polite conversation. Recently, "hell" replaced "heck," "damn" replaced "darn," and grammatical atrocities such as "I go" and "he goes" replaced "I said" and "he said," and so on.

The dialect of television is one of the more interesting aspects of the power of this medium and its effect on a standardization of vocal style in American culture. Announcers, sportscasters, newscasters, and almost everyone else who is not doing character dialect sound exactly the same. Perhaps native New Yorkers, ghetto blacks, southerners, and anyone else with a trace of dialect receive their vocal training somewhere in the Midwest (minus the twang). For media culture the point is that the mass media have established the standard for vocal quality, elocution, and the apparent absence of dialect for the entire society. Dan Rather of CBS news is from Texas, but you would never know it from listening to him on a newscast. While Bryant Gumbel of NBC's today show is black, he lacks the familiar ghetto or southern dialect. This point is not made in support of racial, ethnic, or regional stereotypes, but to illustrate the fact that a homogeneity has been created in an idealized form through television grammar.

PERSPECTIVES

The major perspectives of television consist of stereotyping for simplicity, a range of entertainment strategies, and ideal norms. At the risk of being redundant, bear in mind that each of these constitutes a way in which various phenomena are perceived and defined, so that the meanings of television experience for both media professionals and the audience are shaped by these perspectives.

The majority of television programs are framed in perspectives that embody mainstream American taste, values, and norms. To portray these characteristics in a manner that results in quick identification by viewers, television often deals in simple *stereotypes*. Stereotypes are little more than short-hand categories of belief and typical behavior traits, based sometimes on fact but often on irrational criteria for self-serving purposes.

As a normal process of everyday life, individuals categorize or sterotype other people in order to predict how they may act or respond. The sociologist Gregory Stone argued some years ago that in order to engage in role taking, a person must identify who the other is before he or she can develop the empathy necessary for predicting how that other might act. Since stereotyping permits quick identification through a process of generalization, it follows that accuracy is a major concern in evaluating a stereotype. When generalizations are based on exaggerations, distortions, or even outright fabrication, the act of stereotyping may be a dangerous procedure, and in making these exaggerations, individuals are no better or worse than media. But since television deals with a mass audience, the propensity is to present exaggeration and use superficial generalization for instant viewer recognition. What this means for viewers is that television's view of the human condition is largely stereotyped and superficial as opposed to the more detailed view obtained through specialized media.

To understand how television employs a stereotype strategy, begin with popular entertainment programs, such as the situation comedy, and consider the program's theme or angle and how the main characters deal with that theme. For example, the success of *The Mary Tyler Moore Show* was due in large measure to the fact that Mary Richards,

Lou Grant, Murray Slaughter, Ted Baxter, Rhoda Morgenstern, and Phyllis Lindstrom were all stereotypes we knew and loved. *Three's Company* employed the classic dumb blond, the rational brunette, the flaky landlord, and the burlesque good guy who always gets himself into a pickle. In *M*A*S*H*, Hawkeye is Groucho Marx; Hot Lips, the sensuous shrew; Frank Burns, the inept villain; and Radar, the straight man. In addition, each of the *M*A*S*H* characters is stereotyped in some other manner, such as the sane voice (Hawkeye, BJ, and Colonel Potter) amidst the madness of war, Hot lips as the bureaucrat with an underlife, Frank Burns as the hypocrite, and Radar as the innocent. *Magnum P.I.* took the virile, street-wise 1940s detective, dressed him in casual Hawaiian attire, added a baseball cap for a common touch, and juxtaposed him to a sophisticated but lovable snob (Higgins) and two "boys" for a fun-filled romp through action-packed capers involving the inevitable gorgeous woman.

Television uses every stereotype in the common sociological variables of age, gender, social class, education, and occupation and combines them with various roles, such as the teenager, lover, parent, and so on. Viewers are given little insight into specific individuals, nor are actors allowed to develop their characters much beyond the stereotype. And that is the point: Characterization on television usually ends with the stereotype in a "what-you-see-is-what-you-get" manner.

Entertainment television also goes beyond the exaggeration of specific characters to an over- and underrepresentation of some characters. Young, handsome blond adults are overrepresented while some minority groups are both underrepresented and distorted. Settings are often too comfortable and people rarely are so financially strapped they are forced to do without necessities, such as food and fashionable dress. More important, problems are always solved and with a minimum of effort, particularly on *Love Boat* and *Fantasy Island*.

Problems themselves are stereotyped, usually in a superficial manner. Marital difficulties, especially on soap operas, are often described as resulting from the intrusion of a younger and apparently more exciting woman. Teenagers' problems usually have something to do with honesty and physical attractiveness. Crime is rarely explained; it is just handled. Violence is intolerable only if it is perpetrated by the forces of evil.

Belief that exaggerated stereotypes are a successful mass appeal strategy is evidenced no more clearly than in advertising. Harried housewives are thankful over Mr. Muscle oven cleaner; doting husbands rave over Stovetop dressing; lovers become smugly confident after using the right deodorant, shampoo, and mouthwash; snobbish aristocrats drive off in a Rabbit diesel, and milquetoast accounts are brought to tears before Mr. Goodwrench fixes their cars. Every common role in society is played out with an exaggeration that exceeds absurdity, and yet it goes on and on without complaint from viewers.

Stereotypes such as these fail to reveal the complexity found in real life, but they do present recognizable confrontations that provide the heroes a chance to perform. For example, we take for granted that events in a dramatic program will unfold in a manner requiring the star to solve problems in a superhuman fashion. The climax will consist of a showdown, in which reason is tried first, followed by emotional and physical action. This clearly was demonstrated in episodes of *Star Trek* in which Mr. Spock gave all the rational data available for solving the problem, but it was Captain Kirk's intuition and moxy that saved the day. In *The Incredible Hulk* the sensitive hero tried reason (always in vain) and then tossed villains into walls like so many darts. Viewers have become quite familiar with these formulas as they have not changed appreciably for thirty years. In situation comedy, *Mork and Mindy* is *My Favorite Martian; Diff'rent Strokes* is *Leave it to Beaver; Happy Days* is *Ozzie and Harriet;* and *Gilligan's Island* is every inane sitcom ever made. Such consistency explains why reruns of old programs are still popular with kids today.

Stereotypes are successful at the mass level of television because they are familiar and relate in some way to experiences or concerns common among viewers. Occasionally, there is daring innovation in television, but the rule is to "play it safe" and give people what has worked in the past, changing only the cosmetics. As a result, stereotypes constitute a specific viewpoint that, in turn, becomes an interpretation strategy for media professionals and the audience.

The perspective found in almost every television program including news, documentary, and even science programs is *entertainment.* In developing a strategy to appeal to the largest possible audience, it would seem that a common desire cutting across a large aggregate of people's entertainment. However, entertainment tastes vary, and there is no guarantee that a specific type of entertainment will appeal to a diverse body of people unless they all are receptive to a particular kind of entertainment at that moment, such as the circus audience or a sports crowd. But over the years, every medium attempting large-scale audience appeal has established itself as an entertainment vehicle. This tradition is seen in such examples as Rome, medieval fairs, Elizabethan theater, vaudeville, Hollywood film, radio, and now television. People accept, even demand, entertainment from television as long as it falls within a parameter of middle-American taste. As such, viewers are selectively attentive to entertainment from television at almost any moment they switch on the set.

Television entertainment employs all the characteristics of the entertainment perspective described in Chapter 1: talent is extraordinary, subjects and personalities seem larger than everyday life, close-up photography invites vicarious involvement, and programs are often emotionally satisfying. For example, in the popular sitcom *M*A*S*H,* not only is the situation of war extraordinary in itself, but each character is a highly skilled technician as are the actors who portray them. Also, the camera places the viewer in the scene so that one can often imagine oneself playing the role or feel like a silent participant. The program begins with an episodic problem and always ends with a solution or conclusion to the episode. What ties these facets of entertainment together and gives television its potential impact in holding an audience's attention, is drama, comedy, or both. As in film, television is equipped to dramatize both visual and auditory cues; nothing need be left to a viewer's imagination. In *M*A*S*H* we see almost every detail from the physical environment of the camp to the clear emotional expressions of the characters. Above all else, we watch the unfolding of the story with appropriate dramatic emphasis, climax, and aftermath.

The drama factor in television entertainment is also clearly present in newscasts, talk shows, game shows, and, of course, the epitome of TV drama—the soap opera. Network news is dramatic in several respects. First, the anchorperson projects a serious and authoritative demeanor that apparently only middle-aged people can carry off successfully. Credibility is also dramatically emphasized by staging the newscast inside the newsroom. Background music enhances the serious atmosphere, the rhythm and tempo of speech are matter-of-fact, story length is short, and almost every news event has film and graphics to emphasize visually the drama. Today, there is little difference between a network newscast and the entertainment format used in theater—both employ dramatic staging techniques to frame their subject matter. By contrast, local newscasts in the seventies used a comedy framework called "happy-talk." Newscasters bantered back and forth with short quips, there always seemed to be a remote minicam report with some eccentric character, weather forecasters dressed in clown suits, and the newscast always ended with a humorous bit of irony. Sometimes it seemed the only straight reporting occurred on the sports segment. The entire scene was not unlike the satirical skit "Weekend Update," on NBC's *Saturday Night Live.*

An unfortunate illustration of the entertainment perspective in news occurred in August of 1981 when Christine Craft was removed from her anchor slot at KMBC in Kansas City, Missouri. A viewer survey revealed that she looked "too old, too unattractive, not deferential enough to men, and unacceptable because of her California background." While she was praised as a journalist, her ratings on entertainment and upholding a traditional woman's role were low. Reacting to her situation, Craft indicated she had compromised enough, even to the point of following explicit instructions on how to dress for each newscast. Commenting on the importance of a journalist's wardrobe, Lynn Wilford, a consultant for Media Associates, said that anchors need to know that

> certain fabrics and certain materials do not work on the air. The reality is that TV news is contained in an entertainment medium and the criteria used to judge TV news people are the same ones used to judge people in soap operas and talk shows [Nadel, 1982: 15].

As a strategy for dealing with issues presented on prime-time programs, television utilizes another important perspective—*ideal norms.* Ideal norms are the traditions of hard work, honesty, modesty, fidelity, and so on, which everyone upholds in principle. They are essential in society as they constitute the fundamental moral principles that make the image of social order possible and are ideal in the sense that following these rules is considered the best possible course of action. Despite the occasional and even frequent deviance from these ideals in everyday life, people do not openly challenge their efficacy. This is particularly true at the public forum level of politics. An educator will uphold the ideal of hard work for students learning various skills knowing full well that who you know is often more important than what you know. Clerics expect their parishioners will deviate from the Ten Commandments, but from the pulpit they preach strict adherence to these norms. The same reasoning holds for prime-time television.

The reason television has developed an ideal norms perspective is that it attempts to reach the largest possible audience through what former NBC program chief Paul Klein (1975) called the "Least Objectionable Program" (LOP) principle. Television discovered, perhaps inadvertently, that incorporating ideal norms into the presentation of subjects and solutions to program plots results in a course of action that viewers cannot find objectionable. To illustrate, the continued popularity of the Miss America Pageant demonstrates the American public's support for the traditional role of women, the ideals of youth and beauty, and the value of God and Country (at least at an ideal level). In fact, the Miss America Pageant serves as a television ritual to reaffirm much of what is ideally considered good and sacred about our culture. On the other hand, subjects such as drug abuse by teenagers, pre- and extramarital sex, or general sexual display make up a significant portion of viewing time. But the solutions to these problems, for example, extramarital sex, will follow ideal norms. Watch any prime-time situation comedy, and you will discover an ideal norms moral at the end of the program. Even programs such as *The Dukes of Hazzard,* which openly displays soft porn, grinds cars at an alarming rate, and shows little respect for legal authority, still manage to emphasize basic human rights albeit vigilante style.

Television will, on occasion, titillate the viewer and be provocative on moral issues, but it rarely suggests abandoning the ideal or traditions that form society's moral fabric as to do so would invite the public's wrath. Prime-time soaps, such as *Flamingo Road* and *Dynasty* may seem to openly challenge ideal norms with extramarital affairs and fairly explicit sexual scenes. But these affairs usually occur between evil people or between people who are denied love from their legal spouses. While the sexual expression in these scenes may shock some viewers, the ideal of true love is not violated.

This is not to say that violations of ideal norms do not occur, and two worthy of note occurred early in the 1982 fall season, one on *Magnum P.I.* and the other on *Hill Street Blues.* In *Magnum,* Thomas Magnum ends one episode by reluctantly executing a particularly evil Russian KGB agent who is about to get off scott-free after killing several people. The term "execution" is particularly important as the shot Magnum fired at the agent was not done in self-defense or in the heat of battle. Since Americans have grown somewhat accustomed to the idea that executions are apparently carried out for the sake of national security, the *Magnum* episode is an example of how ideals can be challenged as practical strategies become more acceptable. Even so, witnessing the execution by Magnum was particularly shocking within the context of prime-time TV.

The other example involved the blatant bending of the law by *Hill Street Blues'* Captain Clean, Frank Furillo. In this episode two young men were about to escape a murder charge after they had raped and killed a Catholic nun—inside a church, no less. Furillo maneuvers the legal system to get the two killers released (on a lesser charge) so they would fall immediate prey to the angry lynch mob waiting outside the courtroom. Fearing for his life, one of the youths confesses and Furillo gets his man. While the public understands that justice officials occasionally bend the judicial system as a matter of practicality, Furillo's action is clearly a violation of ideal justice. However, the final scene of the program shows the Captain entering a church confessional and solemnly saying "Forgive me for I have sinned."

Since ideal norms represents the sacred traditions of society, prime-time television is the most conservative of all major media. In this respect television does not mirror society; it lags behind the changes in morality as practiced in everyday life. In fact, change in what is normal or at least acceptable in such practices as premarital sex, homosexuality, extramartial sex, and abortion is occurring so rapidly that television is conservative by contrast. A quick survey of recent popular programs, such as *Dallas, Fame,* and *60 Minutes,* reveals they all share the theme of searching for morality in a rapidly changing world.

However, caution must be exercised in using the ideal norms perspective as an analytical framework for understanding television. In prime-time programs, an appeal to ideal norms is often a means for justifying the T & A, off-color jokes, ludicrous characters, necessary bad guys, and subjects such as abortion, impotence, and prostitution. The plot, character development, and humor of many programs follow the practical norms that appear very liberal in contrast to the moral ideals in society. But at the end of the program, everything is usually placed in a highly moralistic framework—with a happy and moral ending, the end justifies the means. Even rebels such as the Fonz on *Happy Days* can be overbearing outlaws during the program; however, when the climax rolls around, they show good sense and uphold the ideals.

A possible negative consequence of the ideal norms prespective is that it reduces the complexity of problems to a simplistic level, particularly in situation comedies. The complexity that usually characterizes most interpersonal problems is rarely described in television programs. Problems are interjected with humor as a means for avoiding or masking complexity, and characters always manage to maintain self-control. Rarely do TV parents scream at each other; instead, they use quick-witted retorts, never holding a grudge. Parents do not slap their kids; they use psychology or sulk, knowing the kids will eventually come to their senses. People who cause the problems in these fictional accounts either become miraculously self-reflective and see the light or they get their comeuppance. On the dramatic "cops-and-robbers" shows, police are never bigoted; they are intelligent, moralistic, even-tempered, hard working, and altruistic to a fault. Criminals are either saved through sound reasoning by police or friends, or they fall off a ten-story building in a dramatic climax of swift justice. To be sure, the world of prime-time television is a just world.

The format perspectives of entertainment and ideal norms are also commonly employed in most non-prime-time programs. For example, games shows, with their carnival atmosphere, are highly entertaining for many viewers. But, since someone must lose these dizzy contests producers make sure that contestants lose in good grace. Indeed, it is almost embarrassing how gracious, even joyful, these losers appear.

In contrast, soap opera entertainment is similar to peeking through a keyhole into the hidden, backstage of people's lives. Sordid affairs, rare diseases, and other uncommon problems provide viewers with a sense of well-being by comparison. Yet with all the unconventional situations on soaps, they are probably the most moralistic of all TV programs. Through gothic justice sin is always punished in a most fundamental manner and good deeds are eventually rewarded, although the righteous often must endure extreme hardship.

The combination of entertainment and ideal norms in talk shows emerges through a relaxed, informal, patio-type chatter. Small talk is the general rule, although Phil Donahue, Erv Kupsinet, and Dick Cavett often venture into topical issues and bohemian esoterica. Typically, guests, such as Dolly Parton, espouse ideal norms in giving recipes for success and coping. In fact, most guests are actors attempting to make a hit in the mass entertainment market where the ideals of the heartland are essential. Following this format, every talk show host (Johnny, Merv, Dick, and Phil) is either a bonafide Midwesterner or projects the Midwest image.

The combination of entertainment and ideal norms is also a significant factor in the format of newscasts. As mentioned previously, the entertainment perspective in news is found in the portrayal of confrontation and the accentuation of drama. On occasion, drama is carried to such an extreme that mundane affairs of state are made to seem mysterious or that we are on the brink of something cataclysmic. Such has been the case recently with speculation about what the new Soviet leader Yuri Andropov is really like and whether U.S.-Soviet relations will change, as though the foreign policy of any superpower could change overnight.

Ideal norms abound in news format, particularly in the "holier-than-thou" attitude projected by crusading reporters in the wake of some injustice. The reaction of all network anchormen following the successful insanity defense of John Hinckley, Jr., was nothing short of indignation. The same holds true of *60 Minutes* reporters; what could be more moralistic than four noted reporters exposing scams in business and government. Yet *60 Minutes* has not escaped criticism as witnessed in a *Wall Street Journal* article that criticized a *60 Minutes* story on the "Kissinger-Shah [Iran] Connection." Said the *Journal,* it "raised some disturbing questions about TV's penchant for reducing complicated subjects to neat little conspiracy theories" Good, 1980: 40). Despite the occasional criticism, conspiracy theories and the exposé enable news reporters to appear as seekers of truth and crusaders for justice, which plays very well when mixed with a little entertainment.

Regarding other emotional examples of television perspectives, consider the extent to which sports has increased its show-biz quotient and emphasizes the ideals of good sportsmanship. While sports has always had an entertainment dimension, the antics of players, cheerleaders, pregame sideshows, clowns, computerized scoreboards, and game rules designed to increase scoring all expanded after television enter the sports scene. In addition, with nationwide, prime-time broadcasting of sports events came the inevitable emphasis on the ideal norm of fair play. Recently, numerous rules have been imposed by the sports czars (Rozelle et al.) aimed at inhibiting emotional and physical outbursts by players and coaches. Today anything approaching a dirty play is immediately chastized by righteous commentators such as Howard Cosell. Currently the networks clamor for big boxing matches and then blame everyone but themselves when there is a mismatch on the order of the Kim/Mancini lightweight title fight in which Kim died.

In summarizing this section, television attracts and holds an audience through stereotypes, entertainment, and ideal norms, which in turn shape the definitions, interpretations, and solutions that are applied to the subjects and issues dealt with by television. These perspectives are highly compatible in developing the language of television as they are both emotionally satisfying and produce a very low degree of ambiguity. Since the primary aim of television is to sell products to a mass market, television must design clear programs that hold an audience up to and through a commercial message. The language of television must be able to capture a potential viewer at any point in a program and hold that viewer's attention. Theoretically, anyone could turn on the set in the middle of a program and be willing to stay tuned regardless of what he or she missed. As an informal experiment, randomly tune in programs somewhere in the middle and determine how long it takes to figure out what is going on or how long it takes to become attracted to the remainder of the program. The consistency of television language over the years, familiarity with that language, and the low degree of ambiguity in all television make it possible to reach and hold the mass audience.

Media Influence

There is little doubt that television, at present, is the most powerful of all major media in Western society, and it follows that in the overall media culture of our time, television is the primary ingredient. Television has far-reaching consequences, although our understanding of these consequences is often superficial and sometimes inaccurate. As argued previously, mass media, particularly television, should not be analyzed through a model of direct causes producing specific effects. Rather, television is influential because people voluntarily (although it seems unconsciously) adopt the perspectives, images, and grammar employed by television. Through this model, television has a subtle influence in promoting long-term viewing habits and a quite dramatic influence on short-term viewer responses. For example, watching television news with its action/drama format over many years may result in a belief that stories on network news are worthy of attention and are as dramatic and intense in actuality as they are presented on the newscast. In turn, there may be an unquestioned thrust in TV news, as some surveys report that as high as two-thirds of all adults rely on TV as their major source of news. In addition, when people feel that accounts of some event are conflicting, they are more apt to believe television than other media.

An example of the trust placed in television news for a short-run story occurred during the 1980 Republican Convention. After two days of dismal ratings, Republicans were worried they would not build a large TV audience for the convention finale. A meeting was arranged between Ronald Reagan and Gerald Ford for the purpose of creating the impression that Ford would be Reagan's running mate. Given previous relations between the two men, most journalists and politically astute viewers should have considered a Reagan/Ford ticket as next to preposterous since, on previous occasions, Reagan made fairly strong statements opposing Ford's policies and many of his ideas. Nevertheless, CBS with Walter Cronkite pushed the story. By 10:00 p.m. Wednesday evening, July 16, the usually reliable Associated Press had Ford on the ticket. Several newspapers, including the Chicago *Sun-Times*, carried headlines proclaiming Ford's selection by Reagan.

In this example, a media event contrived by campaign strategists turned into a news story accepted by professional journalists who should have exercised more caution and critical analysis. But then it should also be mentioned that CBS led the Nielsen ratings that evening. There is little doubt that trust in Walter Cronkite lent the Ford story credence it might not have otherwise had, although the important point is that television news led the way in influencing other media and the general public. Similar examples occur on a regular basis and should be examined in terms of how television format serves as an interaction form among media professionals and viewers.

Television grammar and perspectives are designed to establish credibility and expertise. We have been indoctrinated with the idea that a television camera does not lie, although people who believe that statement fail to realize that a camera's position, the type of shots used, lighting, and other elements of grammar constitute a subjective viewpoint. However, belief in the objectivity of television and the elements of grammar that seem to give the viewer a close-up view fosters the feeling that what we see on the screen is authentic. The point is that format or form is a way of seeing that lends credibility to the content. If the form of grammar of any type of communication seems appropriate, we often assume the content is accurate. For example, the television program *Saturday Night Live* uses the format of real commercials to satirize various products. Viewers report being conned by the format into believing they were watching a bonafide commercial until the punch line was delivered.

In turn, an anchorperson can gain the appearance of being an expert by appearing within a news format. In fact, as a television anchorman confided to me in a personal interview, "You don't have to know anything about journalism to anchor the evening news." To the media-conscious viewer, the television news format establishes journalistic credibility, entertainment programs establish the attributes of talent, and sportcasts establish a skill level for athletes. These personal attributes are initially recognized through a media format that then may promote a self-fulfilling prophecy by the viewer.

Television also shapes the role of the expert on newscasts, talk shows, and documentaries. Each of these programs uses a grammatical inflection device of keeping stories or statements very short and fairly dramatic. Experts are selected or emerge by their ability to take complex issues and simplify them in short concise statements with punch. A television producer once remarked that Carl Sagan was the perfect science expert as he could explain the "black hole" phenomena in 25 words or less. This is not to impune Carl Sagan, whose scientific skills are considerable, but to point out that experts are selected for their talent in meeting format requirements. The danger in this procedure is not that inaccurate information will be passed to the public, as most experts are drawn from sources where everyone if fairly competent. Rather, the danger is in the simplification and superficiality required in television format and the impression that one expert may represent a unified position in a particular field.

For example, viewers may think that Dr. Joyce Brothers represents a unified view within psychology; viewers may not realize that psychologists with different theoretical positions hold a wide range of interpretations on any issue. This misrepresentation is emerging in many fields as a handful of media experts represent various academic disciplines to the television public. In addition, it should be mentioned that media experts are influential with other media. When Dr.

Brothers appears on a talk show, she is influential with viewers who are also readers, and publishers look to these media personalities as indicators of what the public will buy. Consequently, what gets published is influenced by who appears on television. Indirectly, this influence makes its way to textbooks, funding agencies for scientific research, and personnel decisions in business, government and education.

These examples demonstrate that a significant part of media influence involves the potential of television to create entertainment stars and official experts who become highly influential both within the media industry and with the audience. In a few cases these media personalities seem to exceed mortal status as exemplified in television by Walter and Johnny—with their familiarity, last names are unnecessary. Personalities such as these are not just talented in their respective fields; they *are* television culture. What they represent, advocate, or dislike is often accepted as truth or the right way of doing things. Throughout the short history of television, personalities such as Arthur Godfrey, Milton Berle, Jack Parr, Ed Sullivan, and more recently Barbara Walters, Carroll (Archie Bunker) O'Connor, Phil Donahue, and of course, Cronkite and Carson, have become cultural heroes. What these individuals represent to their audience is the epitome of an ideal norms middle-class perspective. Their enormous influence enables them to sell soap, become experts on politics and child rearing, and establish fashion trends. Consequently, the media personality can generate news, which perhaps is why early in the 1980 presidential campaign, Cronkite was seriously mentioned as a vice presidential running mate to John Anderson.

One of the most frightening results of viewer attachment to television personalities occurs when the lines are blurred between reality and fantasy. Viewers who thought of Robert Young as Marcus Welby and requested his advice on medical problems were turning fiction into fact. This story is not uncommon; soap opera performers often receive letters from viewers warning them of danger from an adversary character in the program. Actors are often addressed by fans in their fictional role names such as Archie Bunker, the Fonz, Lou Grant, and J.R. instead of Carroll O'Connor, Henry Winkler, Edward Asner, and Larry Hagman. Drama series tough guys are periodically challenged in public by viewers who want to see how tough these characters really are.

In these instances viewers are demonstrating the extent to which they personalize their relations with media personalities and the high degree of vicarious involvement that is possible in the viewing experience. Experiences such as these are also enhanced by elements of television grammar that promote intimacy between viewers and performers. Camera close-up shots showing a high degree of eye contact enable viewers to feel they are interacting in an intimate manner with the character on the screen. Soap operas and dramatic programs also show a great deal of the character's underlife or what is normally hidden from view, giving the impression that we have something on these individuals. Indeed, the private lives of television and film personalities are commonly taken as public domain by the audience.

On a less extreme level viewers may adopt media personalities as role models or media mentors. Personalities, interaction styles, personal appearance, and ideas on various issues are taken as behavior guides by some media conscious viewers. Boys play at being Reggie Jackson, girls and young women see themselves as Farah Fawcett, and men attempt to emulate Carson or Tom Selleck. This type of hero worship is not new with our society, but the constant exposure available on television may increase the amount of role modeling and vicarious involvement with these personalities. This might not be considered a negative influence if the emulation is of ideal norms. On the other hand, television's superficiality and simplification makes the world of television and the lives of these personalities appear much easier, uncomplicated, and happier than people normally find it in everyday life. Consequently, a media-conscious public may develop unrealistic expectations, which in turn may increase anxiety and encourage people to live vicariously in the fantasyland of television.

Indications of this have already emerged among men and women who feel they cannot compete with the standards of attractiveness depicted on television. During the golden age of movies everyone knew that movie stars were different; in today's sitcom the purpose is to create the impression that fictional characters are typical or average. Is it all right to be a pimple-face teenage boy when the girls he tries to date have pictures of TV idols plastered all over their rooms? Can a teenage boy find happiness with a girl less attractive than Valerie Bertinelli? How do parents relate to their children when the ideal parent is Ms. Romano or Mr. Brady? While many of us had media heroes when we were young and perhaps still do, media-cultured individuals may make these heroes an obsession and create unrealistic expectations for themselves.

If television reality is more believable and more desirable than everyday life, and if television personalities and characters are more acceptable than people in face-to-face encounters, cultural change is bound to occur. Our culture and heroes are increasingly being drawn from media, particularly television. As this continues, expectations and demands in society may become impossible to satisfy, resulting in increased vicarious involvement with the fantasy of television. Relative to this point a 14-year-old female viewer said:

> It may not be wise to have kids believe family problems [*Eight is Enough*] just work out so nice all the time. There is pain in the world. Some people's problems, you know, just don't go away [Cottle, 1980: 81].

MEDIA INFLUENCE AND CULTURAL CHANGE

In addition to the obvious examples of television's impact on institutions such as politics and sports, there are more subtle ways television is influencing institutional practices. For example, in criminal justice, family life, and our sense of history, television is shaping the reality we expect and even demand in everyday life.

Criminal Justice

The entire system of justice from police detection and apprehension to the court system has and will continue to undergo change as a result of television's portrayal of the criminal justice system in fictional drama, sitcoms, and documentaries. What people see on television is what they have come to expect and demand in actual criminal justice procedures. Following the discussion of television as a legitimizing agent and resource for expertise, many viewers assume that police and court practices depicted in television fiction correspond to actual practice in real life. The so-called accuracy of Jack Webb's detective programs and the appearance of authenticity in attorney programs is at best atypical and in many cases a misrepresentation of real-life practice. However, the public's acceptance of TV reality is pressuring police and court professionals to change their ways despite the dubious value of these changes.

Jack Webb's *Dragnet* and the many spinoffs that followed stimulated the Los Angeles Police Department to recruit officers who fit the image as presented on TV. Officers were required to stay fit and encouraged to look trim and tailored, imitating those familiar crusaders of *Adam 12* and *CHiPs*. While the improved appearance of police officers may be a positive result of television, it may also have promoted an attitude of elitism that is counterproductive in public service. This elitism may be exemplified in the proliferation of SWAT teams, police helicopters, more motorized and less walking patrols, and as some critics have suggested, an increased use of revolvers and other methods of physical force.

While authorities point to the increase in violent crime as justification for these procedures, the fact is that elite police squads and physical force have increased, and these increases coincided with an increase in televised fictional police drama. On this point, evidence does exist that heavy TV viewers have the mistaken impression that crimes of violence, particularly related to drugs and mental problems, constitute a major crime category (Gerbner, 1978). This misrepresentation as fostered by television may be a significant factor in the increase of police units and techniques designed to apprehend the violent offender.

The courtroom is also undergoing considerable change due to fictional television drama and the addition of TV cameras in courtrooms. Relative to jury trials, an article in the *Los Angeles Times* states:

> Faced with TV-fed expectations, some police investigators and lawyers have found it best simply to give jurors what they expect . . . some lawyers put their strongest witness on first and make points in a hurry, just like a TV show [Fergurson, 1980: 5].

The subtlety of the last point must not be overlooked. Television format uses short scenes to increase tempo, drama, and excitement. As viewers become accustomed to this format, they may expect the same procedures in similar real-life situations. As a result, a juror may be more impressed with the form a lawyer uses in court than with the content of his or her argument.

This may already be occurring; many law schools around the country use, as part of their training, video-equipped courtrooms for mock trials. An indirect lesson student attorneys may be learning is the emphasis on form, particularly television format. As suggested earlier, establishing meaning proceeds through a recognition of form to a definition of content. As the media culture of criminal justice continues to develop, the credibility and force of an attorney's argument in court might have less to do with the legal content than with the format used by lawyers.

Family Life

The impact of television on the family and particularly on children has been the subject of research since the early days of this medium. The preponderance of research has focused on the lack of skill development due to the amount of time children spend watching television and the dirct and indirect lessons they learn from TV programs. Familiar conclusions include the finding that heavy television viewers usually do not score well on reading achievement tests, that children tend to model their behavior after TV characters, and that some children may suffer from a retardation in developing imagination and an ability to make abstractions. However, research on these topics is somewhat contradictory, leading to the conclusion that some children are adversely affected by television and others are not. In families where parents exercise control over what their children watch and explain or qualify the material presented on television, children usually show few ill effects. Most young children are emotionally dependent on parents and rely on their advice over other influences. Still, many questions on the impact of television on the family remain unanswered.

One of the more fascinating topics concerning children's use of television is the problem of distinguishing between the reality and fantasy of what they see on television. It is generally accepted that a child's world is dominated by play more than by the serious matter of work and responsibility. Children play out both fantastic and reasonable roles in their pre- and early school years, pretending what it is like to be a father, mother, fireman, race car driver, cowboy, and so on. Unlike adults in similar roles, children are not expected to take responsibility or become committed to the consequences of their acts while at play. For children play is present not future oriented. Play is for the intrinsic enjoyment that may result rather than a future payoff, which is why adults sometimes yearn for the simple and happy days of childhood.

Given these ideas about play, which are based on socialization theories from G.H. Mead, Jean Piaget, Johan Huizinga, and others, it may be hypothesized that while children are at play they recognize the behavior involved need not be taken seriously or adopted as part of their self-concept. In other words, kids at play are not necessarily learning to be violent or demonstrate a commitment to become a cowboy or space pilot. While at play, kids are engrossed in action and having fun with subjects as is the case in watching a cartoon. My own research (1974) on the play world of television indicates that kids make clear distinctions between what they consider reality and the fake world of fantasy. Children see cartoons as fake and know that Bugs Bunny's ability to snap back after being flattened by a steamroller has no relation to real life—but it is fun to watch anyway. Most kids know monsters are not real, but it is exciting when they pretend a ghost awaits them at the bottom of a darkened stairway. On this point a 14-year-old black uban male said:

> See, I don't mind that it's all made up. Stuff has got to fit my mood. I know it's fake. If I didn't watch what my brother calls "the fake and bake," I wouldn't watch the tube. You follow my meaning? When I get into the TV, I want the fake and bake [Cottle, 1980: 78-79].

Relating the play world of children to the play world of television, one of the possible adverse consequences is that kids may extend their play period to a point at which it interferes with learning how to become committed members of society. In examining recent surveys on the television generation, which now extends to people in their mid-thirties, results indicate that the protestant ethic of postponing enjoyment seems to have vanished. Gail Sheehy's (1979) research on this topic shows that while young men still believe in the goals of success in the work world, they are deferring work in order to concentrate on their tennis backhand. The tie-in this may have to television is tenuous, but it is worth considering.

As the age of childhood advances into the late teen years and beyond, will television be a significant part of this play world? In 1982 one of the most popular noon-time activities on college campuses was watching soap operas, in particular *General Hospital.* Despite all its excitingly innovative visual technique, MTV (Music TV) constantly "plays with" or pokes fun at rather serious topics. Although the adverse effects of this may be exaggerated, it is important to determine the role of television among people who are preoccupied with play. Are these people more passive in their participation in society? Are they less concerned with craftsmanship in work? More hedonistic? Less critical and reflective about themselves than the world around them? Since we have no conclusive answers to these questions at this time, we need serious scientific investigation.

One bit of evidence that is quite clear is that most television programs in the recent past are oriented to describing the lives of children, teenagers, and young adults in situation comedies. Middle-age cops, cowboys, private detectives, attorneys, and doctors in serious roles have vanished from first-run programs. Today, sitcoms have children in starring roles and teenagers or adults who act like teenagers. Sitcoms may rightly be called "kidcoms," with the age range of this term extending from preschool to young adult. On college campuses students are not watching just adult humor cartoons or high camp reruns, they are watching modern-day Keystone Cops in *The Dukes of Hazzard* and the lowbrow satire of *Delta House* and *Saturday Night Live.*

With children and adolescents apparently controlling the on/off switch, sophisticated humor has been replaced with crude and rude slapstick and crass one-liners. No doubt some readers will take exception to the castigation of their favorite programs, but the fact remains that most sitcoms are child oriented with wacky humor and innane plots. As the boy quoted earlier comments:

> Hey, what the hell, all of TV is for kids. I don't know a show on TV that's for adults only. Like you can go to the library and pick up a book and read the first two sentences and you know that there's a book for adults only. You don't even get to the bottom of the page before you quit. But TV? Every show they got's for kids. Smart kids, dumb kids, all kids [Cottle, 1980: 79].

Kidcoms may be considered a play form of communication in which the subject matter may not be taken seriously by the viewer. While this is probably true for those viewers who have not succumbed to media influence, it is possible that heavy viewers prefer and accept most television as employing appropriate strategies. Surveys indicate that teenagers are the heavy viewers of sitcoms, and male viewers apparently like those programs that have an anti-authority perspective. While the critical viewer may see the absurdity of certain programs, others may attribute considerably more significance to what they experience with television. For these viewers, sitcoms may be the source of considerable challenge to traditional norms.

The undermining of adult authority is supported in recent research by Joshua Meyrowitz (1983). According to Meyrowitz, not only do children act like adults on TV programs, but through television kids get a peek at the backstage of adult life, learning adult secrets and exposing the adult strategy of keeping certain things secret from the younger set. Monya Katzson (1982) pointed out in an unpublished paper at Arizona State University that adults no longer have control over interpreting to children the history of previous generations. Through reruns of films and TV shows covering the last three generations, children today can interpret the media protrayals of these generations for themselves.

In contrast to the playfully rebellious world of kidcoms are the highly traditional, family-oriented programs, such as *Little House: A New Beginning, Father Murphy,* reruns of old family programs, and many commercials that show the family in a very idealistic manner. These families are adequately prosperous, happy, energetic, and above all, secure. Viewers looking for this type of reality may become disillusioned when their own lives do not measure up to the world described on TV. Children may expect parents to devote all their energy to satisfying the child's desires. Kids may also expect their parents to be youthful, attractive, energetic, and highly skilled in many activities. As a friend's daughter said to her while on a recent vacation, "Mommy, why can't you be more peppy like those ladies in the Pepsi commercial?"

In addition, traditional roles in the family are subtly reinforced, giving support to charges of sexism, racism, and other acts of discrimination. Old people are underrepresented and often depicted as asexual eccentrics. Black and Hispanic people are happy-go-lucky in sitcoms and either evil or downtrodden in dramatic programs. Blacks are overrepresented, especially in the under 25 age group, and Hispanics are severely underrepresented. Women are young, attractive, and still fairly irrational. Men are single and macho. Since television must present subjects understood by all, the format calls for extreme stereotypes. On the other hand, blue-collar family life has suddenly become chic, although sitcoms never show the problems of making ends meet in today's inflationary economy. In short, television does not accurately represent the demographic or personal characteristics of typical people.

In summarizing the impact of television on the family, it seems that at present the strategy is to depict the family through ridicule or unrealistic prefection. Everyday life may be so humdrum for most viewers that sitcoms provide a welcome relief. But the image of the family projected by television is at odds with interaction patterns and characterizations that would promote reasonable optimism in contemporary society. While television supports ideal norms in principle, it also emphasizes ridicule as an interaction strategy and characterizes adults as either inept or unrealistically perfect. As a result, an entire generation is being shown that putdowns are normal and that the negative aspects of their own lives are atypical of how Americans live.

History Through Docudrama

One of the most serious results of television's influence on cultural change concerns the alteration of history and changes that may occur in how we define history. The most significant phenomenon in this process is the television docudrama. In recent years viewers have been bombarded with somewhat factual accounts of black history, political, religious, and sports heroes, significant historical events, and fictional accounts of political life, high society, and ethnic life-styles that are made to appear factual. While the purpose of these docudramas is to relieve history through an entertainment perspective, the result is a very subjective and often distorted view of the past. Can we asusme that heavy viewers or even casual observers will see these accounts as more fiction and drama than historical reality? Are viewers allowing television to reinterpret and distort history for the purpose of selling soap and being entertained?

Historical distortion has occurred in numerous docudramas. For example, *The Amazing Howard Hughes* was in large part an educated guess by writers, the Southern Colonel played by Henry Fonda in *Roots* was fabricated, and the happy ending in the story on former Brooklyn Dodger catcher Roy Campanella was a fraud (Reeves, 1980). These examples are not alarming unless you consider that viewers believe they are getting a history lesson. As evidence that viewers accept the authenticity of docudramas, we only have to cite New York Governor Hugh Carey who placed the fictional character Jane Pittman *(The Autobiography of Miss Jane Pittman)* on his list of Black Americans who had contributed most to their country. After viewing *Roots,* which is based on fact, how many viewers knew that Jane Pittman was pure fiction? The format of both programs was identical, and both received critical acclaim. For many viewers, docudrama is not just another descriptive account; it is reality. As TV critic Richard Reeves (1980: 39) states:

> Televsion may be the major influence on the way Americans live today. Docudrama may become the dominant influence on what we believe and how we once lived and what kind of people we are.

Contrast Reeves's sober warning with producer Alan Landsburg's (*Fear on Trial* and *The Triangle Factory Fire Scandal*) statement:

> I was a practitioner of the pure documentary and found it a frustrating form. Finally, I was delighted to find docudrama occurring as an avenue of being able to communicate more than the existing or shoot-able film allowed. After all, I could film the bloody White House for so long and I couldn't get into the damn Oval Office where the action was, so I was forced to conclude the action going on in the White House is my guess as to what happened. Now, in docudrama, at least, I can mount that guess and can properly see it for the audience [Reeves, 1980: 38].

The key phrases in that quote are "my guess as to what happened," and "properly see it for the audience." Landsburg is not alone in holding this view. Producer Gerald Isenberg (*It's Good to be Alive,* about Roy Campanella, and *The Defection of Simas Kudirka*) says: "Docu-drama is a creative interpretation of reality. It's not reality itself" (Reeves, 1980: 38). Buz Kulik, producer of *Kill Me If You Can* (Caryl Chessman) admits that his intention pure and simple was to make an anti-capital-punishment argument. These men are admitting to creating history, making ideological statements, and doing it with a flair that will capture viewers.

The danger in docudrama is not that television producers use drama and entertainment in presenting history. Those of us who teach know how effective drama can be in teaching almost any subject. The problem occurs when drama obscures fact, and when dramatic fiction is passed off as fact. Gore Vidal made the point very well in a state-ment to docudrama producers:

> Take a moment to think about the delicate line between the facts, as we call them, and the drama which you are obliged to invent, because there is no such thing as cinema verité. The hand that holds the camera is painting a subjective picture. You cannot avoid it. And don't try [Reeves, 1980: 39].

If docudrama alters history through distortion and fiction, how might the long-term use of this method influence the way we interpret history? No culture is known for pure objectivity in interpreting its past, but at least modern historians operate by specified scientific rules designed to reduce bias. Although science is not immune to subjectivity, its findings are subject to continual critique through an open community of scholars. In contrast, network television does not usually encourage the luxury of alternative views except in the political arena. A docudrama may stand as a definitive statement in the minds of viewers, and it has an immediate and forceful impact. Consequently, a historian, parent, or teacher has an uphill battle to correct inaccuracies made by television. Remember, the majority of TV viewers believe the word of television over all other media. In addition, scientific method has a degree of rigor in its procedures that television docudrama lacks. Television follows the strategy of perspectives and an attending grammar. In television, fact is subordinate to entertainment while in science and teaching it is the reverse. The PBS program *NOVA,* produced by WGBH in Boston, is one of the few programs that usually meets the criteria of scientific pedagogy. In *NOVA* entertainment is subordinate to science.

How this might relate to the way we treat history is pure speculation at this point, but an appropriate exercise nevertheless. One danger is that through television we might exaggerate the idealization of our past more than we have until now. For black Americans, *Roots* presented an uplifting, romanticized, positive view of black history. Certainly black Americans have been stereotyped in negative terms long enough, but when the pendulum swings to the opposite end, the problem of subjectivity is just as extreme. Should we make saints out of Caryl Chessman, Private Slovic, and even Robert Kennedy? Perhaps they were heroic and their principles deserve recognition. However, selective cannonization based on decisions by television executives and the idealization of their personal characteristics tends to obscure knowledge of the critical issues that is necessary in order to understand these individuals and make sense of their deeds. It is partially a matter of not seeing the forest for the trees. In turn this may result in chauvinism and misplaced hero worship as opposed to acceptable ethnocentrism and appropriate respect.

It should also be added that television does not encourage viewers to dig deep into the detail of historic events. Stimulated by television, we live in an "instant" syndrome of expecting immediate results for almost everything we do. This is true not just for fast food service, but in education, work, and even personal happiness as well. The docudrama is an example of instant education as it provides the viewer with a feeling that all important material has been covered. As with a happy ending in an entertaining drama or comedy, the docudrama offers that same sense of closure or completeness. The implications for education and recording history may be significant.

TELEVISION INFLUENCE ON OTHER MEDIA

The impact of docudrama on historical reconstruction is just one among many examples of television's potential for influencing cultural change. A more indirect and yet very pervasive example is the effect television has on other media.

Despite a reluctance by representatives of other media to admit television's dominance, it is clear that all other forms of mass communication and many nonmedia areas in society feel television's heavy influence. The reticence in other media to admit to this influence is reflected by the attacks made on television at every available opportunity. Newspaper editorials and columns take network television to task for poor taste in programming, news coverage, and commercial ad styles. Sophisticated magazines treat television as a waste of time or a bizarre form of entertainment that may deserve some attention, but only for curiosity's sake. Film executives fight against pay TV and decry artless editing of films aired on prime time. Satires of television are common features in every medium. Yet television has captured the public and large advertising revenue, and most important, it is the dominant format in the contemporary media culture.

The latter point is critical as other media are beginning to look very much like television whether they admit it or not. Television format consisting mainly of entertainment and grammar characteristics such as condensation, simplicity, rapid tempo, and action is gradually being adopted by other other media. Compare magazines, newspapers, feature films, and even radio of 15 to 20 years ago to the formats they employ today, and the noticeable change over this period is primarily due to television.

In *print media* newspapers follow television in several respects. First, their news coverage has become a detailed support resource for the television viewer. With television basically providing a headline service, people must rely on the press for more detailed accounts. For morning edition newspaper editors this means paying attention to the evening network newscast. Publishers and editors understand that many of their readers have an established routine of watching one or more evening news programs. As a result, the morning edition offers the detail and ancillary stories that television cannot provide.

A second important influence is the format change recently made by a number of major newspapers. The front page of some newspapers reads like a television screen appears. Specifically, boxed inserts are used to capsulize and set off stories. A reader can make a quick scan of the front page for the highlights just as he or she does with television news. In addition, more entertainment or so-called human interest items are appearing on the front page. To maintain circulation publishers are resorting to an increase in nonnews material. Somewhat paradoxically, much of the nonnews or entertainment material is increasingly being presented in a news format. Stories about Guiness world records are not news in a traditional sense, but they are reported on the same page and in the same format as the State Department's latest crisis. As the line between fact and fiction becomes blurred, so does the difference between serious news and games.

Popular *magazines* have made the most noticeable adjustment to television. Some magazines are devoted entirely to a behind-the-scenes description of television personalities, programs, issues in the industry, and video technology. The occasional critical articles in *TV Guide* and the entertainment focus of *People* cover nearly every aspect of television culture. This is not a new endeavor for magazines as they have served the same function for the film industry since the 1940s.

The most fascinating influence of television on magazines concerns changes in magazine format. Open almost any popular magazine and several characteristics are readily apparent. As with the newspaper, boxed inserts are a prominent feature. The insert may be a condensation of the main points in the story, an ancillary story, or a bold-faced line lifted from the text that captures the essence of the author's thoughts. This format conforms to the condensation and telescoping techniques used in television. Television viewers are accustomed to the low abiguity of TV programs and are demanding the same features in other media. *Psychology Today* was one of the first magazines to adopt a television format successfully. Others have followed to the extent that even conservative literary giants have modified their format along television lines.

Other features of magazines that demonstrate television's influence include the short sections usually found in the first few pages. Entitled "Top of the Week" *(Newsweek)*, "Hot Properties" *(Metropolitan*

Home), or "Frontlines" *(Mother Jones)*, the intent is to give readers the "quick-and-dirty" style of television on minor and often entertaining stories. Another feature is the increased use of cartoons, photos, and artist sketches that graphically support textual content. In other words, following the impact of television, magazines have increased the use of visual graphics. Finally, magazine stories have been shortened considerably and are printed as a unit rather than forcing the reader to turn to page 59 and again to 87 and again to 103. Some magazines still force readers to leaf through pages to find missing pieces, but gradually this practice is disappearing.

Books also show television's influence. Glance rapidly through a few introductory-level college texts; the experience is similar to reading a Time-Life publication. Multicolored graphics, photos, boxed inserts, bold-faced type, and summaries provide students the opportunity to get instant knowledge without using a magic marker or even reading carefully. But then as some prophets have warned, reading may be a lost art in the not-too-distant future.

Book publishing in the "trade" editions feels the influence of television in another way. Since book sales are definitely increased by getting exposure on television, publishing houses employ PR experts and agents to get authors on the talk show circuit. Several minutes on *The Tonight Show* can mean a great deal of money to an author and publisher. Consequently, an author who plays well on TV or is a proven media personality has an excellent chance of obtaining a publishing contract.

The *film* industry has offered considerble resistance to television's expansion although it too has been forced to compromise and alter its procedures. The film industry suffered a considerable loss in revenue and control over the entertainment profession after television became established in the 1950s. Despite the increase in total population, weekly movie attendance has decreased dramatically since the peak period of the 1940s. Since the future of visual technology is in video rather than film, in order to survive, the movie industry has diverted much of its production to film for television. Hollywood will produce a few blockbuster films each year, but the bread and butter is in films for TV. In creating films for the television audience, the film industry follows the television format of simplicity, more action and less dialogue, shorter scenes with more jumpcuts, and less innovation in film technique. Even feature films not designed for TV follow the current popularity models in television. Recently we witnessed a rash of sitcom movies in the likes of *Smokey and the Bandit, The Blues Brothers, Caddyshack,* and so on. Creativity is affordable in the film industry only for big-name producers, while following the proven popularity of television format is a safe bet.

Television influences not only other media; it also influences itself. This interaction is partly the result of the continuing ratings war. When ABC vaulted into the top spot a few years ago with sitcoms and *Charlie's Angels,* the other networks followed with more of the same. The intrinsic imitative nature of television prompted spinoffs, with *Rhoda, The Jeffersons, Benson,* and many outright imitations. As one TV executive reportedly said, "If ABC did kiddy porn NBC would follow with adult porn." The imitations rule holds for almost every segment of the broadcast day and every major ratings period. When CBS led off a sweep week (concentrated ratings period) in February of 1980 with *Gone With the Wind,* NBC countered with *One Flew Over the Cuckoo's Nest,* and ABC did a special on Elvis in the same time period. During the Christmas holidays kids take a beating when networks compete by scheduling Charlie Brown, Dr. Suess, and Frosty head to head. With each rating point worth something in excess of $30 million a year in pretax profits, there is no desire for experimentation or alternative broadcasting. Networks run scared and opt for imitation as the safest road.

Imitation and the strategy of "whatever works" can be seen in news, sports, soaps, talk shows, and game shows. Currently there is talk of expanding the nightly news into an hour program—will this mean more in-depth reporting? Sports has been proliferated into prime time on the order of *Battle of the Network Stars*—can Penny Marshall out-macho Bob Conrad? Not only have news and sports expanded into dubious fringe areas, but news and sports combined formats in such programs as *That's Incredible* and *Real People.* In each case, a battery of would-be reporters brings the audience coverage of outrageous sporting and entertainment feats. Like a carnival freak show people get their moment of glory, and the audience waits in suspense for a tragedy or laughs it off.

In these examples the strategy is one of combining several successful programs into something slightly different. A similar strategy has been applied to game shows and soap operas. Game shows have been combined with entertainment variety shows in the form of *The Gong Show, Family Feud,* and a few others. With soaps the strategy has been to pull in teenagers, college students, and blue-collar workers.

Producers simply take the old format and fit it to the concerns of the audience they are attempting to capture. *General Hospital* became the top-rated afternoon soap with the addition of a teenage character, Laura Webber. Within a short period this program drew teenagers and college students at a level that astounded even the experts. The success of these soaps led to the rapid development of many new soaps for prime time, such as *Dallas, Knots Landing, Flamingo Road, Falcon Crest,* and others. The theory is, if people will accept one format, it is a safe bet they will accept something close to it.

The same logic has been adopted by television advertising. Over the years, there has been a close correlation between advertising format and the popularity of television programs. For example, with the recent popularity of soap operas, ads have made extensive use of a soap operalike scene with the hidden camera recording the informal interactions of people using the product. A variation of this approach is the hidden camera in the kitchen, refrigerator, bedroom, shower, and medicine cabinet. Some hidden camera shots are simply gimmicky, but the effect is a behind-the-scenes informal view that soap operas use so effectively. The sitcom skit is also currently popular with people dancing in and out of elevators, supermarkets, and fast food chains. When detective drama was popular in the early seventies, many ads were action scenes of the hero on the go. Testimonials and pseudo-experiments popular in the sixties are still used occasionally, although today the experiment is used mainly to sell detergent, and testimonials use the familiar star in a short dramatization, such as Robert Young (Sanka Brand) and James Garner and Mary Ann Hartley for Polaroid. Products for kids often use the cartoon format, beer ads are turning to sports stars doing funny routines, and the newest ad formats are dare-devil stunts and news. Using news for advertising is one of the most subtle and insidious examples of media culture yet devised. In these ads the grammar of a news report is followed in almost every detail, creating the impression that the ad is really a news report. The same technique has recently been used in magazines and newspapers were ads are made to appear like a feature article or a news column.

Finally, we could make a rather outlandish claim that television has influenced the *vacation industry.* Walt Disney was an extremely farsighted and creative individual, but Disneyland and the proliferation of these instant vicarious experience packages did not become popular until after the media culture of television had taken hold.

Today every major city has a Disneyland-type park somewhere nearby. All the western towns, seaports, and small town sets used on television over the past two decades have been recreated in vacation villages throughout the country. The instant vicarious experience provided through television is now available to vacationing families. Indeed, it seems the difference between the television program *Fantasy Island* and any vacation village is little more than tired feet and a dent in the pocketbook.

Summary

If people will become more reflective about how they interact with television, how they use television, and the interaction between television and other media, they will be sensitive to the direct and indirect ways in which television is a major factor in the ongoing construction of American culture. However, the form of interaction through television and the meanings that are constantly emerging are so taken for granted by many people that a television-created culture has emerged. Television is not simply a source of news and entertainment for better or worse. Television format has become a form of communication that is gradually being adopted by other media, by people in their interpersonal encounters, and in the major institutions of society. Gradually the reality presented by television is becoming the paramount reality in society.

Unfortunately, many people are relatively unaware of what is going on or how the process of producing this paramount reality works. The perspectives and meanings that people are consciously and habitually attuned to in everyday life are increasingly being drawn from media, particularly television. It is not a matter of television causing specific cultural change in a deterministic manner. Rather, people are adopting features of television format and content to interpret and establish meaning in their own lives. The audience is an active, although unaware, participant or accomplice, to a process in which culture is being created through television.

Forecast

None of what has been discussed in terms of developing media influence or the impact of television on cultural change need occur as a *fait accompli.* Television can change its approach, and the audience can change the way it interacts with television. On the bright side, there are indications that change is imminent in both the medium and the audience.

In his book *The Third Wave,* futurist Alvan Toffler claims that a "demassification" of television will occur. He feels we will move from a few images distributed widely to many images distributed narrowly. The new narrowcasting will consist of hundreds of sharply focused channels serving the audience's vastly diverse interests. Viewers will no longer submit to the LOP principle in massification, but will become their own programmers and create their own viewing schedules. This is already occurring through the expansion of cable systems and the increased use of VCR units. At present better than 25 percent of all TV households subscribe to cable TV systems, and in another decade that figure will more than triple. Sales of videotape recording units are increasing dramatically even at their present high price. In the near future the cost of computer and video electronics will decrease relatively to make sophisticated systems easily afford-able. Videotape will become more durable and less expensive, and fiber optics will increase picture and sound quality. Informal and commercial networks of tape exchange are already in existence. It does not take much imagination to see that extensive possibilities for selectivity and control of viewing habits will exist in the near future.

Creativity in television production is also occurring in many sectors. People such as rock star Todd Rudgren are experimenting with video animation and video synthesizers. Teenagers are experi-menting with video just for fun. Video is replacing the old home movie, and teachers are experimenting with video in the classroom.

Recently, psychologists and doctors at a Minneapolis hospital developed a closed-circuit program to communicate with children recovering from surgery. Called the "Electronic Get Well Card Show," children were addressed personally by their favorite stuffed animals and given relaxing images to aid in dealing with pain. Psy-chologist Marian Hall emphasized that the process is not one of mind control but a format that encourages children to take positive action in their own healing process (Berg, 1980). Another experiment tried at several cable outlets is called "video wallpaper," which consists of slowly changing abstract images enabling viewers to relax without the aid of drugs. Similar to white-noise and natural environmental sounds, video wallpaper has potential as a therapeutic device for individuals, mental health centers, hospitals, and even prisons.

On the other hand, some critics point to many current factors in predicting the continuation of the same old wasteland. The cost of producing programs ($600,000 plus for a prime-time hour), technical know-how, public taste (60 percent of prerecorded videotape sales in 1980 were in porno films), the fact that even with cable viewers prefer prime-time pap, and the feeling that the public has been spoiled with sophisticated production work prompted former CBS President Fred Friendly to predict, "In the end the networks will dominate" (Welles, 1980).

This prediction would be depressing if it were not for the possibility that television eventually will operate much as radio does today. No doubt there will always be a mass medium providing a mass audience with LOP-type entertainment. In radio this function is served by MOR stations. Yet specialization has occurred in radio in the form of narrowcasting FM stations, and there is no reason to believe this cannot occur with television. As viewers become more sophisticated in video technology and more reflective about how they use television, there will be an increase in specialized interests and programs to meet those interests. Although we are presently in the apparent grip of a mass-level media culture, there is reason to be optimistic.

CHAPTER 6

FILM
The Emotion Medium

After a three-week absence from the movie theaters, a friend, who is also a well-respected physical scientist, remarked to me, "I'm movie famished." That short phrase dramatically captures the extent to which going to the movies has become such a significant part of contemporary leisure activity.

From the very beginning, American cinema was successful. Movies were not only in the right place at the right time; they provided the American middle class and working class with attractive entertainment to fill new-found leisure time. Thomas Edison and William Dickerson's motion picture camera (1888) and the Edison projection technique called Vitascope (1895) appeared just prior to a significant drop in the urban work week. By 1900, the work week had decreased to an average of 56 hours and in 1920 it had dropped to 46 hours. Suddenly, urban workers had more leisure time than they knew how to use. At the turn of the century, recreation outside family activity was served mainly by reading and an occasional trip to the vaudeville stage. Entering the entertainment scene shortly after 1900, movies were an instant hit as they combined the form of the vaudeville stage with the content of novels at a price nearly everyone could afford. Movies were pure fun, providing a welcome contrast to the drudgery and impersonality of most urban work experience.

As with other electronic media, movies began as a novelty in the nickelodeons and vaudeville theaters. But with films such as the hour and a half French-made *Queen Elizabeth,* starring Sarah Bernhardt (1912), the three-hour Italian production of *Quo Vadis* (1913), the 90-minute American-made *Prisoner of Zenda* (1913), and in 1915, D.W. Griffith's classic *Birth of a Nation,* the film as a major entertainment medium was on its way. My mother once remarked that her parents took her to see *Birth of a Naiton* when she was six years old on the explanation that it was a milestone event. They were right, as with this film the public acknowledged that motion pictures were a major cultural force.

The growth rate of the movie industry was nothing short of phenomenal. By 1910, just seven years after the first one-reel feature film *(The Great Train Robbery)*, there were 9,480 motion pictures theaters in the United States. Only two years later this figure rose to nearly 13,000. By 1914, movie palaces seating up to 1,000 patrons were common in all major cities, and by 1918 the neighborhood theater was the center of community activity in residential areas. Movie magazines appeared in 1911, and by 1914 *Motion Picture Story Magazine* had a circulation of 270,000. The Strand Movie Palace in New York City recorded a weekly attendance figure of 40,000 in 1914. Theaters could not get films fast enough. Spirited competition resulted in no-holds-barred tactics ranging from outright sabotage to price wars and devious contracts.

In 1917, the three major film producers, Paramount, Famous Players-Lasky, and a group headed by Adolph Zukor combined to form a verticle monopoly of producer and distributor, and finally, through the practice of "block booking," they obtained control of theaters. Under this system theaters were contracted to show only those films produced by the parent studio. Although competition was severely restricted, theaters were guaranteed a steady supply of films. In 1918, Paramount, now headed by Zukor, distributed 220 films a year to over 5000 member theaters. By the end of the 1920s the growth and dispersion of the film medium had exceeded everyone's wildest expectations, and the Hollywood-based film industry became the single most important form of commercial entertainment with a yearly gross revenue of over a billion dollars. Reaching a peak in the 1940s, between 250 and 300 feature films were released each year to over 20,000 theaters. At the height of popularity in 1946, average weekly attendance was 90 million.

Following the heyday of Hollywood in the 1940s, the rising popularity of television, increased production and advertising costs, and the Supreme Court decision that broke the verticle monopoly of studios forced a reorientation in commercial film. As weekly attendance figures steadily declined it became apparent that people were not simply "going to the movies"; they were becoming far more selective. By the mid-1960s, the 16 to 30 age group had emerged as the primary (60 percent) movie audience. Studios tried in vain to capture the mass audience with spectaculars such as *Cleopatra* (1963),

Sound of Music (1966), *Dr. Doolittle* (1967), *Star* (1969), *Goodbye Mr. Chips* (1970), and *Tora Tora Tora* (1971), but all except *Sound of Music* were box office failures.

However, small-budget films, such as *Marty* (1955), eventually forced Hollywood to rethink its strategy. According to many film historians, it was *The Graduate* (1967) and *Easy Rider* (1969) that turned things around for the slumping industry. *The Graduate* violated all success-formula criteria as it was based on a minor novel, featured unproven talent, and was a relatively low-budget ($3 million) film. Every major studio turned down Buck Henry's screenplay until Columbia finally agreed to finance the independent production. *The Graduate* established a new principle: a story theme and director could be the stars. Director Mike Nichols took Broadway actress Anne Bancroft and newcomer Dustin Hoffman, an unglamorous lead male, and pop song stylists Simon and Garfunkel and produced a hit that still commands a handsome rental fee. Dennis Hopper and Peter Fonda carried this idea a step further into a highly specialized audience film, and for less than $500,000 produced a hit *(Easy Rider)* that astounded the film business. Independent film companies shooting on location with mobile units, using actors who looked like common people, and telling stories relevant to a youth market comprised the majority of films made in the 1970s.

Yet old success formulas with the lure of huge profits continue to tantalize Hollywood. Spectaculars such as *Towering Inferno* (1974), *Earthquake* (1975), *Jaws* (1976), *Star Wars* (1977), and *Superman* (1979) were profitable beyond belief. On the other hand, *The Great Gatsby* (1978), *Apocalypse Now* (1980), and *Heavens Gate* (1981) were large-budget fiascoes. Despite the high risk involved in making large-budget films, the industry seems bent on continuing a policy that only occasionally yields a big payoff. But look behind the gloss of the spectacular, and it is the bread-and-butter specialized film and films for television that keep Hollywood in business today.

What lies ahead? The answer is probably more of the same, a combination of big-money thrillers and specialized subculture films. Whatever the result, movies will continue as a chronicle of American ideals and popular taste as witnessed from the silent era to the gangster films of the early 1930s, the Fred Astaire/Ginger Rogers dance routines of the Depression, the naive idealism of Frank Kapra's films during the late 1930s, the romantic epics, war films, and musicals of the 1940s, the suspense stories of Alfred Hitchcock and the science fiction films of the 1950s, beach blanket frivolity of the early 1960s, the disaster films of the early 1970s, and the simple morality plays of *Star Wars* and *Superman* of the late 1970s. These mainstream themes represent a crude measure of our collective consciousness and willingness to express this consciousness through a popular art form. But my concern in this chapter is not to discuss movies as art or speculate on the business strategy of the movie industry. Understanding commercial film as a form of mass communication requires an examination of the language of film and the perspectives and genre we have come to know and enjoy.

Film Grammar

To understand the grammar of film it is important to remember that film began as a silent, visual method of storytelling. In fact, when sound tracks were synchronized with lip movement in the late 1920s, some filmmakers and critics were not happy with the change. Producer Jack Warner commented after *The Jazz Singer* debuted in 1928, "Who wants to hear actors talk, it's the music and action we want." Film critic Gilbert Seldes stated in the late 1920s that talkies would force the film industry to give up its visual creativity and appeal to the mass audience (Jowett, 1976: 196). While neither of these comments was prophetic, there was some truth to what they said. People did want the visual action, and silent film was an extremely creative art form with innovations occurring constantly. It was silent film and the grammatical techniques established by these filmmakers that define the structure of film we know today. What these creative experimenters accomplished was to take some of the grammatical techniques found in novels, poetry, and stage plays, such as parallel plots, flashbacks, and time distortion, and adapt them to the flexibility of film. The result was often startling. History came to life with an emotional impact unequaled by other media. The drama of the novel gained a new force when presented on the screen. Even the glitter and excitement of the vaudeville stage gave way to the strange new reality of film entertainment. Everything from nature to everyday life was portrayed with a dramatic visual intensity rarely achieved by other media.

Although the concept of perceiving movement through the projection of still pictures in rapid succession dates back nearly 2000 years, it was not until the electronic age that motion picture projection became more than a toy for the public. But once film technology moved out of the backroom tinkering stage, public reaction was similar to the present day boom in video games. And yet what really shocked and fascinated early nickelodeon patrons was not seeing movement on the screen, but seeing a world they knew from everyday life projected with force, mystery, and drama. Edison's film *The Kiss* (1896) startled viewers with its frankness. Close-up photography gave early moviegoers an intimate relationship with characters that would violate the informal norms of everyday conversation if it occurred in a face-to-face situation. In most societies people dare not stare into the eyes of another for long without suggesting severe emotional consequences. But in the anonymity of a movie theater a person can stare into an actor's eyes as long as the image remains on the screen.

Film techniques made it immediately clear that a reality different from everyday life existed on the screen. A train roaring into the station, ocean waves crashing against the shore, or a horse at full gallop took on new dimensions on a brightly lit screen in a darkened theater. Russian director Sergei Eisenstein of the silent era put it very well in stating that a camera prevents us from seeing too much, so that by eliminating parts of the scene suspense can be created out of the mundane. Eisenstein understood that a good director makes the audience want to see something in a particular way and gratifies that desire at just the right moment. Clearly, the way movies tell their stories is more satisfying than the stories they tell.

Imaginative shaping of the everyday world has always been a major characteristic of film production to the point that audiences willingly suspend disbelief. Motion pictures require a viewer to accept illusion as reality and the commonplace as mysterious. This occurs through selective attention engineered by filmmakers who established a set of rules on what we should pay attention to and how we should organize these experiences. Like a painter who arranges lines, colors, and planes to draw the viewer's eye to an object in the foreground, so a photographer frames a scene to emphasize a tiny object or create the impression of something off-camera that orients the viewer to future action—a sense of an about-to-be-discovered reality.

Yet all this is in the viewer's mind, such as the famous shower scene in Hitchcock's *Psycho* (1960), in which the viewer never actually sees a knife enter the body but imagines it nevertheless. Or consider the suspense created by the camera following the child riding his tricycle down the empty hotel corridors in *The Shining* (1979). The grammar of film has led to a "mind set" or interpretive framework in which illusion is accepted as reality to the point that gross distortion is suspended for the sake of rendering a plot meaningful.

SYNTAX

Most films begin with a scene showing one or more of the principle characters tending to routine affairs, unaware that a plot is about to begin. After several scenes establishing time and locale, the protagonist appears and/or the plot begins. These first scenes describe the characters, and the viewer comes to understand what additional information will be necessary to become involved in the plot. From this point on the syntax generally follows a linear cause-and-effect model of solving the puzzle, building to a climax, and ending with the denouement, which explains or justifies the conclusion.

In a classic example, *Citizen Kane* (1941) begins with the puzzle "Who or what is Rosebud?" We never doubt that the puzzle will eventually be solved. In fact, director Orson Welles supplies significant, although disguised, clues as to the identity of Rosebud at the beginning of the film. While the storyline describing the character of Kane becomes rather complex, Rosebud is the elegantly simple phenomenon that ties everything neatly together. While predictability is important for film viewers, it is definitely not what makes a film interesting. In *Casablanca* (1942) we know immediately that Rick is the key figure and that this independent, cynical loner will probably make a supreme sacrifice before the story ends. What makes *Casablanca* such a great film is the series of events that emotionally involve the viewer.

As with most stories, commercial film follows a simple syntax with a problem statement at the beginning, a sequence of events germane to solving the problem, an inevitable crisis and climax, and a distinct conclusion. Since there is little mystery in the organization or syntax, what makes a film interesting is the uncertainty in knowing what events will be relevant for solving the problem of what obstacles will have to be overcome. We know something will happen, but exactly what and why is the mystery that makes the effort worthwhile.

To add intellectual mystery to a story some producer/directors, as with novelists and playwrights, may not follow the linear syntax of beginning, middle, and end in that order. While cause and effect are all presented, a story may begin at the end and work back through events to show how it all began. In *Citizen Kane,* Welles begins with newsreel coverge of Kane's death and asks the question, "What was this man really like?" Skipping around in the events of Kane's life, through flashbacks and flash forwards, Welles forces the audience to complete the necessary continuity in solving the puzzle. Welles omits no parts to the problem, and like our trust in working a jigsaw puzzle, we know that closure will eventually be reached; it matters little what piece is used to begin the project. While this is an intellectual more than emotional exercise, it adds to the interest of the story. However, the key to success in violating the norm of a temporal sequence of events is to ensure that continuity or a logical blending of events may be constructed by the audience. How this is accomplished is one of the more fascinating aspects of syntax in filmmaking.

To understand how continuity in a film is achieved, examine the most fundamental step in planning a film—the *storyboard.* In constructing a storyboard, an artist and director sketch the composition of each scene and camera shot. The importance of this procedure is that each scene, composed of a series of shots, must be a complete visual experience conveying meaning for the viewer. In contrast to a written narrative, film is composed from shots that are often filmed out of sequence and pieced back together at a later time. This requires that each shot function as a sentence, essentially a nonverbal statement describing an object, symbol, or a human emotion. In this manner, a director's concern in photographing a script is to translate time, space, and screenplay dialogue into visual expression. Whereas a verbal grammarian can diagram a sentence into subject, verb, object, nouns, prepositions, and so on, a director diagrams a visual scene into camera angles, shot lengths, panning and dollying the camera, and various types of edits. In this manner the storyboard and shooting script constitute a syntax designed to organize the viewer's experience into meanings of time, space, characterization, and plot, primarily through visual data.

While each shot on a storyboard is related to preceding and following shots, they also function as independent visual experiences that viewers can make sense of even if they are unaware of the overall context. This is not to say that viewers will infer the context from the shot, only that a general interpretation can be made. For example, a crowd of people, a wheat field, the exasperated expression of a harried housewife, or a couple huddled fearfully in the dark corner are all fairly unambiguous in their own right. While the viewer does not know the precise meaning of each picture, due to a lack of context information, preliminary interpretations may be made. After years of watching movies, an individual develops a repertoire of familiar shots and scenes that are expected or anticipated in various contexts and can be linked together into a meaningful story. Consequently, the syntax of film grammar partially involves taking a series of shots or statements, which like sentences can stand alone or be integrated into a whole just as sentences are integrated into paragraphs. Yet the entire process is visual, accomplished almost independently of the verbal dialogue. To test this idea, watch any movie on television or at the drive-in with the volume turned off. In most cases, a person familiar with commercial film will have little difficulty understanding scenes or even the entire film. Given the primacy of visual grammar in film, verbal dialogue plays a supporting role; statements are short, even terse, and usually follow the emotional expression of the actor.

Visual syntax establishes continuity in that directors group the visual experience of short shots into fairly short scenes, each conveying an anambiguous meaning. Through edits, such as cuts or wipes, dissolves, and fades, each part of the story visually blends together. A dissolve or overlap of scenes through double exposure establishes the fact that one scene is ending and another related scene is beginning. A cut or sharp end to a shot suggests that the next shot is part of the previous shot as in the case of two people talking with each other, cutting back and forth to follow the conversation. As time advances, each cut establishes a new viewpoint for the observer, with an elimination of all irrelevant action within that situation. Occasionally a cut is used to jump to a new course of action, although this is tricky business as the audience may lose the continuity. Instead, a new course of action is usually established through a dissolve or fade. By fading the picture to black or a neutral color, the audience knows that a line of action has ended and a new course is about to begin. These editing devices have become so taken for granted that continuity seems to flow naturally, and we trust that all parts to the story will eventually come together. Again, the point is that continuity is managed visually through camera technique and editing rather than through dialogue or following reality as it might occur in everyday life.

Most technicians employed in constructing the syntax of film grammar were developed during the silent era by such innovators as D.W. Griffith in America and Sergei Eisenstein in the Soviet Union. Griffith prefected techniques of drawing the viewer into the action through a sequence of long shots, medium shots, and close-ups. He varied camera angles from high to low to create impressions of dominance or submission. Griffith also developed the all-important cross-cut edit, which shows parallel courses of action that eventually intersect, such as the band of horsemen riding headlong to overtake their intended victims (cutting back and forth between victim and pursuers).

A recent example of the power of cross-cut edits can be observed at numerous points in *Raiders of the Lost Ark,* especially when Indiana Jones drops into the snake-filled pit containing the ark. Back and forth we jump from a position amidst the snakes to see Jones's terrified expression to a view of the snakes from Jones's position, a sequence that ends just short of becoming boring. The classic example of cross-cutting (one we all associate with silent film), is the fair maiden tied to the railroad tracks by the evil villain wringing his hands in anticipation as the train approaches. Not until the hero saves the day do we actually see the proximity of the train to the victim, but through rapid cross-cutting we imagine the train drawing rapidly closer to the helpless victim. How do we know? Each successive shot is a closer view of the train and victim until all we see are giant wheels turning furiously or the nose of the train bearing down in one shot and the victim's fearful eyes in the other. Through camera manipulation and editing both time and distance are actually created in the mind of the viewer.

Space and time can also be distorted, as Sergei Eisenstein demonstrated in his famous Odessa steps scene in the film (1925) *The Battleship Potemkin.* The film, commissioned by the Soviet government, was designed to portray the abortive revolution of 1905. Eisenstein selected the mutiny on the Battleship Potemkin, stationed at Odessa, to symbolize the revolution. In Odessa, a long flight of steps leads down from the center of the city to the wharf where the Potemkin was moored. As the town people, who have rallied to the defense of the mutineer sailors, advance up the Odessa steps, a squad of the Tsar's Cossack soldiers form a firing line aiming down at the crowd. In this masterful sequence of shots and edits, Eisenstein shows the squad of soldiers firing into the crowd and the brutal aftermath. First we see the advancing crowd from a viewpoint behind the soldiers and the rifle shots. The next series shows individual bodies of bloodied screaming faces, boots of the soldiers as the last object seen by a dying victim, the wheels of a runaway baby carriage, a woman in agony holding her dead child, and so on. Eisenstein made time stand still to promote the viewer's emotional involvement in a frightfully realistic scene.

This technique has become established procedure for extending time, used in countless films, particularly in dramatic confrontations. In *Butch Cassidy and the Sundance Kid* (1969), director George

Roy Hill used the same technique, adding slow motion, to portray the shoot-out between Butch, Sundance, and the gang of bandits waiting in ambush on the South American mountain trail. Familiar violent action scenes in adventure films and artistic seduction scenes, such as *The Thomas Crown Affair* (1968) and *Turning Point* (1972) have been edited to extend time and, most important, to heighten the emotional involvement of the viewer.

Film techniques that change reality by jumping ahead or back in time, by prolonging or condensing time, or by simultaneously showing parallel courses of action, violate the logic of everyday life experience. However, in the magic of the darkened theater, movie patrons willingly suspend the frameworks they use to interpret everyday life and substitute a language relevant for film. While this new reality juxtaposes events and adds backgrounds to events that normally do not occur in everyday life, these scenes become acceptable, in part, because (1) each shot is intelligible in itself, (2) shots are grouped into meaningful wholes (scenes), (3) within a scene shots follow an apparent logical sequence in which it is assumed that each new shot will relate to a previous image, and (4) there rarely is enough time and little in the way of other information to allow for alternative explanations.

Through skillful and familiar edits, the entire visual experience throughout a film appears to have continuity, which is essential to establishing the believability of the visual experience. As long as images are blended smoothly and grouped into segments that should be logically connected, the audience is willing to accept minor distortions in time and space for the sake of continuing the action and heightening emotion. As viewers become familiar with film grammar they even demand distortions in time and space and expect edits that establish continuity and encourage involvement. As this syntax comes to be taken for granted, viewers instantly know that a dramatic confrontation between two people will involve close-ups of facial expressions, that a chase scene will use cross-cut edits to show the parallel lines of action, that a panning camera is about to disclose something critical for the plot, and that a fade signals the end to a major segment. We know that a moment of suspense will be prolonged and that irrelevant space and time will be eliminated. We also trust that a crisis will develop, a climax will occur, and that denouement will be suggested. All this experience is the result of a visual syntax in which filmmakers selectively organize space and time, direct attention to particular visual phenomena, and blend shots and scenes into something meaningful for viewers.

INFLECTION: RHYTHM, ACCENT, AND TEMPO

What brings the syntax of film grammar to life or gives syntax its verve are those devices that add rhythm, accent, and tempo. In fact, Robert Gressner defines cinema as "the creation of rhythms amid illuminated objects and to accompanying sounds to express meaning and emotion (Huss and Silverstein, 1968: 40). For film, *rhythm* refers to the visual patterns occurring with regularity, *accent* places emphasis at particular points in the patterns, and *tempo* is the pace or quickness in the occurrence of those patterns. Each of these components of grammar adds interest through the emotion it evokes from the viewer, and, as such, they are essential to how the viewer relates to the subject matter of the film

Rhythm

In music, rhythm is the pattern of time, as in the 4/4 time of most popular hit songs, the 3/4 time of waltzes, and so on. The rhythm of poetry is measured in meter, as in the Trochaic (stress on first syllable) Octameter (eight beats per line) of Edgar Allen Poe's engaging poem "The Raven." In each case, the regularity of time adds a beat or a feel to the communication as in dance, music, and poetry, where rhythm makes the exercise enjoyable. As a nonverbal form of communication, rhythm can be visualized in the variations in styles of walking. Some people strut, others dance, some walk with a slight hitch, others drag their heels, and fashion models seem to glide on air. In each case we are concerned not with the pace but with the pattern that people establish in how they walk.

However, rhythm in film is often more subtle, playing an essential but supporting role to syntax. What is deceiving about rhythm in film is that once it is established, viewers become involved in the plot and cease to notice how rhythm influences the overall structure and mood of the film. Yet viewers would notice immediately if the basic rhythm of a film were suddenly to change without warning. Such is the case with several of Federico Fellini's films (e.g., *8-1/2* [1963] and *Amar-*

cord [1974]) and many so-called art films, which are designed to force the viewer not to take anything on the screen for granted.

Rhythm is achieved through several techniques: camera work, which establishes a sense of movement; editing, which fosters the basic sense of time through impulses of action; music, which provides an auditory beat and often employs a reoccurring theme or refrain; and lighting, in which a director constructs patterns of visual contrast.

Although rhythm can appear in a still picture in the form of juxtaposed lines, curves, shadings, and colors, there is a more pronounced sense of visual rhythm when movement occurs. In a stage play, patrons see movement by actors relative to their fixed position in the theater and the fixed background of the stage set. While the patron's position is still fixed in a movie theater, movement can occur in three ways: by the characters, the camera, and the movement of the background. When a camera moves with an actor, the viewer obtains a sense of flowing with the action. In this action viewers can experience the changing patterns of the scene and the rhythm of the actor relative to the scene. For example, watching an actor move suspensefully through city streets places the viewer at the advantage of understanding the rhythm of the scene itself. By placing the camera momentarily in the position of the actor relative to a changing background, such as sailing on the open sea, the viewer can experience the rhythm of the scene as it is experienced by the actor. Given the potential combinations of these movements, viewers can experience a multiplicity of rhythms, although care must be taken by a director to ensure an overall harmonious effect. The main point is that through camera, actor, and background movement, the viewer can feel actively involved in the scene, moving in harmony with the visual rhythms established by the filmmaker.

To understand the effect of editing for rhythm, a distinction must be made between editing for rhythm and for tempo. Since rhythm is concerned with patterns rather than how fast those patterns occur, edits for rhythm follow a sense of beat or visual arrangement of patterns. For example, comedies usually have a staccato rhythm quite distinct from the suspense film or love story. Rhythm may follow a beat similar to ocean waves, periodically rising to a crescendo and then beginning again. *Raiders of the Lost Ark* seemed to follow this pattern with waves of action reaching a climax, only to have the action begin again immediately, leaving the audience exhausted at the end. The key to understanding rhythm as a function of editing is simply to determine whether the film seemed to have a smooth flow regardless of its tempo. A viewer should never quite get to the point of saying "It's time for the scene to change." If the edits follow an established rhythm, the viewer feels ready to move on to the next scene exactly at the time the scene changes. Cross-cutting between parallel actions or a chase scene has a visual rhythm much like the meter in poetry or two dancers working together.

Although visual rhythm is a bit more complex than has been described here, the main point is that establishing rhythmic patterns through editing is a critical device for involving the audience in the flow of the action. A film audience follows the action through repeating patterns just as a dancer follows a musical rhythm, moving to a new position or visual image with each beat. As in dance, the rhythm in film creates a fluidity of time and space that elicits emotional involvement.

As a device for establishing rhythm, the musical score of a film also plays an essential role. Since the days of silent films, the musical theme, refrains, short groupings of notes, and even particular instrument have become identified with images and actions on the screen. One of the most simple and yet dramatic uses of music was the three-note (B, A, B) theme from a composition by Bach in the silent horror film *Phantom of the Opera* (1926), starring Lon Chaney. Other well-known examples include *The Third Man,* (1949) the *Superman* films, and *The Pink Panther* series. In each case the musical refrain was a baseline or reference point that initiated or completed various scenes, thus adding to a sense of the rhythmic flow of the story. Music may also provide a general beat throughout a film as was done so effectively in *Easy Rider,* with its substitution of hard-driving rock music for dialogue in many scenes. As Ernest Lindgren (1963: 189-190) states in *The Art of Film:*

> Music, where it is used, has to advance the action, to link one dialogue section to another, to establish associations of idea and carry on developments of thought. To intensify the lyrical and emotional relief. . . . It should be noted, however, that it is not the intrinsic quality of the music in a film that is so important as its dramatic appropriateness and proper synchronization between its rhythm and the visual rhythm of the film.

Lighting is probably the least noticed of the three rhythm devices and yet people often comment on the effectiveness or beauty of photography in movies. What captures the attention of these viewers is not just pretty pictures, but how shots are framed and the use of lighting or contrast. Lighting is used in three principle ways: direction, or the part of a film frame that receives the most light, intensity, and the amount of diffusion and tone of the light.

To establish rhythm through lighting, each of these three techniques is used in combination. An extreme example of this approach, in a film that did not use other methods for establishing rhythm, was employed by Andy Warhol in *Empire* (1974). In *Empire,* Warhol aimed a stationary camera on the Empire State Building in New York City for eight consecutive hours. The film consisted entirely of changing light values on the building itself. Of course, given the time span of this visual experience and the normal audience expectation of a plot, the film is boring to the point of absurdity. In a more normal example, Sanley Kubrick's *Barry Lyndon* (1976) was photographed entirely in soft, available light, resulting in a romantic rhythm of tranquility. *The Third Man,* a black-and-white masterpiece, consisted of many high-contrast scenes, establishing a suspenseful drama through visual rhythmic patterns. In fact, most mystery, detective, and war films made during the 1940s used high-contrast black-and-white photography for a rhythm of suspense and action. *Body Heat* (1981), a remake of those powerful femme fatale films of the 1940s (Lana Turner, Rita Hayworth, Veronica Lake, John Garfield), was filmed in low light with flesh tone accent to establish a sensuous slow-beat effect. The entire film played like a torch song sung in a dimly lit night club. Lighting can aid in establishing a steady rhythmic flow, as in *Body Heat,* or one of varying rhythms, as accomplished by Woody Allen in *Interiors* (1978), in which he juxtaposed brightly lit scenes with pale scenes of pastel hues and darkly lit scenes, foretelling deep emotional conflict. Spliced together these scenes jolt the audience through a powerful rhythm of sharp contrasts. As with camera movement, editing, and music, lighting may create a sense of rhythm that is emotionally engaging, serving as legitimation or the "right feel" for the characters and the plot as it unfolds.

Accent

Accent is not distinct from rhythm; it is a rhythm device requiring special attention. Since rhythm is the pattern of regularity that brings syntax to life, accent serves to focus attention in a manner that evokes emotional involvement. Camera angle, edits, music, and lighting, as discussed in the previous section, become rhythm devices insofar as they function to accent various phenomena. In brief, inflection or accent aids in sharpening the emotional focus in communication. The grammarian defines accent as the stress placed on particular syllables of a word; as Rousseau said over 200 years ago, "Accent is the soul of speech." For visual film grammar, this term may be interpreted as the stress or accent placed within a shot as analogous to the syllable of a word, within a scene as analogous to a sentence, and in the climax of the plot, where we expect to experience the greatest accent.

Accent is particularly important in establishing a perspective necessary to comprehend a film's story. In comparing silent film-maker D.W. Griffith to the Russian realists (Vsevolod Pudovkin and Sergei Eisenstein), we get clues as to how accent affects the perspectives that emerged in their films. As a romantic idealist similar to the romantic poets of the early nineteenth century, Griffith involved the audience in the emotion of the story through shots and scenes that flowed in continuous movement. By contrast, the Russian realists took Griffith's techniques and used them to focus dramatically on specific aspects of action and objects to the point of exaggeration. The Russians discovered that in dramatically emphasizing particular shots they could drive home their ideological message with simplicity and great clarity.

Griffith is credited with perfecting at least three editing techniques that aided significantly in establishing particular perspectives for the viewer. In *parallel editing* he used cross-cuts to show the parallel unfolding of several scenes or subplots concurrently. This suggests to the viewer a historical perspective for integrating all parts of a story leading to a particular conclusion and interpretation. The recent film *Ragtime* (1981) used this technique to show the changing times of early twentieth-century urban America. In *attraction editing* he juxtaposed images to underscore the interaction of characters or elements in a scene. For example, juxtaposing an angry sky with facial expressions aids in establishing an emotional perspective for interpreting future action. Finally, in *accelerated editing,* Griffith distorted time by making each shot in a scene progressively shorter in length. This technique obviously is an action perspective that quickens the tempo and involvement of the viewer. As described earlier, Eisenstein reversed this procedure to extend or prolong time in his Odessa steps sequence. In addition, Griffith was not above using a bit of trickery, such as masking the top and bottom or sides of each frame of film in a shot to create special illusions. For example, a battle scene in *Intolerance* shows a soldier falling from a fortress wall. Griffith masked one-third of each side of the film to promote an illusion of the wall's height. In this example, Griffith created a physical perspective and set the stage for the multiplicity of special effects we take for granted in films today.

Camera angle constitutes an accent device through such means as establishing dominance (from a high angle), submission (low angle), and equality (eye level). In *Citizen Kane,* a low-angle long shot shows the character Jedediah (Joseph Cotton) framed by the towering V-shaped legs of Kane standing in the foreground, clearly inferring the dominance of Kane over his one-time friend. As many TV viewers will recall from the 1950s, this same shot was the opening scene for *Gunsmoke,* with Matt Dillon's legs framing the villain about to be gunned down in a shoot-out. Another famous shot from *Citizen Kane,* this time a high-angle view, shows Kane's wife Susan after she sunk to the depths of drunken despair. In a single camera movement (a Welles innovation) the viewer is carried upward toward a billboard picture of Susan as an operatic singing star. The shot continues to a rain-drenched rooftop, through a depressing neon sign, and down through a skylight to a condescending view of the woman. In a single shot with a slow-moving rhythm, Welles suggests her successful rise and total collapse. In addition, the use of low light reflected by rain, the flickering neon sign, and the modulated volume of background music all add to the inescapable perspective that Susan is "down and out," ruined by the manipulating Kane in his quest for power.

In contrast to the complexity of accent as used by Welles in *Citizen Kane,* a simple and very common device is the slow zoom to an extreme close-up during an actor's dialogue. A dialogue might go on for 15 to 30 seconds without placing particular emphasis, especially if the camera and actor remain in a fixed position. But when the camera begins to zoom in slowly to an extreme close-up, we know the dialogue is about to reveal something very significant. This simple device is a cue for the audience to pay attention.

A very engaging example of how inflection and accent may establish a perspective occurred in Woody Allen's *Stardust Memories* (1980). The scene depicts Allen's former lover, now in a mental hospital, in an eye-level, head-and-shoulders shot. Through a rapid succession of jump cuts and momentary freeze frames (stopping the action) of the woman's face, we witness her neurosis and instantly know how to interpret any future reference to this character. The entire scene is shocking as it is totally unexpected. In this case, camera angle and edits produce an unmistakable accent that instantly becomes the form for a new interpretation—an interpretation accomplished entirely without dialogue or background props.

Despite the importance of accent in establishing an analytical perspective for the viewer, the bottom line is still emotion. Any form of communication normally associated with a high degree of emotional involvement, such as music, dance, poetry, and fictional prose, it is accent that elicits emotional involvement. It is the accented beat in music that provides the driving force in dance or the toe-tapping, foot-stomping action of listeners. In other words, the structure of the song and its content are largely irrelevant if you do not feel the beat. Stretching the point, the statement "seeing is believing" also implies "feeling is believing."

Music is particularly important in establishing accent, as any filmmaker will testify. In *Body Heat,* the wailing alto saxaphone effectively aided in establishing the rhythm for the torrid love scenes, which virtually steamrolled off the screen in sultry impluses. In *The Big Sleep* (1946), a Raymond Chandler mystery with Howard Hawks directing Bogart and Bacall, the use of brass horns cued the audience to an action scene and accented the rhythm throughout those scenes. Most everyone is familiar with the musical sounds and sound effects associated with violence, suspense, love, and even routine situations. So familiar are these sounds that each could be played independent of a visual image, and the movie fan could conjure up the correct imagine and attending emotion.

Lighting has a powerful emotional impact, particularly as a means for modulating a scene. Slowly altering the intensity and direction of lighting in a scene can change the mood from cheerfulness, to sorrow, to fright, or to any other emotion. One of the most pleasing scenes that modulated the light source occurred in *The Last Picture Show* (1972), directed by Peter Bogdanovich. In the scene, actor Ben Johnson, who won an academy award for his performance, is seated on a log by a pond in the Texas panhandle reminiscing to a young lad about one of his old girl friends. Filmed in black and white, the background lighting for Johnson's dialogue changes from one shade to another in slow modulation, accenting his statements and evoking a feeling of genuine warmth for the man. For many viewers it clearly was the high point in the film. Another, less-pleasing yet effective use of light modulation occurred in *Apocalypse Now* (1979), when the psychotic face of Marlon Brando was shown in firelight changes from subdued to bold, harsh tones. Other familiar examples include the sinister effect of low-angle lighting in old horror films. By contrast, love scenes normally are shot with very soft, diffused light to accent skin texture and soften any harsh features that would distract from the mood. While I could go on at length describing devices that establish accent, the major point is that the integration of many accent techniques is critical to establishing the moods that accompany the basic rhythm and syntax of a film.

Tempo

Tempo is primarily achieved through editing. D.W. Griffith discovered the importance of editing in establishing tempo when he gradually shortened the lengths of shots during a chase or heavy action scene. As the shots grow shorter in time duration, the effect is a quickening of the pace, similar to watching a basketball game. When the players are in a stalling strategy, the spectator's view if fixed on one spot for a fairly long period of time. When the teams move to a fast-break strategy, the spectator is forced to watch the action move rapidly back and forth. While the action on the basketball court is real, the film experience of rapid movement is created entirely by the rapid change from one scene to the next. In fact, in the film experience a viewer might easily grow bored with movement by an actor if the camera did not appear to change positions. For example, a viewer could watch a cowboy ride at breakneck speed across the open plains and quickly lose the perspective of the speed if it were not for a rapid succession of edits showing the cowboy from different angles and cross-cutting to other objects of relevance, such as the maiden in distress. On the other hand, the suspense scene uses prolonged shots or fewer edits, as in *Alien's* suspenseful climax, where the hero played by Sigourney Weaver is confronted by the monster in the space shuttle. In a series of prolonged close-up shots and cross-cuts from Weaver to the alien, time is extended in agonizing suspense as she slowly struggles into a space suit in preparation for jettisoning the monster.

Tempo is also controlled by how one scene is blended with another. As described in the section on syntax, making a transition from one scene to another is accomplished by one of three general means as described earlier; the dissolve or double-exposed overlap, the abrupt cut or wipe, and the fade. Since the dissolve blends one scene into another it often is used where tempo is low or moderate. In contrast, the cut or wipe is best used in the staccato, up-tempo pace of a chase scene or fast-moving dialogue. The fade, in which the scene fades to no picture at all, brings the action to a momentary halt and allows the viewer to relax before the next sequence and perhaps a new tempo in the story begins.

In addition to editing, music establishes and supports tempo by adding to the underlying rhythm with its own tempo. In one of the opening scenes to *Honeysuckle Rose* (1980), singer Willie Nelson takes off with the band in his make-shift bus to the up-tempo accompaniment of "On the Road Again." While the bus is in no particular hurry, viewers get the pace of the film almost entirely through the music's tempo. Similarly, viewers experience the change in tempo from a scene in which Superman flies around the night sky with Lois Lane in hand to his solo flights to engage Lex Luther or the evil trio from Krypton. In each case, the music tells the tale through its tempo.

While much could be added to a discussion of tempo, the main point to remember is that pace in film is primarily a matter of how action is made to appear through the camera, editing, lighting, and sound. The interesting film is usually one that varies tempo within the general rhythm, adding to the significant points in the story. As such, tempo is one more strategy for involving the viewer emotionally in the film, Anyone interested in examining the subtle use and variations of tempo in film should study the artistic films of Joseph von Sternberg (*Salvation Hunters* [1928], *Docks of New York* [1928], *The Case of Lena Smith* [1929], and *The Blue Angel* [1930], which introduced Marlene Dietrich).

VOCABULARY

The vocabulary of film is less obvious than might be assumed. Verbal dialogue is certainly an important part of film grammar, but so is nonverbal communication and the details of set design.

Beginning with verbal dialogue, it must be emphasized again that what an actor says out loud is often secondary to the visual impact and background sound of a scene. Quoting Ernest Lundgren (1963: 143): "The fact remains that it is the visual part of film that leaves the deepest and most lasting impression on the great majority of people, and those films are most effective that appeal primarily to the eye and only secondarily to the ear." In this regard, film dialogue at its best is often terse and well refined. Rarely do we hear verbal padding as usually occurs in everyday speech. Gone are the long pauses, stammers, filler words, redundant explanations, and four-letter slang terms, unless they serve to accent an emotion. Missing also are long statements or extended verbal exchanges between characters. The power of Gary Cooper on screen was in large measure due to his ability to deliver the short lines of screenplay dialogue with an emphasis that supported nonverbal gestures and the scene's visual power.

To understand the requirements of film dialogue, recall the importance of the storyboard in planning photographic strategy. Since a director's main concern is to present a visual narrative, the dialogue necessarily is represented visually before words are spoken, and it follows that viewers will make definitions of a scene prior to hearing oral dialogue. Therefore, of major interest to the viewer is whether the dialogue is appropriate for expectations already formed on the basis of visual information. We make harsh criticism of film dialogue when speech interferes with visual impressions already formed; redundancy is unnecessary, or worse, speech may detract from the emotional impact of visual sensations. To test out this idea, examine any particularly pleasing scene in a film and note how first the visual setting is established by the camera, followed by the actor's nonverbal gestures, then verbal dialogue, and perhaps concluding with more nonverbal gestures.

In examining films by the Marx brothers, S.J. Perelman wrote extremely witty lines for Marx's dialogue, but as Roy Huss and Norman Silverstein (1968: 149) note:

> What would Groucho's puns be without Groucho's concomitant raised eyebrows, bobbing cigar, and slouching gait? A competent director like Leo McCarey knew how to energize visually the incessant verbal flow from Groucho and Chico by shifting from close-ups of facial expressions to middle shots of body movement or to punctuate the scenes of dialogue with the silent antics of Harpo.

Describing nonverbal vocabulary could take an entire volume in itself, but since we are all experts on reading and evaluating nonver-

bal cues in interpersonal interaction and in film, only a few points
need mentioning. First, a number of studies demonstrate that the eyes
and mouth, in that order, are parts of the body that people usually
notice first. Ray Birdwhistell's works on kinesics describe many
other significant gestures, such as hand movements, torso posture,
head movements, walking and sitting styles, and so on. What is
important in reading these gestures is that most people consider these
nonverbal cues as proof of the real intentions of a speaker. Run
through a list of favorite movie actors and determine how many have
very expressive eyes and mouth, enabling them to convey a full range
of emotion. Silent film stars such as Charlie Chaplin, Buster Keaton,
Mary Pickford, or Greta Garbo all had enormously expressive eyes.
Even less-attractive actors such as Humphrey Bogart or Donald
Sutherland have dominating eyes, resulting in their ability to capture
immediate attention from the audience. Given the number of close-up
shots demanded in film grammar, facial expression is crucial for skillful acting.

A second point in the nonverbal film communication is the actor's
ability to hold expressions long enough to convery the intended meaning to the viewer. This skill requires training, as people in everyday
speech rarely hold an expression for more than an instant. On this
point, compare an amateur home movie of friends or relatives to a
commercial film and note the difference in the length of time various
facial and body expressions are held for the camera. This point is
inutitively understood by most people, as evidenced when they mug
for the camera in a home movie, deliberately drawing out and exaggerating an expression in a manner similar to professional actors.
Extending the time duration of nonverbal communication in commercial film also adds to the fluidity of scenes. The ability of an actor to
hold an expression throughout a shot or for an entire scene aids in
establishing the mood and continuity of the film. The audience must
obtain a clear understanding of the actor's mood and also see these
moods connected in a rhythmic and logical sequence in order to prevent ambiguity or awkwardness. On this point, French filmmaker
François Truffaut said that actors of both gender need to have a good
deal of femininity (not to be confused with effeminate styles). It may
be assumed that Truffaut was equating feminity with grace, poise,
and perhaps class.

Whereas nonverbal gestures are critical in establishing the
emotional validity of a movie plot, the details of set design, props,
wardrobe, and personal grooming establish the authenticity of a story
and the characters. While it may seem strange to claim that details of

set design, props, and so on qualify as vocabulary characteristics of film grammar, these objects constitute the nouns found in any novel. Just as gestures are nonverbal adjectives, visual details of a scene are the proper and common nouns.

Beginning with set design, a film is portrayed in a historical time frame and locale that is understandable to the typical viewer. To establish this time frame and geographical locale, an attempt is made to approximate the situation through natural environment and props that convince the audience or at least do not distract through a look of phoniness. While exact authenticity is often unnecessary, a filmmaker must at least satisfy the viewer's stereotypical expectations of the story's time and place.

The importance of authenticity and detail is a longstanding tradition in the film industry as demonstrated by Erich von Stroheim in filming *Foolish Wives* (1922), in which he held up shooting a costly outdoor scene for hours, waiting for smoke from a chimney to rise at just the right angle. Similar examples are legion in film history as directors wait for the right light, cloud conditions, and other environmental phenomena that cannot be controlled artificially. Hollywood is also noted for its elaborate methods of creating the appearance of authenticity. Everything from miniaturization of action scenes to the small detail in personal props for actors are given careful attention. The considerable cost and effort are not wasted, as the more convincing a set, the less suspension of disbelief is required by the viewer to become involved in the story. For example, in *The French Lieutenant's Woman,* the story shifts back and forth between the present and 100 years earlier in England. To instantly reverse or project the viewer's time frame, set design had to be accurate to minute detail, a feat accomplished with astonishing success. In futuristic settings, such as *Star Wars* (1977), there must be no present-day artifacts that might tip off the viewer to the fact that the time frame is a fraud. Even in present tense, middle-American settings, directors must take care to ensure that all props are consistent or appropriate for the region, social class, age group, and cultural lifestyle of the people being portrayed. To this extent, set designers must be historians as well as sociologists in knowing what the audience will notice and how these objects will be perceived in interpreting a scene.

No doubt the most important vocabulary detail in the visual scheme of a film is costuming. Contemporary film audiences have become accustomed to a high degree of authenticity in wardrobe, as clothing is the most important symbol in establishing identity in today's urban world. Since the majority of people live in an environment of relative anonymity, we recognize and identify the social class and subcultural membership of people by the clothes they wear. Today it is not enough to identify a hero or villain by his or her hat color—there must be an authenticity in shape, style, and signs of wear and tear.

However, there are limits to what film fans will accept in authenticity—limits that end when it comes to make-up and grooming of romantic actor/heroes. Since a large part of going to a movie involves indentification with a leading actor, these individuals must remain within a style of appearance that will evoke our emotional attachment during the film. For example, Robert Redford can wear the costume of a slick hustler in *The Sting,* set in the 1930s, but his hair length and style cannot be as short and straight as that of a typical grifter during that period. Audiences demand detail for the sake of making the film more believable, but they still want to feel comfortable with the actor in terms of contemporary standards of personal grooming.

Make-up is probably the least-noticed detail in the visual vocabulary of film and yet is quite important for establishing characterization and variation in moods. Again, if the actor does not look the part, his or her dialogue will probably not overcome any deficiency in appearance. Skin tone, hair color, eye shadow, and so forth are all part of establishing the look of innocence, cheerfulness, boredom, sadness, or downright depravity. Lighting alone will not capture the intended "look." It takes proper make-up interacting with lighting and camera angle to achieve the desired emotional tone. For example, the cosmetics of violence, such as blood and bruises, constitute a detail that can make or break the authenticity of a scene. The art of make-up has become such an important detail in film that some actors have been known to spend five or more hours in make-up to achieve the right effect. Even gimmicks, such as Marlon Brando's use of cotton in his cheeks for the *Godfather* role, are examples of attention to detail that we often take for granted, and yet these gimmicks might be just the details that make characters believable.

Since people notice detail in the everyday settings of home furnishings to jewelry, clothing, and personal grooming, it follows that deviations from expected detail or lack of detail will call into question the impressions people are attempting to establish. Some errors in detail pertain to the general quality of a film, such as the failure to synchronize the lighting of a dark room with the act of turning on a light switch, shots that are out of focus, or worse yet, the appearance of an overhead microphone in the picture. More often, authenticity of a scene and the ability to become emotionally involved are hampered by discovering an artifact, such as a gun, an article of clothing, furnishings, a toy, and so on that simply did not exist in that time and place. A common error in many films of the 1940s was to depict common folks with material possessions they could not possibly have afforded or obtained even if they had the money. This lack of realism could be overlooked in such details as characters who never slept, ate, or attended to other biological functions, but when they wore the same clothes day after day and always seemed to have ready cash it grew tiresome. Even sophisticated children would laugh when a six-gun in the hands of a singing cowboy fired ten shots. These same heroes rarely were injured, and when they did suffer a minor bruise it miraculously healed by the next scene.

These details did not go unnoticed, even in situations defined as play or nonserious activity for the viewer. As a result, films during the 1950s became more realistic, especially in the genre of Westerns following the film *Shane* (1953). This film was the first in my recollection, to show the terrifying power of a Colt-44 handgun and the terrible bruises resulting from a fist fight. After *Shane,* Westerns were forced to give new attention to detail, especially in scenes of violence.

Finally, a specialized vocabulary characteristic in film that requires at least brief attention is the "special effect." Although special effects also qualify as accent devices, they constitute a specific aspect of film grammar that is more than accent. The special effect is not only a descriptive statement: it is a visual experience that surpasses the descriptive accounts found in novels. In conveying a new experience, words are often restrictive in terms of the vocabulary limitations of the participants. Words also require a fair amount of cognitive work to visualize what may be attempted in a descriptive passage. But a pictorial special effect is immediate both in terms of shock value and the range of meaning that can be conveyed in this visual experience. For this reason the special effect is a very unique descriptive vocabulary as it is astounding in its immediacy and emotionally charged in involving the viewer in the experience. Special effects provide the illusion, the flight into fantasy that, to date, film does better than any other medium.

Film Genre

From the beginning of commercial film in the nickelodeon parlors, movies have focused on basic moral themes and human struggles. The search for love, happiness, success, and the conflict between good and evil was played out in stories that encouraged a viewer's emotional involvement with the plight of screen characters. Perhaps the little of Pauline Kael's book, *Kiss Kiss, Bang Bang* (1965), says it all. Whether the film is a love story, an adverture, or a human interest biography, the theme is moralistic and the plot is the trial of defining right against wrong and surviving or finding happiness and success in the process; sex, action, and violence are thrown in for emotional embellishment. But within these larger concerns, certain kinds of films have become so popular they have become standardized in their perspectives and grammar—standardized into *film genres*.

Entertainment movies, which are loosely organized and analyzed through categories or genre such as Westerns, detective crime films, adventure-thrillers, and musicals, constitute a perspective or set of perspectives for dealing with common norms and values. The love triangle occurs in many films, but it will be dealth with differently in the Western, the detective genre, or the musical. For example, in a romance genre the perspective is one of focusing on the tension in making a choice between the two competing members of the triangle. Or take "the chase" as a particular perspective within the genre of comedy compared to the suspense-thriller. In *It's a Mad Mad Mad World* (1963), the chase frames the routines of burlesque and slapstick comedy. By contrast, the chase in a war-torn country with a life-and-death struggle and intense interaction results in the suspense-thriller. Therefore, a genre may integrate several perspectives into one standardized set of expectations for how the content of the film should be interpreted. Through repeated exposure, viewers develop preferences for particular genres and use their criteria for evaluating films within that genre. Of importance for media influence is that a genre may become a preference for dealing with a particular theme or morality issue.

WESTERNS

The Western is by far the all-time favorite movie genre for the American film audience, and its popularity is explained quite simply. In Westerns, the basic existential questions of life are posed pragmatically and answered with clarity. Personal freedom, honor, and control over personal destiny are concerns met squarely through clear-cut issues and instantly recognizable and predictable characters. Although other genres meet the same existential problems, none seems to accomplish the task with such passion, intensity, and uncomplicated heroics. But perhaps most important of all is the fact that Westerns function as historical legend and mythology, describing the stuff that Americans claim to be made of. The struggle to tame a lawless, expanding frontier was accomplished by people with a passion for personal freedom, a disregard for a person's past deeds, a strategy of self-reliance, and above all, a commitment to courage and honor. Despite the fact that Westerns depict a period in history lasting less than thirty years, this period represents all that is idealized in the American spirit. And that idealization is epitomized in the Western hero.

Few people who take seriously the basic ideals and history of Americana do not at least secretely admire, respect, love, and vicariously emulate the Western hero, captured so thoroughly in characters portrayed by John Wayne, Gary Cooper, Randolph Scott, and Alan Ladd. Unquestioningly, the king was John Wayne, a veteran of over 200 profitable Westerns from 1929. Wayne always represented a man willing to face tremendous odds for the sake of freedom, honor, and the basic moral naiveté of good versus evil. The Western hero often paid the price of loneliness for demanding that others accept him on his own terms. He often appeared awkward in interpersonal relations, especially with women, yet he always acted decisively in the inevitable struggle. Temptation or a sordid past might dog the Western hero, but when the chips were down, virtue, sensitivity, and great inner strength emerged in ways that inspired lesser people. The Western hero was a leader par excellence, a mythological character that still motivates people to think and act with optimism.

The uncomplicated Western hero is aided by a simple plot, transparent characters, and situations that are replicated with only minor variation in every film. Viewers can count on the villain who exudes evil intention, such as Jack Palance in *Shane,* the town doctor who has good sense in everything but liquor, the rancher baron who buys loyalty and craves power, the good-hearted saloon girl who loves but never gets her man, the eastern society lady who either succeeds or fails to become "westernized," the well-meaning but pragmatic sheriff, the dandy cardsharp, the comedian sidekick, and the hero, the mysterious stranger who ultimately is forced to save the day. John Ford's classic 1939 production of *Stagecoach,* starring John Wayne, cast the die for Westerns. It not only featured these standardized characters and props (the gun symbolizing power and the horse symbolizing freedom) but established the scenery (Monument Valley) and the scenes so familiar to us all—the range war, cattle drive, hanging party, poker game, Indian attack, and showdown shoot-out. None of these characters or scenes requires intellectual or cosmopolitan understanding. In every respect, the Western is predictable and perhaps intellectually boring, but its emotional appeal has been cathartic for several generations of movie fans.

DETECTIVES

The detective film is the urban counterpart of the Western. Aside from the obvious scenery differences, the detective film offers an intellectually stimulating plot of "whodunit." But for many fans of this genre, the challenge of figuring out the puzzle is not the major appeal; rather, like the Western, the appeal lies in the emotional satisfaction of the chase and observing the wits of a hero who needs "street sense" to outmaneuver the opponent and triumph in the showdown. While the detective needs a large degree of cosmopolitan experience and cunning to meet the challenge, in every other respect this character and the Western hero share much in common—courage, honor, self-reliance, decisive action, and control over personal destiny. Like the Western hero, the detective is also uncorruptible, placing a higher value on honor and freedom than on material gain and upward mobility. Sam Spade, Lew Archer, Mickey Spillane, and others never become rich or famous because they never sell out; they are a rock of integrity if not the model of decorum. As Wayne epitomized the Western hero, Bogart is the detective—a study in contrasts— cynical but optimistic, tough but suave, chauvinistic but chivalrous, unhandsome, yet very attractive. Like Wayne, Bogart was a tough guy who meant well and could always be counted on in the clutch. Recently, the detective was replaced by the secret agent and the undercover cop, but with few exceptions they are simply the detectives of the 1940s set in modern times.

The gangster, as an apparent antithesis of the Western hero and detective, actually shares much in common with the two law-abiding heroes. Gangsters are tragic characters who easily could have been bonafide heroes had circumstances been different. Caught in the web of poverty and oppression, the high achiever turns to a life of crime to gain personal power, wealth, and fame, something that elicits empathy among many in the audience. The ganster simply is too expedient, fails to see beyond the glitter, and turns to the easy power of the gun. He (most often a male) is that irrational side of all people, a part of us that should know better but fails. Still, we admire the gangster's rejection of unconventionality and covertly respect the symbol of power in America—the gun. Gangsters usually are not cowards, although their bravado is a bit hollow behind the gun, nor do they lack honor or intelligence. What they lack is good sense, and for this they are pitied.

In all three cases—Western hero, detective or undercover cop, and gangster—the emphasis is on the ideals and traits of the American character. Clearly, the focus in this genre is on vicarious involvement, following the character rather than the story.

ADVENTURE-THRILLER

By contrast, the adventure-thriller is just that, an accent on action encountered by a superhuman individual or group demonstrating great physical prowess in pulling off an impossible mission. The objective in the mission is of little importance; it is the action that attracts the audience. What distinguishes the adventure-thriller from a Western may be a fine line, as the heroes in both genre are indestructible outsiders who display great courage. But adventure-thrillers focus on what the heroes do in confrontations rather than who they are and what they represent. The adventure film is heroic in machismo and action rather than for principles. In fact, the main character(s) in these action-packed, thrill-a-minute escapades are often amoral love 'em and leave 'em, take-the-money-and-run opportunists. Western, detective, and gangster films are usually morality plays, while adventure-thrillers are just plebian fun. Since the adventure thriller is based almost entirely on action, filmmakers become entrapped by a strategy of "can you top this" heroic feats and special effects. We are treated to a linear progression of heroes from Flash Gordon to James Bond to Superman, and dazzling special effects including epic battle scenes, super explosions, terrifying chase scenes, colossal wrecks, and cosmic marvels. A wide range of films is encompassed by this genre, from war stories (old, new, and futuristic) to the improbable heist or capture and the great escape. There are many subgenre in this general category, but the primary focus in all is action and thrill for the moment. The audience wants the grist of action and violence, something Sam Peckinpaw (*Straw Dogs,* 1971) and Walter Hill (*Southern Comfort,* 1982) have found quite profitable.

MUSICALS

Musicals, which include courtship-romance, musical biography, and comdedy, have periodically enjoyed huge success on the screen, particularly when society seemed to need a light-hearted lift. Note the most profitable and popular musicals and the years of release: The Gold Digger films (early 1930s), *Top Hat* (1935), numerous musicals during the 1940s, *Singin' In The Rain* (1952), *Sound of Music* (1966), *Cabaret* (1972), and *All That Jazz* (1980). (The last two are rather cynical views, perhaps reflecting the malaise of the 1970s.) In the vast majority of these and other memorable musicals the story line is basically a success story of love and/or theatrical fame; a chance meeting between a male and female performer, a hit duo, blossoming into love, rejection, or a misunderstanding with each going their separate way, and a happy reuniting building to a grand finale. While it may sound a bit corny on paper, this story, almost devoid of plot, has and will warm the hearts of millions when set amidst the splendor of well-choreographed song and dance productions. The combination of success story and song and dance seems to be a sure-fire hit when society is mentally depressed or afraid.

Although success is expressed in all film genre, it takes on a special enchantment through colorful and sparkling dance routines and joyous song. Traditionally, song and dance in Western theater are a nonthreatening, nonintellectual, and nonideological form of communication. It is pure fun and happiness even to the point of being a ritual designed to promote good feeling. In fact, some forms of music, such as bluegrass, never express depressing subjects or demeanor. Comic Steve Martin once commented after Watergate that if Richard Nixon had played the banjo he might have been spared political ruin. While this is a bit far-fetched, the basic point is well taken as it is simply impossible to engage in serious or anxious thought while involved vicariously or overtly in jubilant song and dance. Even during the late 1960s, the counterculture regularly engaged in song to instill feelings of comaradarie and happiness during political protests. Indeed, throughout Western history, song and dance have been the communication form most frequently relied on to quell pessimism and evoke optimism.

HORROR

Horror films were pioneered by German filmmakers during the silent era, employing techniques from expressionistic theater, such as distorted sets, bizarre makeup, moody lighting and allegory. The classic film *The Cabinet of Dr. Caligari* (1919), *Waxworks* (1924) and Fritz Lang's *Metropolis* (1927) laid the foundation of form and content for the entire genre of horror and science fiction monster films we know today. Whether it is a recent Brian DePalma shocker or an old Dracula film, the focus in this genre is on excitement and terror in the nightmare world of our deep-seated fears. While people may be reluctant to admit a secret liking for horror films, they continue to enjoy popular and apparently timeless appeal. Some analysts like to argue that a subconscious force is behind the popularity of horror films, but the fact is that all people have nightmares and harbor secret fears on a conscious level. Horror movies function to legitimate and even normalize this nightmare world by placing it before the masses as a common cultural characteristic. Since the fears that emerge in nightmares are vivid visual experiences, they make ideal subject matter for the darkened movie theater.

Horrible night-stalking evil creatures compelled to kill irrationally or gone berserk with rage instill the fears that audiences demand. Through a grammatical form of placing the audience in the role of searching for and confronting the beast, viewers are willing and defenseless victims, anticipating but not knowing when the attack will come. Similar to the Greek myth of being turned to stone by Medusa's eyes, the audience seems compelled to look. If executed well, these horror scenes stay with a viewer long after leaving the theater, as exemplified by *Psycho* and *Jaws*.

The key photographic and editing strategy in horror films is to encourage suggestibility through ambiguity. The source of fear is usually exposed through glimpses in dimly lit settings, as once the source is out in the open, especially in broad daylight, the audience sees the monster as they would see everything else in their familiar and ordinary world. To prevent the appearance of ordinary experience, the filmmaker casts the horror in a physical setting that approximates the nightmare world, keeping the source of fear hidden in the shadows. In *The Creature From the Black Lagoon* (1954), early scenes of the creature are shocking compared to those after the creature is shown out of water and in full view. By contrast, Count Dracula is always menacing because he is known to change form and mesmerize his victims. Once the sun goes down the vampire is omnipresent. The recent film *Alien* (1979) used the same technique quite effectively, never showing the monster in a complete form until it was jettisoned from the spacecraft in the final scenes.

The horror film also accentuates fear in the viewer by alluding to a dark, irrational side of human nature. Supposedly all people have the propensity or weakness for evil and violence if conditions are right. The werewolf films are examples of a classic confrontation of the average person enslaved by an evil presence—that violent side of the split personality that may emerge when the moon is full. In a similar vein, *The Shining* (1979) portrayed a typical, practical American father slowly possessed by evil until his sole purpose was to murder his family. These demonic forces and deranged monsters continue to emerge in the fears of viewers because by definition a phenomena this irrational cannot possibly be dealt with through ordinary means. At any moment demonic possession might occur and in the most unsuspecting situations, as described in *The Exorcist* (1973). And yet it is precisely the excitement offered by such an unpredictable though familiar enemy that draws the viewer's attention. And when the climax in the film passes, familiarity with this monster seems to elicit a sense of sympathy from the audience, as both beast and audience share in common the experience of being victims of circumstance.

While excitement through fear and shock based on irrationality and lack of adequate defense is the content of the horror film, the science fiction counterpart deals with a source of fear external to the viewer's known world. To overcome this threat, viewers learn that it is necessary only to acquire knowledge about the alien world and defeat it through logic and reason. In the "sci-fi" monster film of the 1950s, the audience was spared the premise of inner irrational fears and was concerned only with the shock of confrontation; once the external threat had been defeated, the situation returned to normal. These films may be intellectually interesting but rarely did they evoke the terrifying fear of the true horror film. The Japanese sci-fi films and *Star Trek* are cases in point. In contrast, *Alien* combined the intellectual approach of the science fiction film with the beast of a horror movie. In *Alien* it was clearly established that no known scientific means were available to kill the monster; the only hope was escape.

As true horror genre, with a sci-fi mentality, *Alien* was an excellent example of fear generated through suggestibility and ambiguity, a case of what is not seen and cannot be known being the essential ingredient of terror and intellectual curiosity.

Perhaps the 1980s will witness a combination of sci-fi and horror genre in which the beast will mirror our innermost fears and, at the same time, require a sci-fi mentality to understand and overcome the phenomenon. Examples already include a remake of *The Thing* (1982) and *Poltergeist* (1982). On the other hand, the adventure-thriller is currently quite popular, and films such as *Blade Runner* (1982) combine sci-fi and horror genre with a wrap-around of the adventure thriller. What is interesting about *Blade Runner* is that it also uses the film noir (dark color and emotional tones) detective genre of the 1940s and the classical German expressionism of the silent horror films (e.g., *The Cabinet of Dr. Caligari*). While *Blade Runner* has a very thin plot, it is a visually engaging film with its grotesque physical artifacts, lighting, and characters. The contrast between a futuristic world of high technology and a deevolution of human relations and trashy street life is an unnerving terror itself. *Blade Runner* may well become the prototype of a new film genre, a synthesis of traditional forms and newly considered existential questions.

The four genre discussed in this all-too-brief section (see recommended readings) by no means exhaust entertainment film offerings. Intrigue and suspense as the intellectual side of adventure-thrillers, the love story set in a variety of genres, message and morality films on specific social issues, fantasy, films about films, and esoteric products from subcultures and foreign countries (e.g., new wave) all add to the vast array of genres and subgenres available to the movie fan. But the four genres discussed above capture the more popular films and provide enough evidence to make the argument that genres constitute a perspective that is emotionally charged.

Media Influence

Influence from film is a result of the meanings filmmakers and viewers attach to their screen experiences and how they relate those screen experiences to life outside the theater. Although this chapter concentrated on the language factors and perspectives that contribute

to understanding commercial movies, significant factors not discussed include organizational matters that affect production, the star
system, the social stratification of the film industry, and various
ideological factors that influence the selection of film subjects. While
these factors are important for understanding the total culture of
filmmaking, the concern here is to analyze how the communication
strategies employed by filmmakers influence the perception of reality
as seen by both film professionals and the audience.

Within this framework the discussion of media influence will touch
on four categories: (1) the emotional relationship with a medium that
emphasizes visual information, (2) the influence of Hollywood film
on everyday life, (3) our sense of history resulting from film genre,
and (4) stereotypes as presented in film and their apparent consequences. In general, it is suggested that movies may become an
experience every bit as meaningful and significant as other
experiences in one's life. Can the lingering fear of taking a shower or
swimming at night be explained without reference to *Psycho* or *Jaws*?
Are fashion and standards of physical attraction influenced by Hollywood? Do visual images of ancient and recent history result from
entertainment films? And where are various stereotypes reinforced?

EMOTION

Earlier it was stated that interaction in urban society requires
considerable facility in reading visual cues from other people. For the
urban public, movies have become a rich resource of information and
a vicarious training gound for visual communication from formal
to intimate interaction. Noting the importance of studying the
consequences of visual bias in film, Garth Jowett and James M.
Linton (1980: 104-105) argue in their book *Movies as Mass
Communication:*

> The advent of a new mode of communication, such as the movies, alters
> the basic way the society perceives itself. In altering the balance
> between the various forms of communication, the introduction of a new
> channel of information also restructures the agenda of those things
> which we deem to be important. An obvious example of this type of
> cultural restructuring would be in a society where the visual media
> (movies and especially television) have become the dominant forms of
> communication. In this case the authentic "visual experience" becomes
> more important than the more personal, internal "mind images" created
> by written material.

Adding the element of emotion to the visual bias of film it would seem worthwhile to explore the extent to which visual information through a visual grammar becomes associated with various emotional states. The argument that a visual dramaturgy of settings, props, and other visual data is critical for establishing meanings in urban social relationships has been discussed and documented by Erving Goffman, Gregory Stone, and others. But to date, little has been done to analyze the association of visual properties in interaction with the emotions of participants. Hypothetically, a major aspect of media influence in film is that people expect particular emotions to follow the presentation or manipulation of particular visual information. The question is, are particular visual experiences, such as scenes or settings, physical appearance, and nonverbal gestures, associated with feelings of love, anger, anxiety, or tranquility?

Through constant exposure to love scenes in movies, viewers may come to associate feelings of romance with soft light, comfortable surroundings, and a particular body language. Movie patrons have learned that when the stage is properly set and other visual images are presented, feelings appropriate to romance follow actions on the screen. While this occurs in other media and also in everyday life, Hollywood films emphasize this process to such an extreme that people may accept what they see in films as the ideal or ultimate expression. That is, movies may be the most extreme and perhaps the best source of information on emotional experience of any mass medium.

Although movies have been a source of intense emotional portrayals for over 80 years, it is not enough to argue that film is influential only through repeated exposure. The question to answer is, what do people pay attention to in these repeated exposures? Following the discussion of film grammar it may be hypothesized that syntax in such situations as romance, action, or suspense in various movie genres may establish a sequence of how these situations and behaviors should unfold. For example, film fans learn that there are gestural and situational preliminaries to a romantic kiss, that suspense or suspicion involves a sequence of events and gestures, and that adventure requires repeated trials and obstacles with appropriate expressions by the participants. In other words, a condition for establishing a mood requires an appropriate sequence of visual performances for an actor and visual information for an observer. In addition to a visual syntax, movies use editing, music, and lighting techniques to establish rhythm, accent, and tempo, which are additional aides in constructing moods. Finally, the visual properties of a setting and nonverbal gestures provide evidence for the authenticity of emotional states associated with whatever action is taking place. For a movie fan, romance may not be emotionally satisfying or even seem legitimate unless it occurs within settings and through nonverbal gestures similar to those portrayed on film. When dark streets or a dark house becomes a situation for suspense, knowledge of the forms used in horror films may become the framework through which the darkened street or house is interpreted.

As with our discussion of other media, it is reasonable to suggest that people set stages and act out behaviors designed to elicit feelings through forms learned from film, and they interpret scenes and behaviors in everyday life through the resource of film. In this respect, the fantasy world of film becomes the basis for expectations and definitions in life outside the theater.

Scientifically testing the influence of film is not an easy matter as the confounding variables are difficult to identify and control. However, on an intuitive level, some of these ideas should make sense simply because most people take them for granted. People recall from their childhood experience particular films that were resources for play activity. The Westerns, crime movies, war shows, sports biographies, and horror films all supplied situations for imitation in play. But to make the play reenactment authentic, all participants had to follow the script and wear approximate costumes. What is imitated in this play is the visual drama more than verbal dialogue, as kids and even adults rarely recall the exact lines spoken on the screen. But most everyone recalls what it looked like to ride the horse, fight, run with the ball, be scared, and so forth. Even if kids cannot replicate the exact emotions on the screen, they at least know how these emotions were expressed by actors.

THE INFLUENCE OF FILM ON EVERYDAY LIFE

The second category is an extension of points made in the previous section. Since movies are a repository of visual information and emotional guidelines, viewers are likely to pay attention to the perspectives in films that are immediately relevant for their daily lives. It was no accident that silent films prior to World War I dealt with the trials and tribulations of the common working person. During the war years and into the 1920s films catered to the middle-class audience, showing how the affluent, especially women, lived and handled various situations. In fact, female characters were so common during the first quarter century of film that a studio credo was "Movies that don't appeal to women don't make money" (Jowett, 1976: 63). From the Depression years through World War II, musicals supplied an optimism and helped support the attitude that this period was a temporary setback in the inevitable fulfillment of the American dream. In these films, and in those of today as well, people obtain support for basic ideals and values along with practical information on lifestyle and material culture relevant for their immediate and long-term future.

Not only do entertainment films support ideals and values; they also provide leaders and heroes who represent these ideals and values through their actions on the screen. The classic symbol is the Western hero who rides into town, protects the innocent, saves the ranch, and rides off having demonstrated that altruism, courage, self-reliance, and freedom are alive and well. Never mind that it may never have happened in real life; it should and it could, and that is all that matters. As discussed earlier, John Wayne was not just a good actor for Western genre; he symbolized American ideal culture and made it come alive on the screen. As a friend once remarked, "If John Wayne doesn't stand for what America is all about, then why not?" The media influence of this phenomena is that movies continue to reestablish this symbol, and in the process this symbol lives on in our ideals to the extent that in 1980 Americans elected a president who was successfully identified with the genre. Viewers' demands for these symbols are so intense that once an actor is accepted by the public as a particular symbol, that actor may be typecast in that role from that time on.

Films also create personified symbols for more mundane situations that are relevant for both the daydream fantasy world and everyday life. For kids growing up in the 1940s, where did the idea emerge that cowboys and Indians do not cry, or that it is alright for a soldier to be scared but not a coward? What many people recall from their youthful days at the movies are visual screen images and emotions that constituted a library of how to act, believe, and feel in situations that some day might occur. Furthermore, is an adult film experience much different than a child's? Certainly the relevance of screen experience will change as adults are concerned with romance, norms for the practical encounters in parenting or on the job, and the like. Nevertheless, the visual imagery and emotional expression of modern urban women or men in situations such as midlife crisis may be every bit as powerful and suggestive to adults as were the Western heroes of their youth. People can participate or use movies to generate a variety of meanings ranging from full vicarious participation in film characters and stories, to using visual scenarios and emotional expressions witnessed on the screen as a repository of information for self-comparison and as guidelines for behavioral strategies. The visual appearance of emotions such as the suspicious glance, the menacing stare, the seductive pose, the flirtatious eye, and many more thave been standardized if not actually created through film. The phrase "as they do it in the movies" is not an empty statement.

In addition to the personification of symbols in film, fashion and standards of lifestyle have been a part of the media-conscious culture for years. Everyone is familiar with standards of physical attraction for women and men, the orientation of youth in our culture, and fashion trends established and supported through motion pictures. If a teenage girl lacks the physical characteristics of Brooke Shields, she can achieve an approximation through clothing and hairstyle. Back in the 1950s, the model of physical appearance for many women was Natalie Wood and Brigitte Bardot and for men it was Tony Curtis and Robert Wagner. Throughout the course of motion picture history numerous minor and major fashion trends have been set off or popularized through particular films. Examples include Theda Bara's "vamp" look in the 1920s, Jean Harlow's platinum hair, Clark Cable's mustache, Betty Grable's spiked heels, Brando's leather jacket, Travolta's jeans, and most recently Indiana Jones's (Harrison Ford) hat in *Raiders*. The simple point is that people leave the theater enthralled with a character or some aspect of the story and immediately think of how they can prolong the image and feeling enjoyed and legitimatized by the film. These fashions may be short-lived if others do not follow suit or respond favorably, but it does indicate the power of the film's visual and emotional impact beyond the context of the theater.

FILM GENRES AND HISTORY

The power of film to shape our perceptions of history can be illustrated, in part, by examining the standardization in film genres and its impact. Over the years, characteristics of various genres have become so standardized that it is foolhardy for a filmmaker to tamper with the expectations viewers have formed. The most popular films over the years are those that either established or epitomized a particular genre, while films that violate genres formulas or mix the formulas of several genres often fail at the box office. In 1981, the film *An American Werewolf in London,* failed by not making it clear whether it was a comedy or a horror film. On the other hand, Mel Brooks made it quite clear from the start that *Young Frankenstein* was strictly a comedy. In addition, he conformed to audience expectations of the horror genre by placing it in the proper historical and geographical content, shooting the film in black and white, and using all the lighting, camera angles, and music we associate with this genre. If the parameters of a genre are this standardized and audience expectations this rigid, there should be little doubt that any genre that is associated with a historical period will influence our perceptions of that historical period. The Western and the late nineteenth century, the gangster film and the Depression/Prohibition, and the musical and the 1940s all have rather specific historical perspectives ingrained in their formulas. Think of a particular "period" genre and certain historical images immediately come to mind. Reverse this process and think of a particular historical period and one or more films may come to mind.

The influence of film and specific genre is particularly acute in dealing with those historical periods that contain considerable conflict and drama. For example, Biblical and Roman epics, the medieval age of knights and chivalry, the royal courts of eighteenth-century Europe, the age of swashbuckling pirates, the Civil War, the Westward expansion, World War I, the Roaring Twenties, Prohibition, World War II, the pop explosion of the 1960s and the counterculture—every dramatic conflict period in Western civilization has been portrayed in entertainment films. And because Hollywood revels in action, intrigue, and romance, that is precisely our view of these historical periods.

Ask the avid movie fan to describe the Roman Empire and you are likely to get a description of *Ben Hur.* The Civil War is *Gone With the Wind,* and Prohibition is *Scarface* and *Little Ceasar.* The image nearly everyone in America and the world over have of the American West is covered wagons drawn in a circle fighting off crazed Indians, cattle drives, range wars, shoot-outs, dusty, board-walked streets with no traces of horse pollution, the crowded saloon with a parking place always available at the hitching post, buxom dancehall girls, and so on. These images are so well established in the present-day populace that in recreating these old western towns for public amusement, the design must follow the movie set rather than an authentic replication. If Old Tucson in Arizona were actually built the way it looked in 1870, nobody would recognize it or accept it. Of critical importance is the fact that for many people movies are their primary source of historical knowledge. Whatever distortions and emphasis occur through Hollywood's interpretation become fact for these viewers.

STEREOTYPES

Finally, historical images may be surpassed in impact only by the numerous *stereotypes* and role models created through various film genres. Almost every major stereotype in American culture has either been established or perpetuated through entertainment films. Take the example of the *Star Wars* series, a simple story of boy rescuing girl from the clutches of an evil tyrant. To establish the visual impact of the story, viewers need to see the beauty and virtuousness of the girl, the innocent sense of justice, basic courage, and zeal of the rescuer-hero, the power of the evil tyrant, the battle, and the happy ending. Since this is a basic struggle between good and evil, viewers also need cues for recognizing the protagonists on each side, and since the film is an adventure thriller, viewers do not want to be bothered by any ambiguity in figuring out who is on which side.

On a more serious level, Hollywood stereotypes are so extreme they have become the basis for prejudice and discrimination in everyday life. From the Uncle Tom and other subservient and degrading images of minorities and women, there is sufficient reason to attack Hollywood's complicity in prolonging racism and sexism. Images of Italian gangsters, efficient German automatons, well-mannered but bungling Englishmen, drunken Indians, black beeboppers, Southern rednecks, and Midwest towheads have all resulted in prejudicial attitudes and discriminatory practices. The fact that Hollywood's film stereotypes are so powerful was dramatically illustrated when Marlon Brando refused an Academy Award for best actor (1973), stating he objected to Hollywood's negative portrayals of American Indians. If Brando had not been right, the reaction against him by his peers and many fans would not have been nearly as strong as it was. And yet Hollywood has recently attempted to reverse some of these negative images, particularly with respect to blacks and women.

However, people will cling to old stereotypes, just as they love old movies.

On the whole, Hollywood operates in concert with American society, upholding mainstream beliefs even when those beliefs might seem outmoded or deleterious to society's welfare. As Jowett and Linton (1980: 109) have suggested:

> Popular U.S. films operate as dramas of reassurance. The beliefs, attitudes and values presented in Hollywood films tend to resonate with the dominant beliefs, attitudes and values of American society. In other words, the dominant ideology of a society tends to be reinforced by the ideology presented in its films.

This does not mean that films reflect society. As argued earlier, the act of making and viewing a movie is an act of constructing meanings, not of reflecting them. On this point it is instructive to examine the work of experimental filmmakers such as Norman McLaren.

Experimental filmmakers are not to be confused with those making art or cult films. The experimental film is an experiment with film communication itself, as exemplified by Norman McLaren's very powerful work entitled *Neighbors* (1953), a film using live actors made to appear animated through a jerky motion of many still shots pieced together as a motion picture. McLaren forces the viewer to concentrate on what becomes the shocking effect of violence in a fight between two neighbors. He has taken animation, which normally is used in harmless cartoons and fairy tales, to present violence, and the unaware viewer is not prepared for the effect. In addition, the use of animation requires the viewer to see each part of a violent act in rapid freeze-frame motion. This rhythm, accent, and tempo are extremely uncomfortable, as viewers are forced to see real violence rather than smooth-flowing action. Films of this type are powerful examples of how grammatical structures and perspectives may be mixed and manipulated to yield surprising results. In Hollywood films, the manipulation and negotiation process is fairly subtle. But in experimental films we learn how extreme this process may become.

Summary

No one doubts the significant impact of Hollywood on American culture during the twentieth century. But most people understand this to mean that movies shape attitudes and serve as subject matter for imitation, especially among impressionable youth. While evidence for shaping attitudes and imitation is claimed by many, a more fundamental consideration is the extent to which film affects our perception and experience. A common argument is that technology not only changes environment but also alters how we experience that environment. But instead of focusing on the technological hardware of film and other media, the argument throughout this book has been that language grammar and perspectives working as quasi-theories constitute a framework that influences how people perceive and experience phenomena through mass media. And since film relies heavily on visual information that provides vivid images, attention comes to be focused on the emotional component of interaction. It seems almost logical to suggest that most people will find it easier to become emotionally involved at a movie, as with distraction at a minimum a private view of a fascinating visual world unfolds in a darkened theater.

Given the intensity of emotional involvement afforded by movies, the genre and content of films develop a powerful potential for influence. Everyday life behavior patterns, historical interpretation, and stereotypes can literally be created through film. But all this depends on a willingness among filmmakers and viewers to use and accept a grammatical structure and perspective without reservation or critical reflection. The influence of film is not automatic, nor is it inevitable if the grammar and perspectives of film are understood and acted on critically. With this in mind, consider the remarks of film analyst Alan Casty (1973: 411):

> There has developed a widespread sense of deeper purpose for the film as art and as humanist voice. A new social forthrightness and complexity of psychological probing and understanding have given the film a wider scope of concern, a deeper, denser insight, a richer, more fully human meaning. At the same time, a growing stylistic sophistication has ... been marked by greater emotional and sensory intensity. ... Ours is a self-conscious age; our film art is now self-conscious, knowing and knowledgeable, to the extreme, even, possibly, to a fault.

Let us hope Casty's optimism is warranted.

CHAPTER 7

THE POWER SOURCE

It is commonly believed that the amount of time people spend in contact with mass media is sufficient to explain media's power. Proponents of this claim point to such examples as the success of advertising, the inability of some heavy media users to differentiate between what is portrayed through media and the external reality of everyday life, and the lack of reading and writing skills among contemporary youth. While there is some truth to these finds, they do not account for the fact that some heavy media users do not fall victim to media influence or fail to develop traditional communication skills.

Other critics of media claim that media's power lies in the subjective bias of what is presented to the public. These critics lay blame on bias in slanting news stories, hiding the full truth in advertising, and the insidious appeal to so-called prurient interests in sex and violence. The underlying assumptions in this critique include the notions that every story must have a basic truth or "objective" reality, that ideological concerns motivate vested interests to slant stories to their advantage, that all people harbor unconscious needs, and that repetition is a powerful strategy. The dominant position within this critique is that the media industry operates with a political and economic bias favoring big business. Remedial strategies would, therefore, require a reduction in the control of media by big business while at the same time educating the public about the influence of these vested interests.

While there is good evidence to support the contention that vested interests attempt to mold public opinion and action for their own benefit, there is also good evidence to show that the media are not ready and willing handmaidens of these vested interests. In addition, the assumption that an "objective" truth exists for every story is naive, and the notion of unconscious need is tenuous at best. This popular criticism of media power diverts attention away from an exacting analysis of mass communication by focusing attention on factors that cannot be empirically verified, such as unconscious needs, and on factors that may be of minor importance to media culture, such as the influence of vested interests. This is not to say that vested interests are unimportant in assessing media power, but we must be careful to avoid attributing too much significance to their influence, neglecting other sociological analyses and an analysis of the communication process itself.

In examining the mainstream of sociological analyses of mass media, we find evidence that routine organizational activity in the media industry has an impact on the kinds of information passed on to the public. For example, a newspaper occupies a position in a community that requires interaction with other organizations in order to keep the community operating on a day-to-day basis. A local newspaper interacts with local business, government, religion, education, and sports organizations to provide information that keeps each of these institutional sectors alive and well. In addition, within a media organization, professional communicators follow routine work patterns that also affect the kind of information that is passed among themselves and to the public. Through an analysis of these social networks media influence is seen as the consequence of formal and informal behavioral strategies, such as the status hierarchy within a particular newspaper. Certainly, media professional with high status, authority, and personal power will influence other workers in the media industry. The fact that these professionals interact with powerful people in business, government, religion, education, and sports will also have an impact on the content of media. But as we have seen in previous chapters, there is more to this problem—namely, that mass communication occurs through grammatical forms and perspectives that are largely independent of vested interests and constitute an additional dimension of organization dynamics. On this last point, it is not enough to study the social networks within a newspaper or television station and find the patterns of person influence. We must also consider that basic forms of communication strategy and craft perspectives orient the interaction in these social networks.

Both the popular critique and the social organization analysis are primarily concerned with how the agenda of a medium is selected, and both assume that content is something fairly concrete that is either accepted or rejected according to various interests and routines. The agenda-setting approach has merit in that media content will have certain consequences for the viewpoints obtained by an audience, and these viewpoints may be quite narrow or distorted. But the agenda-setting approach is limited as it focuses more on how content is selected rather than how that content is constructed, shaped, and presented. By focusing on ideological and sociological (e.g., organizational) factors that influence content selection, the agenda-setting approach does not consider that more fundamental factors in explaining media influence lie in the linguistics of mass communication and the perspectives (which until recently have been overlooked) used within each medium to interpret information. Understanding media influence from a linguistic and interpretive perspective approach relegates ideological factors (such as big business) and organizational factors (such as bureaucratic routine) to a secondary level in the overall explanation of mass media influence.

Recalling material from the chapter on television, this medium stresses a linear/visual syntax of events, a fairly rapid tempo in presenting information, and a very simple vocabulary and explanation. Beyond this, and interpretive framework of entertainment and ideal norms in television will influence the kinds of information (so-called facts) selected and how they are presented. The language of television news may further dictate that selection of information will be based on whether it shows conflict between sectors of society, whether it is naturally visual or subject to visual presentation, and whether it can be subjected to a television grammar that heightens the drama. The language of the specific station will operate within this general framework, electing to place greater or less emphasis on what caused an event, the tempo of the story, the drama, and the degree of complexity. In this manner, the stories selected by the reporter, the facts obtained, and the angle used are a consequence of the language and perspectives of television, television news, and the specific station.

Understanding that media tailors information according to linguistic criteria, sees issues and events through particular perspectives, and even creates events or culture out of these perspectives is gradually being recognized in some circles. Several news reporters, including Peter J. Boyer of the *Los Angeles Times,* suggested that TV news coverage of the El Salvador crisis early in 1982 overemphasized spectacular combat scenes—"bang bang" as it is known in the trade—and placed the El Salvador question within "another Vietnam" framework. Of the possibility that saturation television coverage might intensify the crisis in El Salvador, ABC News Chief Roone Arledge said, "There's always that danger." But admitting that danger with a readjustment in how a story is interpreted and presented is little more than arrogance. At least columnists such as Peter Boyer recognize that pressures within television to emphasize spectacular visuals and frameworks (such as seeing El Salvador as another Vietnam) are significantly influential in shaping public opinion as well as government policy.

Hollywood films such as *Network* (1976) and more recently *Absence of Malice* (1981) are also examples of an increased awareness of influence through media linguistics and perspectives. In *Absence of Malice* the author, a former newspaper journalist, sees the problem of media power but fails to understand what actually occurred. The film is a story of an overzealous newspaper reporter (played by Sally Field), who discovers what she thinks is a bonafide federal criminal investigation of organized crime. While there is an investigation under the direction of another overzealous but minor Justice Department official, there is no solid evidence for a grand jury indictment. In an effort to flush out evidence for an indictment, the Justice Department investigator leaks a suggestion that the nephew (played by Paul Newman) of a known crime boss is being investigated in the disappearance of a local union leader. The enterprising newspaper reporter proceeds to run a front-page story on the apparent investigation. Through the legitimacy accorded to the press it now appears that evidence actually exists, when in fact it does not. Given the news framework of looking for mysterious, dramatic, and conflict events, the newspaper easily falls into the trap of developing this into a major story. The story proceeds on the angle of when will we find out that Newman is guilty, not is he guilty or innocent? Readers of the story would become involved in the drama and mystery of waiting to find out when charges against Newman will be filed—his guilt is already assumed. Indeed, this is what happens in many media treatments of criminal trials—rarely does the drama focus on guilt or innocence; rather, it is on conviction or acquittal. Returning to the film, naturally a number of adverse things happen in the life of Paul Newman following Sally Field's story, but he devises a way to retaliate with success. Since the so-called fact of an investigation has become a fact in the minds of all concerned, including the newspaper and Justice Department officials, Newman feeds them information that under other circumstances would appear quite innocent. But given the orientation toward Newman as a guilty party, the information he provides makes him and others appear more guilty than ever. All he has done is to turn the strategy of the newspaper and the investigators to his own advantage, and they hang themselves.

Absence of Malice demonstrates that the appearance of truth may be as solid as silly putty, and by applying the model of media linguistics and perspectives, we know why this can happen. But it was not simply a matter of an overly zealous reporter doing slipshod work by failing to check out her sources, as some critics of *Absence of Malice* would have us believe. The value in this film is that it illustrates the fact that news media are quick to run stories that fit their perspectives, and they present these stories through a grammar that lends itself to particular kinds of interpretations.

An instant replay of the *Absence of Malice* plot occurred during the summer of 1982, when the press and network television news made a major story out of alleged cocaine use and kinky sexual activities by members of Congress. Despite the lack of hard evidence, the news media treated the story as a sensational big event. Similar to the *Absence of Malice* scenario, all the news media had were several second-hand accusations and word that an investigation was being developed. Actually, the investigation seemed to respond more to the media stories than the reverse. News media created the basis for an investigation by making the story a big event and then reported on official responses to their (media) stimulation. A better example of how news frameworks create news is hard to find, although the following story on David Stockman (President Reagan's director of the budget) is both instructive and humorous.

During the fall of 1981, David Stockman was reported in the November issue of the *Atlantic* to have said that his economic policy ("supply-side economics") was a trojan horse. This was taken to mean that supply-side economics might not be what it appeared to be. Given their strategy of looking for targets out of which drama and conflict can be generated, the media quickly seized on the angle that Stockman's credibility was in question, particularly with his boss, President Reagan. Never mind that supply-side economics might actually be a trojan horse and that Stockman was simply being quite candid. Instead, the media targeted Stockman as a credibility problem for his candor and then proceeded to act on that definition in a series of stories that posed the following questions: "Will Reagan ask Stockman to resign?" "Is Stockman going to resign?" "Why doesn't Stockman resign?" "He should resign!" Never once did we find out what President Reagan actually thought about Stockman's behavior.

This is a classic case of creating a definition that is consistent with the perspectives and strategy of media rather than reporting and analyzing the meaning of what was actually said. In fact, it was dangerously close to what George Orwell described in *1984* as "doublethink." By taking an ambiguous statement or a real event and jazzing it up with mystery and drama and suggesting causes or simple but unwarranted interpretation, the ambiguous statement may look quite clear and the real event may appear as a critical part of a puzzle—a puzzle created by the media out of media perspectives. While the entire process is little more than creative storytelling, few people either in media or among the public see the fact that media perspectives govern how events are interpreted to the public. In failing to see the problem, both communicators and the audience aid in stabilizing and standardizing media strategies into the appearance of normal routine and a paramount truth. In other words, the daily routine of mass communicators may be uncritically taken for granted as the only reasonable way to gather and present information to the public.

Switching to the audience side of interaction through mass media, the audience member acts in a manner quite similar to the process followed by professional communicators. The media professional acts within a network of social relations that serve to validate or support their own self-concerns. These professionals attempt to achieve the reputation of good journalist, successful script writer, or popular actor among their peers and with the audience. Likewise, audience members use their contact with these media professionals to support their own beliefs and other self-concerns.

Recall that one of the functions of radio is to give the listener proof that society is ongoing with all the vitality most anyone could desire. Reading the newspaper becomes a routine that maintains contact with the social world of politics, economics, sports, or the problems other people must face in their personal lives. For more specific identity concerns a person turns to media that provide contact with others in specialized subcultures, obtaining the information and emotional moods appropriate to those groups and their activities. In seeking to maintain personal identities through media, people in the audience may orient to a specific communicator, such as a film director, actor, newspaper columnist, or talk show host, or at the extreme they may become immersed in the total environment of the medium, losing touch with everyday reality. In any case, the purpose is to determine the extent to which audience members rely on media for identity maintenance and the extent to which the meanings that emerge in this process are controlled by media (see Appendix A).

To understand media influence from the audience perspective, visualize a continuum that describes their use of a media-created environment. At one end is the case of an individual who becomes completely immersed in the media environment, even to the point of transferring that environment to the everyday world or redefining everyday life through the experience obtained in media. Consider the murder trial of Ronny Zamora, a 15-year-old boy in Florida convicted in 1977 of shooting and killing an 83-year-old woman.

Zamora's attorney argued that Ronny was insane at the time he committed murder because of "involuntary subliminal television intoxication." This defense strategy is important for at least three reasons. First, it indicates the extent to which many people believe they are controlled by influences beyond their ability. This point should come as no surprise as most theories in behavioral science rest on the assumption that causes for behavior are determined either by uncontrollable internal forces, such as genetic heritage and subconscious impulses, or by external forces, such as society (social structure) and people who can manipulate others through conditioning techniques. Since the behavior of an individual is largely explained by causes that are beyond an individual's control, the logical implication is that an individual can easily avoid taking responsibility for his or her own behavior. Since the Korean War in the early 1950s, this propensity has increased due to the popular belief in the efficacy of "brainwashing," subliminal and overt advertising, and drugs. Consequently, Zamora's defense on the basis of insanity due to television makes sense as it is based on both scientific theory and popular belief.

Therefore, the second significant point of the Zamora case was a recognition of the power that television is believed to have in determining behavior, especially deviant behavior. The belief among some is that, like drugs, brainwashing, and subliminal cues, the content of television can stimulate people to commit immoral acts, or at the very least, to adopt lifestyles that are superficial and buy products that are useless or downright harmful. In this case, the argument suggests that external forces are not just influential in determining behavior; they can be subversive as well.

On the other hand, Zamora was convicted of his crime, which suggests that the jury refused to accept something as extreme as insanity by virtue of subliminal television intoxication. The point here is that a strong ideal of individualism runs through American culture, an ideal that seems antithetical to the behavioral theories that expose deterministic causes for behavior. Yet this apparent contradiction is not irrational, as the ideal of individualism allows society to weed out misfits and deviants by invoking the rationale that they should know better. This rationale was used successfully in the war crime trials at Nuremburg following World War II and in countless violent crime trials including the Zamora case. At the same time, a belief that social environment can mold the individual allows for the belief that elements of society can be controlled for society's well-being.

What is of significance for a discussion of media influence is the belief that under certain circumstances people can be held accountable for their own behavior despite the fact that strong external influences are present in society. This is akin to having one's cake and eating it too, as at times we can blame television or some other factor and at other times the individual for a failure to take individual responsibility. In effect, this enables people to protect their own identities (blaming others or impersonal sources of influence such as television) and also to seek retribution in a manner that seems more emotionally satisfying (holding someone rather than something accountable). As a result, a third significant point suggested by the Zamora case is that he was acting in a manner consistent with his conception of self and that a major source of his self-conception was located in television, particularly in the world of television crime. Using this approach enables us to see Ronny Zamora as acting voluntarily but from a rather unrealistic premise.

As described by his mother, Ronny Zamora often watched television into the early morning hours. His hero was Kojak, a tough television police detective played by the charismatic Telly Savalas. Zamora's attorney argued that Ronny probably thought he was Kojak when he shot the elderly woman. That television viewers may adopt identities of television characters is not unknown, although it is an extreme case when the individual transfers the vicarious television identity to activity in everyday life. The more typical example is a vicarious involvement with a media character while engaged in the media experience followed by a return to the mundane world after that experience is completed. But adopting a media-created identity and transferring it to the nonmedia world can happen and probably did in the case of Ronny Zamora, as well as with John Hinckley, Jr., who attempted to kill President Reagan. Nevertheless, this does not excuse these people from their criminal acts, for their decision to take on a fictional identity can be defined as a conscious and voluntary act.

The point is that people relate to media on the basis of personal identities and then use media as sources of information and situations to play out those identities. Media's influence is that it serves as a repository of information and situations for voluntary action by audience members. Therefore, media influence should be understood not as a cause beyond an individual's control but as something consciously used by people to varying degrees. The media world can become an environment for total immersion, a world tempered by critical evaluation, or an aspect of culture almost totally rejected by an individual. Using a theoretical approach that focuses on establishing and maintaining identity through an interactive process places the ultimate responsibility for behavior squarely on the individual. Yet as most people know, choices often appear limited and often are difficult.

Moving from the extreme of total immersion in a media-created culture to a situation in which a media-created environment is used for establishing and acting out real-life identities, consider the relationship developed between a radio listener and broadcaster. Radio personalities may achieve popularity among listeners simply by being associated with the subject matter of a particular subculture, such as rock music, sports on a sports talk show, or as a humorist in serving a particular urban lifestyle. As described in the chapter on radio, these personalities may become sources of information, a contact with a subculture, or even a role model to emulate in achieving an identity within a subculture.

A more extreme case of consciousness through radio occurs when the radio broadcaster forms a unique club around his or her personality so that listeners feel part of a select group. An example of this emerged in Phoenix, Arizona, in 1981 when a young disc jockey, Jonathon Brandmeier, took over the morning drive-time show on station KZZP. Through his crazy antics he established an identity for his listeners as *"loons"* and for these listeners, Phoenix became the "valley of the loons." During broadcasts, he inspired listeners to "loon-acy" with such activities as the traffic-jamming "mystery phonebooth," in which listeners were directed to a street corner with orders to arrive wearing underwear on their heads. At a specified time, Brandmeier called a nearby phonebooth to talk with one of the loons and give away one of his prized "loons" t-shirts. He called listeners in the early morning hours screaming at them to wake up, phoned public officials asking them to comment on issues in the valley of the loons, and during the marriage of Prince Charles and Lady Diana he called a McDonald's in London to get an eye-witness account. He composed and recorded satirical songs dealing with local issues, such as "Dead Donkeys" and "Horse with No Legs," and "Red Snow in Idaho" (a satire on the extermination of rabbits in that state). Success with those songs led to the formation of a rock group called Johnny and the Leisure Suits, which drew 10,000 screaming fans at a shopping mall concert. He created special features including the weekly "Take This Job and Shove It" open phone line, in which listeners could phone in and tell off their boss. When his irreverant style of humor offended conservative sectors of the community he seized on the conflict to enhance the uniqueness of his loons and increase the social solidarity of the group. In effect, Brandmeier personalized contact with listeners by creating an identity for them, instructing them how to act out the identity, providing symbols for identification of group membership with bumper stickers, coffee cups, and t-shirts, and finally by validating the loon identity through his daily antics on the air. This strategy was so successful that within a year he became the top-rated radio program in Phoenix and was almost a daily conversation topic among thousands of people age 12 to 40.

The key to understanding Brandmeier's success is not his communication skills, his crazy antics, which relieved boredom, or his energy. Brandmeier took the desire among listeners for achieving a sense of uniqueness and belonging and the audience's comfort with a media-created environment and worked them into a successful formula. In this example, the identity of loon was created through media and existed mainly in a media context. Listeners were loons primarily when they were in contact with Brandmeier's radio program or his personal appearance. In addition, it must be understood that listeners were not vicariously taking on Brandmeier's identity, as Zamora apparently did with Kojak; rather, they were members of his group. Yet both Ronny Zamora's immersion in media culture and becoming a Brandmeier loon are fairly extreme examples of the potential for involving one's self in a media-created environment.

Media make strong enticements and present powerful images to people seeking to develop and maintain a sense of place and meaning in today's world. It may become an easy matter for some people to substitute media experience for everyday life or to become involved in media-created social worlds. In addition, given the ready availability of mass media, it should be expected that people will not only use these media for their own conscious interests, but will come to define their own experience through media-created images. Such is the case with the individual who accepts media images as the standard for evaluation and comparison.

To illustrate the acceptance of media-created images as a norm of acceptability, a sadly humorous example was reported in a human interest column of the *Arizona Republic*. A 45-year-old recently divorced, childless male made it known that he was "hung up on wanting a woman who conforms to the perfection of a *Playboy* centerfold."

> It was a real shock to me to learn after my divorce that most women had stretch marks. I think magazines like *Playboy* and movies or television series that feature scantily dressed perfect women like Loni Anderson do women a disservice. They give them a model they can't possibly live up to. And they give men an idea that women are supposed to look like that. Then they feel let down by women who don't measure up [Hutton, 1981: H-1].

Similar examples can be found in almost any social setting portrayed in media from sports to politics, as most media tend to present ideal images and foster the impression that these ideals are attainable. From physical appearance to communication skills, audiences are continuously presented with crème-de-la-crème images to the point that a media-created ideal seems to be commonplace. That the media-world, ideal image represents the rare extreme is a fact obscured by the constant and easy availability of these images. What once were fantastic images existing mainly in the movies are now images that appear routinely. This indicates the potential for media to create and standardize criteria by which identity achievement and self-esteem are measured in everyday life. Whether reference is to the fantastic image of the *Playboy* centerfold or to learning what occurs through more mundane media presentations, the result is that standards are established by mass media.

Since an understanding of media influence must not be limited to such extreme cases as magazine centerfolds, we should also examine the subtle images and information constantly available through mass media, such as knowledge of how to dress, what constitutes appropriate verbal and nonverbal communication skills, the form and content of lifestyles, and how to handle various problems that occur in everyday social relations. People use media as a source of information on descriptions of social issues and problematic interpersonal situations that have immediate relevance for their own lives. Although a great deal of this information is obtained within the context of entertainment, there is nothing to prevent learning serious lessons while being entertained. Knowledge of age groups, social class styles, occupations, sex roles, sexuality, subcultures, and a great many common personal problems are dealt with daily in mass media. Rich detail, both subtle and direct, is provided on how to understand and act in each of these sociological categories.

For example, children learn how they are supposed to act, dress, and even think in middle-class society and what to expect from parents and other authority figures by watching such programs as *Leave It to Beaver, The Partridge Family,* and *Diff'rnt Strokes.* On a slightly more exotic level, kids growing up during the 1940s learned by watching Westerns how cowboys should ride a horse, shoot a gun, rope a rustler, treat an adult woman (Yes, Ma'am, No, Ma'am), and, best of all, how to fight. Although most of the information was useless and some of it false, we learned it because of our fantasy desires. *Laverne and Shirley*'s popularity during the 1970s was in part due to their appeal to working women. Although *Laverne and Shirley* is a slapstick exaggeration, it strikes home on points related to sharing an apartment, paying the bills, and dealing with men, parents, the boss, and kooky neighbors.

Teenagers acquire a great deal of information—both good and bad—on sex roles, sexuality, sophistication, and the like from all those "fan" magazines and teenager-oriented films. People in all age groups and across the social class spectra obtain information on dress styles and communication skills from watching soap operas and talk shows. In fact, communication skills may be the most potent of all media influences, particularly for children, as evidenced by such examples as *Sesame Street,* cartoons, and television sitcoms. Recent tests of communication skills report that children at all grade levels have fairly well developed vocabularies but rather poorly developed written skills, indicating the increasing dominance of visual and oral media over print media.

The fact that media provide an enormous amount of information on all aspects of modern life should be no surprise. However, this point is often challenged by those who focus only on the negatively defined content of the major mass media. What these critics overlook is that communication or interaction may occur within several forms simultaneously. In analyzing television cartoons, adult critics become worried that children will fail to see the difference between reality and fantasy. While some children may make this error, most do not simply because they understand that the actions of cartoon characters occur within the form of the "cartoon." However, the cartoon form operates within a more encompassing form of everyday language skills and cultural values and norms. A cartoon creater cannot expect an audience member to understand a cartoon unless there is considerable similiarity between the language and perspectives of the cartoon and the life of the child viewer. Therefore, cultural values, norms, and communication skills relevant for everyday life are established in the cartoon while at the same time using a form that tells the child that this is all occurring within a fantasy or play context. As such, liberties can be taken, particularly with physical action and the physical environment. Since children are oriented to play more than are adults, they are cognizant of both the form of fantasy and the form of everyday life within a cartoon.

Lessons relevant to everyday life may or may not be learned from a cartoon, but they constitute a potential nevertheless. The point is simply that to make a communication intelligible to another, the communication must present images or information that is understandable to the other. This strategy requires working within the other's social world as he or she understands it. Consequently, it should be no surprise that a great deal of information on all aspects of modern life is provided by mass media.

As discussed in the chapter on television, a teenager who aspires to become or emulate a sports star learns from watching televised sporting events how a sports star dresses, walks, talks, and even thinks both on and off the playing field. In emulating a role model, the audience member is actually learning how successfully to sell him- or herself in situations similar to those witnessed on television. In turn, a child watching a cartoon learns how to relate to parents, peers, and villains. Watching *Laverne and Shirley,* we learn that unattractive people and jokesters have feelings too. Every aspect of maintaining social relationships is presented in the course of fantastic television drama or comedy, radio music, Gothic romance novels, horror films, and others.

While a considerable amount of this information is an authentic representation of everyday life or is useful for managing situations in everyday life, critical evaluation by audience members is required to differentiate between what is accurate in the media environment compared to what is contrived according to media linguistics and perspectives. For example, kids seem to understand that cartoons are partially a fake world, but do adults understand that newsreel film often leads to an exaggerated perception of events? On the other hand, adults may realize that the *Brady Bunch* is an overidealized description of the American family, but do children understand that many parents are not that competent nor do they get along that well?

Audience members seem to be critical of mass media in both form and content when they have first-hand information from the real world. But when first-hand information is unavailable or limited, which in some cases is due to an overexposure to media itself, there is a compelling tendency to rely on media for meaningful information. Alvin Toffler, in *The Third Wave,* argues that media have given us so much information that we feel the need constantly to increase our appetite. Given the attractiveness of mass media, it is reasonable to assume that we will continue to turn to media rather than other sources for this information, although Toffler feels the tendency to rely on mass media is decreasing. In Toffler's defense, we know commonsensically that many people are critical of media, make critical comparisons between media portrayals and everyday life experience, and use media selectively for self-interests. These people occupy the other extreme of a continuum describing individual involvement in the media environment. But even people who are critical users of media may miss the enormous influence of media perspectives and languages on the institutional character of Western society, an aspect of media influence that deserves everyone's attention.

REMEDIAL EFFORTS

There is no doubt that life in contemporary urban America is lived to a great extent in a media environment. This means that not only do we rely on media for a considerable amount of the essential and nonessential information used in all institutional sectors of society; meanings that become an established part of our urban culture are created within the environment of mass media as well. Quite simply, we have created a media culture and that culture has been created through a willing participation of people on both sides of the communication process—professional communicator and audience member.

This participation is motivated by individual interests that have immediate relevance for all involved parties. Therefore, an implicit argument is that the personal identities of communicators and audience members serve to orient their communication strategies and media use. People select information in the course of their communication activity that has relevance for who they are or want to be at that moment. Television producers are concerned with ratings in order to elevate their prestige and increase their earning power. Actors are concerned with recognition and acclaim from the audience and fellow actors. A newspaper columnist feels a bond with readers and desires the respect of fellow journalists. A radio listener may desire the companionship provided by a station offering information on a subculture lifestyle. A film buff may seek out vicarious involvement in an adventure film, and a person returning home from work turns on the TV to relax. Regardless of whether media are used for a very general or specific purpose, they are selectively used with something in mind, even if that something would be defined as useless or banal by someone else. Media culture is something that, for better or worse, we all create in a ongoing, dynamic process.

But to understand how media culture is created and how media influence occurs involves not just knowing something about why people intentionally use media as they do. In fact, knowing the intent of a communicator or audience member may be of minor importance in understanding the meanings that eventually become established in the course of interacting through media. Regardless of a speaker's intention, a recipient can always nullify that intention by making a definition or response that does not coincide with the speaker's intent. For example, a freelance magazine writer may design a story to stimulate public action on an environmental issue only to find that most readers simply enjoyed the article as entertainment. A television viewer may watch a sitcom for relaxation only to become embroiled in the emotion of declining parental authority as it is depcited in the story. Why and how this occurs involves a complex meshing of many factors that have yet to be assembled in a paradigm acceptable to a majority of social scientists. While no all-inclusive paradigm is being offered here, the effort in the previous chapters has been to identify a set of factors (grammar and perspectives) and an orientation that should be incorporated within any comprehensive theory of the mass communication process.

Recalling that believability of TV news is a consequence of the grammar of news, news perspectives, and an acceptable physical image of an anchorperson demonstrates how the form of a communication affects the believability of the content. Would viewers accept as newsworthy a story read by a bald, overweight, cigar-smoking, aging male, wearing a loud checkered jacket and a bow tie? Would people stay tuned to a news program devoid of visual graphics, on-site film footage, and lengthy stories? Only that small PBS audience who watch the *MacNeil/Lehrer Report* would even consider such a format as news.

Yet audience members and even most professional communicators rarely bother to consider critically how forms of mass communication are strategies that affect how events come to be acceptable and believable. While some people recognize that entertainment has become a form that has made education more enjoyable, do these same people realize that many serious community issues are now also being presented by the press and television through the form of entertainment? For example, do antinuclear demonstrators realize the extent to which they put on a "show" for TV cameras in order to make their presence felt? Do sports fans realize that the ballpark has become a media entertainment arena with the trappings of a circus? These and many other examples discussed in previous pages are testimony to the impact of media forms and the taken-for-grantedness of these forms by the participants. To understand how the process of interaction through media works and to participate intelligently in that interaction requires recognition and evaluation of the linguistic properties and perspectives used by all participants.

If we are to achieve media enlightenment and possibly change media culture, the audience must *not* rely on the media industry to act responsibly for the welfare of the audience, nor should media professionals use the cop out that it only gives the people what they want. Each party must recognize its complicity and accept responsibility for what occurs. But before responsibility can be assumed, people must first recognize what is occurring, e.g., that news is being presented through perspectives of entertainment, drama, conflict, and so on. If people decide after recognizing and critically evaluating the entertainment character of news that entertainmentized news is what they want, so be it.

Specifically, what remedial steps can communicators and the audience take? Initially, it may help to ask why people communicate in a particular manner and why people accept and even trust in particular communication strategies. In examining mass media we do this to the extent of recognizing economic and personal prestige motivations, but these motives rarely stimulate an interest to delve further into the matter; what remains is a rather superficial understanding of motivation. Then, again, knowing why people select particular strategies may have little to do with the meanings that ultimately are established. But asking the question "Why?" may be a good starting point if it results in a further explication of how things are done. That is, the fundamental remedial question is, how does communication strategy work? Once a strategy has been accurately described it may be irrelevant to know why it developed; knowing how something works enables people to avoid its potential influence and possibly bring about a change in the strategy. In short, knowing how something works debunks its mystery.

For example, in 1982 Hodding Carter III (aide to former President Carter) designed a television series (Inside Story) aimed at critically analyzing network news. In a program devoted to how network news presents news on the economy, it was concluded that all three networks followed the same strategy. First, they simplified economic news with continual reference to a few statistics, such as Dow Jones averages, inflation, unemployment, prime interest rates, and the prices of gold and the dollar on foreign exchange markets. Somehow all these figures added up to the current state of the economy. Second, news stories were developed around families, say in Peoria, who were having a rough go of it. This brought the story down to a common level that most viewers apparently understood, particularly on an emotional level. Third, economic news usually was framed in terms of White House policy, fostering the impression that the U.S. economy is managed by the president. The fact that the U.S. economy almost defies analysis was rarely mentioned. Also lacking were references to the importance of banking policy, insurance company investments, foreign investment, heavy industry (except the auto industry) production, and other indicators routinely presented in the *Wall Street Journal*. Instead, the television viewer was led to believe that the current president could do something about the economy and do it quick if he had the right answers. Finally, network news made the economy a continual drama, much like a soap opera or sports event.

The question always seemed to be: What's the latest in the inflation rate and what is the president doing about it?

Understanding that TV news on the economy is oversimplified and even distorted may not make a viewer feel any better about the state of the economy, but at least these viewers would have the basis for taking this "news" with a grain of salt. In addition, this knowledge provides a foundation for debunking the political campaign rhetoric of potential office holders who claim they can easily correct economic problems. Understanding TV strategy on economic news may also lead viewers to question how other news is presented. Knowing why the networks use these strategies may be only an academic exercise for learning how the strategy works, but it should result in a significant degree of freedom. Gaining freedom through knowledge also destroys the bliss of ignorance.

To say that ignorance is bliss does not mean that ignorance is always a lack of information; it also means that something significant is being ignored. Here the argument is that both mass communicators and audience members ignore the habitual or taken-for-granted linguistics and perspectives they use in the course of interaction through mass media. Sociologists such as Harold Garfinkel argue that everyone follows norms or strategies in everyday behavior that are taken for granted or considered unnecessary to explain explicitly. For example, the polite greeting "How are you" is usually not meant as a question inquiring about the state of a person's health; it is simply a polite recognition of the individual's presence. As a form of interaction, "small talk" is not directed at substantive issues; rather it is what Georg Simmel referred to as a form for achieving "sociability."

For mass communication, it seems reasonable to assume that communicators and audience members have an implicit understanding of many of the forms discussed in previous chapters, such as entertainmentized news, event-centered press journalism, and subculture radio. As stated repeatedly, news is not considered news unless it appears through familiar forms. This is akin to saying there is a body of knowledge that almost everyone seems to know about but does not or cannot talk about. Over time, a body of knowledge may become relegated to such a habitual occurrence that it is difficult to articulate; it is seldom or perhaps never the object of critical reflection. As an example, a movie director thinks in terms of visual grammar but may not articulate that knowledge when describing how a film is made. A radio listener may expect a disc jockey to be ebullient on an early morning program without reflecting on why this expectation exists. However, when news of the Falkland Islands showdown (prior to the first loss of life) was presented as a dramatic adventure or sporting contest, people were ignorant of the extent to which they were placing a potentially serious event within a play context. In other words, ignoring a form of communication, coupled with a tacit understanding of that form, may have future substantive implications if the significance of that form continues to be ignored.

To rememdy the practice of ignoring habitual strategies is not an easy matter as the emotional base for such strategies is often quite strong. Nevertheless, if we are to become free and at the same time develop critical reasoning, we must be self-reflective. Playing the "devil's advocate" is a well-known device for seeing alternative perspectives, as long as the substance of devil's advocacy is taken seriously. Perusing alternative literature, such as a liberal who reads the *National Review,* may also lend itself to self-reflection. In fact, anything that disrupts habitual routines may result in a reexamination of that routine and, it is hoped, of its underlying perspectives. Put another way, we should occasionally debunk ourselves to expose our hidden perspectives and determine the extent to which those perspectives coincide with media-generated perspectives.

If this seems difficult or even obscure, begin by examining the interaction among different media to see how their perspectives are similar to each other. By comparison, we as audience members may see how our perspectives are similar to those used in media. For example, it was suggested that a television grammar of low ambiguity through visual clarity and oversimplification has been adopted by newspapers and even college textbooks. Now college students seem to expect texts that require little effort in understanding "facts," and they complain about the ambiguity or subtlety that often marks complex issues, critical thought, synthesis, and comparative analysis of theoretical viewpoints. It is not that the TV generation cannot read; they simply prefer reading material that offers quick and simple results like those obtained through most commercial television. Commenting on this problem, John Vandeling of Saunders College Publishers of Philadelphia stated, "The student's ability for straight concentration has changed, so we need picture-crammed books to hold their attention." Prentice-Hall editor Ed Stanford even claims that "today's students won't use the dictionary. They'll skip the word or sometimes the entire paragraph." Sociologist Ralph Turner, at

UCLA since 1948, adds, "Students today are a lot less tolerant of difficult books than they were when I started teaching." However, he added, "This change in student attitude is good because faculty members no longer can get away with assigning difficult texts that only a handful of the best students can understand" (Trombley, 1982). Turner's point is well taken. It is not that students today are less smart; it is that they are less tolerant of what they consider an outmoded print format.

In comparing sports and television perspectives we find that new games, such as the indoor soccer (MISL) league, were created with TV in mind. As a MISL official said in a *Newsweek* interview:

> What you've got to realize is that the game was literally built for TV. You've got a bright red ball traveling on a nice green background and goals designed for better camera angles. Heck, we went so far as to structure the game to allow for the maximum number of commercials [Leerhsen, 1982: 65].

Sports fans now expect continuous action and visual drama all within an easily understood game. This entertainmentized TV format is graphically demonstrated by such pregame hoopla as the Baltimore Blast indoor soccer team's entrance to the arena via a mock smoking spaceship and Phoenix Inferno players erupting out of a volcano. When people say that baseball is boring, they may be applying a perspective and expectation that coincide with the new TV generation of sports. Remember, baseball was developed and popularized before electronic media were invented. Perhaps it has survived relatively unchanged (unlike football or basketball) because of its contrast to modern TV-hyped sports. Then again, the baseball park of today offers stereo music, clowns, spiffy uniforms, contests, pregame entertainment, fireworks, talking computerized scoreboards, and cute usherettes who sometimes double as waitresses. With an entertainment perspective amalgamated from the amusement park, television, and a bit of Hollywood, the new ballpark attracts patrons who would not ordinarily find a baseball game engaging. In this respect, the audience plays a willing, if not totally aware, part of the synthesis and adoption of perspectives among popular media.

Once audience members become aware of their complicity in the process of media influence and are willing to disrupt their own media routines, they have a readiness to explore the considerable variety of choice among media alternatives. Narrowcasting, as a concept denoting specialized audience interest service, is already well-established in print media, FM radio, cable TV, and a segment of the film industry. If Alvin Toffler and other futurists are correct, we can expect mass media to become even more specialized as the century draws to a close. However, a word of caution is in order. Without critical attention and action on the part of audiences, the similarity of media perspectives may invade the entire media spectrum to the point that real choice among media alternatives may only be an illusion. On this point, film director George Lucas decried the imitation of film scripts by studios making TV movies. "They can get their TV versions out before the feature film is ready for the theaters. You get a cheap, milquetoast, badly done version of your film, and audiences go, 'Oh, hell. I'm not going to pay five bucks to see the same thing.'" However, Lucas also notes that regional filmmakers are supplying fresh new ideas and films that "don't have that ingrown, cocktail-party attitude that you get from Los Angeles" (Thompson and Tuchman, 1981: 76). To prevent standardization, audiences must be diligent in critical examination of media perspectives and active in demanding compliance from the media industry. Real choice among form and content of media service is presently available and will continue, but only if it is demanded by the audience.

As a remedial measure, choice among media alternatives enables audience members to make critical comparisons. Obviously a person who augments his or her television news diet with daily press coverage and popular news and magazine articles is able to obtain some variety. But the seriously critical individual will also consult more specialized media, such as public television and radio news programs, commentary periodicals *(The Nation* and *National Review),* and analytical periodicals *(Columbia Journalism Review* and *Wilson Quarterly).* While each of these media sources may have a particular point of view, the critical observer at least forces him- or herself to make decisions.

The same point also applies to the media professional. The journalist who relies on only a few select sources for interpretation of events, such as reliance on official sources, is severely limited in understanding the total context of a news story as well as the frameworks available for interpreting the event. For example, seeing street crime from the standpoint of the local police department perspective may result in seeing crime strictly from a defensive law-and-order perspective rather than from more sociological perspectives of inter-group conflict, class conflict, racial conflict, political strategy, and the like. To this end, media professionals must also consult a variety of media sources, including scientific literature, if they are to become aware of the perspectives that dominate their routines. Filmmaker Francis Coppola underscores this idea in telling George Lucas, "Look, if you're ever going to be a director, you're first going to have to be a writer." (Thompson and Tuchman, 1982: 76).

In fairness to media professionals, critical self-examination does exist within the media community, and some of this information is readily available to the public. *TV Guide* is a surprisingly good source of self-criticism in the television community. Almost every issue carries an article that examines how commercial television deals with subjects from prime-time entertainment to the news. For example, the May 1, 1982, issue of *TV Guide* printed an article on how TV personalities are selected by publishers to write books that are then hyped on TV programs by these same personalities. What if the TV personality cannot write? "So what," says Mark Greenberg of Warner Books. "We get somebody to write it with [him or her]" (Townley, 1982: 44). Occasionally, television programs themselves are devoted to media self-criticism, although most of these appear through the PBS system. Media will also criticize each other; editorials and commentary in the press criticize television and vice versa. As print reporter Bob Greene said in a *TV Guide* article (1982: 11), "I have spent most of my professional life looking slightly askance at TV reporters."

But all too often these critiques deal with the content rather than the form of mass communication. With few exceptions, media self-criticism has not as yet recognized the importance of the form of communication as a factor in shaping content. For example, broadcast journalists readily admit that as a headline service, network news passes too little information to the viewer. What they need to realize is that the form of these headlines limits not just the amount of information but the kind of information as well.

A few comments should also be directed to the groups in society who think that media-use problems lie only with those people who lack education, are economically dependent, or are not part of the middle-class mainstream. Based on information of television viewing habits as compiled and reported by the A.C. Nielsen Service in 1981, the average amount of time a TV was on each day in a television household (98 percent of all households) is increasing; for the 1980-

1981 season the average was 6 hours and 44 minutes, up 9 minutes over the previous year. Perhaps a surprise is the fact that income was not an important factor in accounting for this figure. Also, as the number of adults in a household increased, so did the amount of viewing time. This indicates that social class and the number of children present may not be major factors in TV use. In addition, the family viewing periods of Sunday, Monday, and Friday evening are the most popular, along with sitcoms, feature films, and general drama. Teenagers spend the least amount of time watching TV, and women over 55 the most. The most popular program for men over 18 was *60 Minutes* and for women it was *Dallas*. While blacks generally watch more TV than nonblacks, they prefer programs featuring black actors, particularly sitcoms.

While this survey provides no information on so-called media effects, it does indicate that TV viewing habits vary more by age and sex than by income or education. Therefore, media critics should beware of directing remedial efforts on TV use and other media only to those groups that have been defined as economically dependent, uneducated, or outside mainstream middle Americana.

AN OPTIMISTIC NOTE

Analytical treatments of mass communication tend to be quite critical of the media industry; indeed, these organizations make easy and almost willing targets. While much of the discussion in previous chapters may have implied a villain role for media, this implication is not intended. As stated previously, audiences must bear responsibility for meanings that emerge through their interaction with media. Although media grammar and perspectives are presented to the audience, the audience is responsible for recognizing these strategies and their implications. Also, the grammar and perspectives employed by the media industry are largely taken-for-granted procedures rather than deliberate manipulative techniques designed to hoodwink and mold public opinion and action. That big business and government may be compatible partners with the media industry does not change the fact that business and government are affected as much by the perspectives and grammar of media as are other sectors of society.

It also must be noted that some media have a stabilizing influence in society as witnessed through the ideal norms perspective used in prime-time television. These ideals uphold values that are a fundamental part of our moral order, an essential part of the process in preventing the appearance of chaos often accompanying rapid social change. On the other hand, some media foster innovation in both ideas and technology. The integration of television and computer technology is stimulating new approaches in education, and specialized print media have found a home with the burgeoning specialized interests of individuals enjoying increased leisure time. Together, the stabilizing influence and innovative stimulus of media have enabled this industry to become a major legitimation agent for our ever-changing paramount reality.

A case for optimism with media may also be found in the media's role in socialization, fostering a sense of community, providing a feeling of belonging, and transmitting a plethora of practical information for everyday living. On socialization, the lessons from *Mr. Rogers, Sesame Street,* and other children's educational programs need no futurer elaboration here. But the fact that *Three's Company* and *Laverne and Shirley* were favorites among teenagers in 1981 indicates that they may be using these programs as lessons for the next stage in their progress toward adulthood. Certainly these programs offer a low-brow humor that has teenage appeal, but they also show how young adults work out interpersonal problems of living together as equals. Soaps function in much the same way for adults of all ages. The idealism of young parents today may have been assisted by the perhaps all-too-idealistic descriptions of family life portrayed in *Father Knows Best* and *Leave It to Beaver* a few years ago. Today, kids are getting a bit more realistic picture through the likes of *Fame* and *St. Elsewhere,* and perhaps may be better prepared to deal with the complex problems of modern adulthood and parenthood.

On community integration, the local newspaper is often overlooked as a source of information and activity in every major community institution from religion to business. Even a cursory reading of a daily newspaper provides a sense of the viability of community life. The same holds true for subculture life through radio and specialized magazines. Radio listeners, TV soap opera viewers, religion audiences, and older people who use media for companionship are gaining a sense of social participation that might otherwise be difficult to obtain. Richard Simmons is not a popular TV personality just because of the zany entertaining antics he performs on his exercise show; he also projects a sincere, caring attitude to his audience. This sentiment is echoed over and over again by radio talk show listeners.

Finally, the importance of media for working out emotional problems in a vicarious manner has been a well-known function for some time, although reaction has been mixed as to whether this is a positive or negative function. As a case in point, a magazine advertisement on Harlequin Presents romance novels reads:

> You don't just read it. You live it. . . . Let your imagination roam to the far ends of the earth. You'll meet true-to-life people and become intimate with those who live larger-than-life. Harlequin Presents romance novels are the kind of books you just can't put down . . . the kind of experiences that remain in your dreams long after you've read about them.

Whether the safety afforded by vicarious or fantasy emotional experience is beneficial or counterproductive may be impossible to ascertain. What can be said is that since people seek emotional experience from media, they are at least attempting to do something positive as they define it. And this holds true for any reason or motive that individuals offer to justify their use of media. From reasons such as relaxation or fun, to obtaining practical information for solving serious problems, media are used because they are potentially valuable, even essential. As discussed in the chapter on radio, listeners seek mood enhancement and change through radio. People watch soaps and movies to gain a temporary feeling of romance, excitement, or relief from boredom. That twenty million people watch soap operas daily, even to the point of scheduling other activities around their favorite show, indicates that something emotionally significant is going on in this passive physical activity.

Since mass media serve a number of positive functions in society, optimism as a frame of reference for media use should not be overlooked in scientific analysis. All too often scientific research of the media begins with the assumption that something harmful to the audience will occur. If audience members do not feel they are being harmed, then perhaps scientists need to consider this as a significant factor in the meanings that eventually develop through interaction with media. We can suggest that audiences debunk themselves in their use of media, but in the process we must be careful not to destroy any primary optimism that may orient their desire to use media. After all, as social scientists, we must have a humane concern for developing both a harmonious and enjoyable social environment.

APPENDIX A
Social Psychological Dimensions
of Communications

The implicit communication model in this book follows from the theoretical principles of symbolic interaction, an approach that is steadily graining favor among students of human behavior. Symbolic interaction dates back to the work of philosopher G.H. Mead at the University of Chicago during the 1920s, and refinements of this approach are constantly appearing in academic literature. Symbolic interaction is not complicated, and it makes few assumptions about human behavior. But before describing the application of this approach to communication, it may be instructive to identify what symbolic interaction does *not* assume about the nature of human beings and their conduct.

In contrast to B.F. Skinner and other behaviorists, symbolic interaction does not assume that people are motivated in a mechanical manner by rewards or conditioned response. In contrast to Freud and proponents of psychoanalysis, symbolic interaction does not assume the existence or causal impetus of an unconscious level in the mind. Nor do symbolic interactionists assume that individuals are driven by instincts, such as aggression or a territorial imperative. Ideas from sociobiologists on the genetic mapping of behavior are set aside by symbolic interactionists until conclusive evidence is obtained. In fact, anything that essentially explains behavior as necessarily determined or involuntary is rejected or held in abeyance. This also includes the rejection of a social structural determinism in which aspects of a social system or powerful groups are believed to mold behavior and opinion. In contrast to these deterministic models, symbolic interaction views the individual as a creature of voluntary action, who in the process of action creates meaning in concert with others and through a symbolic system we call language. It holds that meaning about everything is created by people through verbal and nonverbal communication, and communication is what is studied.

It is through communication or a symbolic representation of phenomena that reality of any kind is developed. Conceptions of the physical universe, philosophical systems, and everyday life are fundamentally words and sentences. The task of the symbolic interactionist is to examine the dynamic process through which people symbolically construct the meanings that inform their lives. The language of mass media and how those languages are used to create individual meanings and culture in a broader sense have been the central concerns of this book.

What remains to be accomplished in this appendix is a brief overview of why people follow particular strategies, develop particular meanings, and defend them. At a naive level the question seems to be, what motivates people to act? While this question is unanswerable in a causal sense (we cannot determine the "real" reason behind an act), we do know that people give reasons for their behavior. And when people offer reasons for their own behavior and the behavior of others it always seems to come back to personal identity. People act to establish, maintain, and defend their sense of self, as fundamentally "self" is the most important meaning or set of meanings a person has. For example, when a student is questioned by a professor in a classroom setting, the student will attempt to respond in a manner that takes into account the identity or identities that seem most at stake at the moment. If the student respects the professor and defines him- or herself as a serious student, she or he will respond with an attempt to elicit a positive response from that professor. If the student is also concerned about impending reactions from fellow classmates, he or she will, in all probability, also attempt to elicit favorable responses from those peers. Therefore, people act to elicit future responses from others that will validate identities or identify relations considered important at the moment.

If we can assume that identify and corresponding self-esteem are the most important meanings to an individual, then *identity establishment and maintenance is the nexus of all social relations whether they occur through overt interpersonal relations or a mass medium.* To articulate this process, begin with the definition that identity is a statement about one's self in both rationalistic and affective terms. A person is an adult, a female, a sister, an accountant, a tennis player, unmarried, a Republican, and a soap opera fan. This person is also compassionate, usually happy, patient, enjoys being alone, and is attracted to blond men. Each of these descriptive terms is an identity statement that as a composite is represented by the person's name. Relating these to the individual's behavior, each of these descriptive statements becomes an action framework; the individual acts as an adult, a female, an accountant, and so on.

However, to establish and maintain these identity definitions requires contact with and response from other people; the statement "no person is an island" represents a common-sense understanding that we need other people to survive both physically and socially. This means that a major part of the process of acting as an adult, a female, and so on requires negotiating with others for responses that will support or coincide with the intentions of the actor. Yet as most people know quite well, negotiating for desired responses from others is not an easy matter as it requires both role taking and role making. In role taking an actor places him- or herself in the role or position of the other in order to anticipate how that other might respond. In role making, the actor engages in behavior to elicit or call out specific, desired responses from that other. Obviously, negotiating out of identity concerns requires considerable time and effort.

Relating the identity establishment process to research on mass communication, it may be argued that people use mass media as both an information source for their identity maintenance strategies and as a source of validation for existing identities. With the former of these two functions, a person may seek news from the press, television, and radio because that person defines knowledge of current events as important for the identity of being an adult involved in community affairs. With the latter, a person may carry out a vicarious affair with a media personality, such as Gunner Stenbeck on the soap opera *As the World Turns.* Gunner may be imagined as a source of validation (significant other) for a female viewer's attraction to blonde men.

In the use of media for both practical information and the establishment of relationships with media personalities, the audience member is selectively attentive to particular kinds of media and media content for the purpose of validating personal identities. Now the question may be asked, to what extent do personal identities and the perspectives that inform these identities originate from media itself? For some people, media may define what it means to be an adult, a female, an accountant, and so on. In addition, media may supply the identity achievement strategies and the sources for validation that are used by the audience member. When this occurs media have reached the zenith of influence, and we may speak of people as having developed a "media consciousness" within a media culture.

On the communicator's side of the mass communication interaction, people involved in creating the content of media also establish and maintain identities with each other and with the audience. Essentially, they behave no differently than an audience member, as they seek favorable responses from their professional peers and the audience in such forms as awards, rating points, product sales, circulation figures, and words of praise, encouragement, and satisfaction.

For example, a television news reporter's identity includes being a professional broadcast journalist, a reporter for a specific station, someone within the status hierarchy of that station, and perhaps a reporter who gathers particular types of news stories, such as crime, human interest, or political news. Each of these identities is established through specific interpersonal relations with co-workers, such as other reporters, editors, photographers, and other personnel at particular television station, rival stations, and professionals elsewhere acquainted with the reporter's work.

In reference to an audience, the reporter receives letters, calls, and casual comments on the street. The reporter's assessment of those responses will depend on the criteria being used to evalate his or her performance and the judged importance of the other who makes those responses. For our purposes we also need to ask to what degree are the reporter's identity-establishment strategies and criteria derived from the perspectives and grammar of television in general, television news in the particular, and the specific characteristics of the station's format? The extent of which this occurs indicates the extent to which the reporter, like an audience member, is caught up in a media consciousness and development of media culture.

In communicating with an audience, the media professional must be continually sensitive to audience response. It is this point in the analysis of mass communication that has received considerable research attention, i.e., audience feedback. The typical explanation of the interaction between mass communicator and audience member is that feedback from the audience is absent, delayed, or indirect. While this is true, communicators must find ways to deal with this problem so that they feel viable and significant to the audience at any particular moment. While market research and past experience provide some information of value on anticipating audience desires and responses, each communicator must also create images of what the target audience member will accept at a particular moment. These images are usually based on a common-sense knowledge of what the audience member will be receptive to at a particular time, day of the week, season of the year, and so forth.

While some communicators are better than others at role taking with an imagined audience, the point is that all communicators practice this strategy just as everyone engages in role taking of others in everyday life. Therefore, even though audience response or feedback is delayed in mass communication, the communication process is much the same as it is in face-to-face relations. Both mass communication and interpersonal communication are interactions using basically the same social psychological procedures. This does not negate the fact that communicators attempt to manipulate an audience. In fact, it is argued from symbolic interaction theory (as Erving Goffman does) that a primary characteristic of the negotiation process in interpersonal interaction is the attempt to manipulate others into making responses desired by the actor. After all, to say an individual attempts to elicit response that will validate an identity is just another way of saying that people attempt to manipulate each other into making desired responses. Consequently, the process of mass communication is no more manipulative by design than is interpersonal interaction.

In summarizing the previous points, mass communication and face-to-face interaction follow similar social psychological procedures in that communication in both situations involves the attempt to establish and maintain identities; identity formation strategies involve perspectives that result in selective attention to identity relevant information; and role-taking and role-making negotiation results in attempts by each party to manipulate the other. In the case of mass communication, the critical question is whose strategies—communicators's or audience's—will prevail. Theoretically, neither party necessarily has more power. But, since mass communication is often evaluated in terms of audience response (ratings, product sales, and the like) the perhaps surprising conclusion is that the audience has the final word. The audience can comply with the communicator's strategies, they can redefine or reinterpret the communicator's message, they can ignore the message, or they can attempt to change the communicator's strategy as was accomplished in the attacks on television violence. Mass communicators can use every strategy they can think of, and if the audience fails to comply, the power of media is nullified. Yet in many rather significant examples, audiences have not exercised their potential power. While this may be because of a lack of information and alternatives from media, the fact remains the potential power lies with the audience.

APPENDIX B
Advertising

Advertising is a subject that people assume is intuitively understandable. Through repeated exposure and the use of a few time-honored psychological techniques—such as testimonials, sex appeal, and fear arousal—people will buy the product. This taken-for-granted understanding of advertising seems to rest on a loose combination of theory related to stimulus response and unconscious need gratification. The resulting belief is that advertising triggers consumer behavior, and as long as this belief persists, the multibillion-dollar advertising industry will go unchallenged.

That advertising works cannot be disputed, but how it works is open to debate. The failure of advertising to decrease the percentage of foreign auto sales in the past decade should be sufficient evidence to suggest that a simplistic understanding of advertising as a triggering mechanism based on a naive psychology is in error. Something far more important than appeals to sex, fear, hero worship, and hard sell repetition is involved in explaining why some ads work and others do not. In part the answer lies in discussion in Appendix A on identity establishment and in understanding the concept "motive." In addition, we must also consider the matter of emotion.

The belief that emotion is an important factor in advertising is no doubt correct. But for many people, this belief rests on the assumption that emotion is not only a primary cause of behavior but that it is also a rather irrational and uncontrollable force. Popular literature such as Vance Packard's *Hidden Persuaders* and Wilson Key's books on subliminal suggestion argues that advertising circumvents the rational process, allowing irrational drives, instincts, or needs to govern behavior. Believability in the *Star Trek* character Mr. Spock rests on the notion that to develop a superior rational being requires suppression of irrational emotional drives. This theoretical approach results in a fear of emotion and a belief that little, if anything, can be done to control its effect once it is unleashed. Consequently, there are laws against subliminal advertising and constant outcrys against other unfair emotional appeals in advertising, campaign rhetoric, and the like. And as long as people believe in the efficacy of irrational forces, advertisers who use such appeals have an edge. The situation is similar to a belief in baseball about the spitball. As long as the hitter thinks the spitball will be thrown, the pitcher has an advantage.

From a scientific standpoint there is no empirical evidence that emotion is a causal force in behavior, although people continually use emotion as a reason to justify their behavior. In fact, the use of emotion as a justification for action is a longstanding, taken-for-granted, acceptable justification. In addition, there is no empirical evidence that emotion is basically irrational or that it resides at some unconscious level in our psychological make up. But again, people believe this to be true, and there certainly are many examples of action that appears to be very irrational. What empirical evidence does show is that people define certain behavior as irrational and assume that an emotional force underlies and causes these irrational acts to occur. What this means scientifically is that people use emotion rather than emotion using or governing people. Put another way, the evidence is that people use emotion as a reason to justify their acts as opposed to emotional ruling or causing behavior. Rather than being an irrational process, the appeal to emotion is quite rational.

Knowing that emotion is used as a powerful justifier for behavior is knowledge that advertisers use effectively. They realize that emotional appeals constitute an acceptable reason among consumers to buy products. "Ring around the collar" does not appear too dumb to a person who wants to avoid the embarrassment of looking dirty in social circles that place cleanliness next to godliness. The same holds true for body odor, dandruff, soiled clothing, and pearly white teeth. That a skid-row bum could not care less about personal grooming only indicates different priorities. Seat belt ads and antismoking ads that have failed to significantly affect behavior do not indicate ineffective emotional triggering. Rather, the results indicate that people have ignored or overruled those appeals. Emotion is not something that circumvents the rational process; it is part of a rationalization process used to justify a past or impending action. This does not mean that emotion is any less significant or real; only that we should recognize its rationality and its pragmatic utility.

Suggesting that emotion is a justification or rationalization for behavior has implications for the concept motive. As with emotion, many people understand motive as a matter of motivation—a force that impels people to act in some manner. The venacular expression of motivating students, athletes, children, and sick people to act in recommended ways rests on the assumption that something can trigger or condition a behavioral response. Find the correct "motivator" and a child will learn to read, an athlete will perform, a sick person will get well, and so on. But again the question arises: Is behavior involuntary or do people select reasons to justify a course of action? Do people react, or do they act and then justify when a justification seems appropriate or necessary? Anyone who accepts the former as true will not agree with the approach to advertising taken here. If the latter is accepted, the result will be an understanding of advertising as a matter of supplying motives or justifications for buying products. In short, advertising does not motivate people to buy a product; it supplys motives or reasons for doing so or having done so. Why is it necessary to have motives or reasons? Because other people ask us for reasons or challenge our behavior, and we define those people as significant enough to warrant a response to their question or challenge.

In an article entitled "Situated Actions and Vocabularies of Motive" (1940), C.W. Mills argued that motives are statements that people offer in response to challenges. In turn, the content of these motive statements is based on what is considered to be acceptable and appropriate given the nature of the social situation in which the challenge occurs. For example, "I purchased the car because I got a great deal" is a motive that indicates the appropriateness of establishing bargaining ability and/or frugality. This motive would be offered to people who place importance on frugality or bargaining ability or in a situation in which demonstrating economic wisdom is an important topic. In another situation or with people who care nothing for the price of a car at that moment, a different motive would be offered, such as the cars appearance, status, handling ability, or speed. The question of which motive was most important for buying the car is relevant only in terms of the challenge and the situation in which the challenge occurs. In other words, Mills argues that motive is a statement of appropriateness within a social setting, not a cause that necessarily precedes the act to which the motive refers.

This same line of reasoning was used by Marvin Scott and Stanford Lyman in article entitled "Accounts" (1968). What they add to Mills's idea is a detailed description of the kinds of reasons (motives or accounts) that people use in particular situations. For example, in one situation an excuse is offered for behavior that could not be helped. In this situation the person's motive is a request to be relieved of responsibility. In another situation responsibility for the act is accepted, but the attempt is to define the act as inconsequential. In both cases an account or motive occurs after a challenge or question occurs, not before, as in a cause-and-effect relationship.

If advertising provides practical and emotional motives for buying products, the next question concerns how to select motives that will be accepted by the consumer. On this point some students of advertising offer the importance of needs, either conscious or unconscious. Indeed, the recent "Needs and Gratifications Approach" to understanding mass media (Blumler and Katz, 1972) is an attempt to show that audiences select media information on the basis of personal and/or structurally induced needs. While the emphasis on audience selectivity is correct, the idea of needs is too general and perhaps inaccurate.

Following from the discussion in Appendix A, it may be argued that a consumer is selectively attentive to those products and advertisements that are considered significant for particular personal identity concerns, or at least are not unsupportive or insignificant. A person may buy a car that fits the image of how that person wants to see him- or herself. On the other hand, a person may buy a bar of soap because he or she likes the color or because there is no negative implication about the soap. In both cases, personal identity becomes the basic criterion for making a decision. In turn, motives are linked to identities as justifications or supports for those identities.

To summarize the argument, people are selectively attentive to information they deem significant to establish and maintain various personal identities. Motives and emotional expressions aid in achieving and supporting identities or salvaging them when challenges occur. Based on this model, what should an advertiser do? First, an advertisement must project an identity and suggest the importance of that identity for the consumer. Second, the ad may establish a situational context and/or mood consistent with that identity. Third, a product is associated with the identity and the situational context.

Finally, a motive or justification is offered to explain why the product is necessary for achieving or maintaining that identity.

Consider several examples of broad identity concerns. Sociologists have demonstrated that people's interests, values, and norms vary by age, gender, and social class characteristics. Advertisers use these demographic and class characteristics to classify large groupings of people as potential users for specific products. Adult women are more likely to pay attention to food and clothing ads, kids zero in on toys and junk food, and young adult males are oriented to sporting goods. While people in these categories are not all alike, the majority share common concerns. Consequently, advertisers can make appeals with fairly predictable results simply because the identity concerns and the situational contexts in which they occur are well established. And since these categories are so well established, advertisers often do not bother with establishing motives for their products. All that is necessary is to announce the general identity category and place that identity in a familiar situational context, and the consumer takes the motive for granted. Middle-aged women take for granted that cosmetics are designed to make them look younger, and all teenagers want to know about pimple cream is that is works. However, when prompting a radically new product or dealing with changing identity concerns, establishing a motive may be essential to the success of the product.

For example, when Miller Brewery introduced its low-calorie Lite beer a few years ago, it was a big gamble as beer drinkers traditionally select their brands on the basis of taste. While Miller wanted to appeal to diet-conscious, occasional beer drinkers to expand their market, they knew a low-calorie beer could easily fail if regular beer drinkers rejected the product. Prior to the introduction of Lite, low-calorie beers had been tried and rejected because of poor or thin taste. What Miller accomplished in their highly successful advertising campaign was to create an image of Lite as consistent with the existing identity of beer drinkers and their common drinking situations. Jocks and other beer drinker stereotypes were seen in bars and other beer-drinking situations arguing over two important aspects of the beer drinker's identity: taste ("tastes great") and the ability to drink enough to keep pace with the gang without losing face ("less filling"). Miller did not change the existing identity; it provided a motive for Lite that was consistent with the existing identity and the situational context in which beer is often consumed. On the latter point, the humor in the Lite ads is consistent with the expectation of having fun in situations where people drink beer, especially with "the boys."

An example of dealing with changing identity can be seen in the shift over the past decade to more energy-efficient products. Fifteen years ago compact cars appealed only to a small group of super rationalistic and perhaps innovative people who rejected status appeals in favor of efficiency and economy. Automobile advertising continued to stay with the tried-and-true appeals to status and comfort in cars but was caught short by the gas shortage during the early seventies. After the gas shortage the automobile identity of many Americans changed abruptly, and Detroit did not have a product that met the new demand. Since Japanese and German auto makers were already geared toward fuel-efficient cars, they capitalized on Detroit's misfortune. Today auto ads meet the new identity of the American auto owner by emphasizing fuel efficiency over all other aspects of the product. It does not matter if a Fairlane looks like a Mercedes; what matters is the price at the pump.

On the other hand, there is a segment of the population willing to spend large amounts of money on the automobile. This group has an identity that rejects economy in favor of just the opposite. Monster pickup trucks, vans, gas-guzzling speed chariots, and outrageously priced luxury cars represent people who practice role distance with the trends toward economy. For these people the identity appeals and motives focus on being macho, super cool, and extremely affluent. Owners of Corvettes, hi-rise 4×4 trucks with bulldozer tires, or Porsche Targas never talk of gas mileage and neither do the advertisements for these machines. What these ads emphasize is mood within a particular lifestyle, and a lifestyle is what buyers of these products are trying to achieve.

In addition to the requirement that advertising demonstrate an association with an identity, place the product in a situation relevant to that identity, and articulate a motive (if necessary), it must also consider the situation in which the consumers are located when they experience the ad. This is easily documented by examining an issue of a typical newspaper. While reading the sports section, men may also be receptive to automobile and maintenance ads, and women will be receptive to fashion ads while reading local news. In addition, their concerns also vary by the day of the week. Sunday morning finds an interest in real estate, Wednesday is for grocery shopping, Thursday is clothing, Friday is recreation, and Saturday mornings are for home fix-it and gardening. Turning to television, we find beer, automobiles, tires, and hardware sponsoring sports events, oral hygiene on the nightly news, soap for soap operas, junk food and cereals on cartoon shows, and used cars on the late, late movie. Recently the J. Walter Thompson USA, Inc., ad agency designed an ad for Kawasaki motorcycles exclusively for the Warner-Amex MTV (music channel) cable system. As quoted from *TV Guide:*

> It was 104 seconds long—a kind of cinema-verite microdocumentary soft-sell art film with an original "heavy metal" rock and roll score . . . so precisely forged and aimed was the commercial that—as one J. Walter Thompson executive put it—"We wouldn't dare run it on any other channel" [Hickey, 1972: 38].

Fitting the product to the situation, including the specific identity and mood of the consumer, increases the probability that consumers will pay attention and accept the emotional and practical rationale suggested by the ad for the product. This is precisely what much of the advertising found in specialized magazines, subculture radio, and specialized television attempts to accomplish. In doing so, these ads almost always follow the grammatical techniques employed by the medium in which the ad is presented, although often these techniques are exaggerated enough so that the message will stand out.

While this discussion has omitted much of the specific techniques in advertising, such as hardsell, softsell, humor, contests, serious messages, testimonials, experiments, and so forth, it has outlined the basic strategy of understanding advertising as a process that follows the social psychological dynamics found in everyday life. There is nothing really mysterious about advertising and nothing to fear about its techniques. The person who is at all self-reflective and somewhat analytical should see through any advertising technique, even if that person is a child. Sufficient evidence demonstrates that you cannot sell a person a product they really do not want and you cannot convince them to change their mind if their commitments are already quite firm. People are open to suggestion only if they chose to be and that responsibility should not be taken away from the individual.

REFERENCES

ALBRECHT, M. (1956) "Does literature reflect common values?" American Sociological Review 21, 6: 722-729.

ALTHEIDE, D. L. (1982) "Three-in-one news: network coverage of Iran." Journalism Quarterly 59 (Autumn): 482-486.

———(1981) "The failure of network news." Washington Journalism Review 3 (May): 28-30.

———(1978) "RTNDA news awards judging and media culture." Journalism Quarterly 55 (Spring): 164-167.

———(1976) Creating Reality: How TV News Distorts Events. Beverly Hills, CA: Sage.

AVERY, R. K. and D. ELLIS (1979) "Talk radio as an interpersonal phenomenon," in Gary Gumpert and Robert Cathcart (eds.) Inter/Media. New York: Oxford University Press.

BAGDIKIAN B. H. (1979) "Newspaper mergers—the final phase," in Alan Wells (ed.) Mass Media and Society. Palo Alto, CA: Mayfield.

BERELSON, G. (1949) "What missing the newspaper means," in Paul Lazarsfeld and Frank Stanton (eds.) Communications Research, 1948-49. New York: Harper.

BERG, S. (1980) "TV healing power in kids' hospitals." Los Angeles Times (August 3): 49.

BIERIG, J. D. (1979) "Contact: the radio talk show as a substitute for interpersonal communication." Master's thesis, University of Illinois.

BIRDWHISTELL, R. L. (1970) Kinesics and Context. Philadelphia: University of Pennyslvania Press.

BLUMLER, J. G. and E. KATZ (1974) The Uses of Mass Communication. Beverly Hills, CA: Sage.

BOORSTIN, D. J. (1961) The Image. New York: Harper Colophon.

BORDEWICH, F. M. (1977) "Supermarketing the newspaper." Columbia Journalism Review (September/October): 24-30.

BOYER, P. J. (1982) "TV's effect on Salvador war." Los Angeles Times (March 24): VI-1.

BRAESTRUP, P. (1978) Big Story: How the American Press and Television Reported and Interpreted the Crisis of Tet in 1968 in Vietnam and Washington. Garden City, NY: Doubleday.

BRISSETT, D. and R. P. SNOW (1970) "Vicarious behavior: leisure and the transformation of *Playboy* magazine." Journal of Popular Culture (Winter): 428-440.

BURNETT, H. and W. BURNETT (1975) Fiction Writer's Handbook. New York: Barnes & Noble.

BUSBY, L. J. (1975) "Sex-role research on the mass media." Journal of Communication (Autumn): 107-131.

CASTY, A. (1973) Development of Film. New York: Harcourt Brace Jovanovich.

COTTLE, T. (1980) "Three youngsters explore their dependence on TV." Panorama 1 (September): 78-81.

COUSINS, N. (1981a) "Editorial." Saturday Review (June): 7-8.

———(1981b) Human Options. New York: W. S. Norton.

DAHLGREN, P. (1980) "TV news and the suppression of relfexivity." Urban Life 9 (July): 201-216.

DAVIS, D. K. and S. J. BARAN (1981) Mass Communication and Everyday Life." Belmont, CA: Wadsworth.

DREIER, P. and S. WEINBERG (1979) "Interlocking directorates." Columbia Journalism Review (November/December): 51.

DIRECTOR, R. (1980) "One minute can make or break a series." TV Guide 28 (August 23): 38-44.

DOUP, L. (1978) "Social worker of the air." Phoenix Gazette (October 13): E-1.

FERGURSON, E. B. (1980) "Media hype for fun and profit." Los Angeles Times (July 20): Part VII, 5.

FIEDLER, L. (1968) The Return of the Vanishing American. London: Jonathan Cape.

FOLLET, K. (1981) "A Moscow mystery." Saturday Review (April): 66-67.

FRAYN, M. (1973) [1965] The Tin Men (London: Collins). Also pp. 191-194 in Stanley Cohen and Jock Young (eds.) The Manufacture of News. Beverly Hills, CA: Sage.

GERBNER, G. and P. GROSS (1976) "The scary world of TV's heavy viewer." Psychology Today (April): 41ff.

GERSON, W. and S. H. LUND (1971) "*Playboy* magazine: sophisticated smut or social revolution?" Journal of Popular Culture (Winter): 218-227.

GILDER, J. (1981) "Tom Wolfe." Saturday Review (April): 42-44.

GOFFMAN, E. (1981) Forms of Talk. Philadelphia: University of Pennsylvania Press.

———(1959) The Presentation of Self in Everyday Life. Garden City, NY: Doubleday.

GOLDBERG, M. with T. GOLDBERG (1980) "Doctor shows are good medicine." TV Guide 28 (August 23): 20-22.

GOOD, P. (1980) "Why you can't always trust '60 Minutes' reporting." Panorama 1 (September): 38-43.

GREENE, B. (1982) "Need a plane? No problem." TV Guide (January 30): 10-12.

HAAS, C. (1978) "Invasion of the mind snatchers." New Times (July 24): 31-36.

HICKEY, N. (1982) "In search of the 100% zap-proof commercial." TV Guide (May 8): 37-42.

HOCHSCHILD, A. R. (1979) "Emotion work, feeling rules, and social structure." American Journal of Sociology 85, 3: 551-575.

HORWARTH, D. (1981) The Voyage of the Armada: The Spanish Story. New York: Viking.

HUSS, R. and N. SILVERSTEIN (1968) The Film Experience. New York: Dell.

HUTTON, G. (1981) "Reflections." Arizona Republic (November 21): H-1.

JOWETT, G. (1976) Film: The Democratic Art. Boston: Little, Brown.
——and J. LINTON (1980) Movies as Mass Communication. Beverly Hills, CA: Sage.
KAEL, P. (1976) "Trash art and the movies," in Joseph F. Littell (ed.) Coping With Mass Media. Evanston, IL: McDougal, Littell.
——(1965) Kiss, Kiss, Bang, Bang. Boston: Little, Brown.
KATZSON, M. (1982) "A sociological analysis of children's television: the Wallace and Ladmo Show." M.A. thesis, Arizona State University.
KAZANTZAKIS, N. (1971) The Last Temptation of Christ. New York: Bantam.
KESEY, K. (1962) One Flew Over the Cuckoo's Nest. New York: Viking.
KLEIN, P. (1975) "The television audience and program mediocrity," pp. 74-77 in Alan Wells (ed.) Mass Media and Society. Palo Alto, CA: Mayfield.
KRIEGHBAUM, H. (1973) Pressures on the Press. New York: Thomas Y. Crowell.
LEERHSEN, C. (1982) "Indoor soccer: good as goals." Newsweek (February 15): 65.
LINDGREN, E. (1963) The Art of Film. New York: Collier.
LITTLEJOHN, D. (1975) "Communicating ideas by television," pp. 63-79 in D. Cater and R. Adler (eds.) Television as a Social Force. New York: Praeger.
LUDLUM, R. (1978) The Bourne Identity. New York: Bantam.
MALONE, J. (1981) "Recent slipups grist for new attacks on media accuracy." Christian Science Monitor (May 15): 5.
McLUHAN, M. (1964) Understanding Media: The Extension of Man. New York: McGraw-Hill.
MENDELSOHN, H. (1964) "Listening to radio," pp. 89-98 in A. Lewis Dexter and David M. White (eds.) People, Society, and Mass Communication. London: Collier-Macmillan.
MEYROWITZ, J. (1983) "Television and the obliteration of 'childhood,'" in Sari Thomas (ed.) Studies in Mass Communication and Technology. Norwood, NJ: Ablex.
MICHENER, J. (1982) The Covenant. New York: Fawcett.
——(1978) Centennial. New York: Fawcett.
——(1959) Hawaii. New York: Random House.
MILLS, C. W. (1940) "Situated actions and vocabularies of motive." American Sociological Review 5: 904-913.
MORGAN, T. (1982) "Sharks: the making of a best seller," pp. 122-132 in Robert Atwan et al. (eds.) American Mass Media. New York: Random House.
NADEL, L. (1982) "Dressing up the news." Columbia Journalism Review (September/October): 14-15.
O'HARA, M. (1954) Novel-in-the-Making. New York: David McKay.
Panorama (1980) "Television and politics—part 2." Vol. 1 (June): 16-20.
REEVES, R. (1980) Docudrama." Panorama 1 (March): 37-39.
RIBLET, C., Jr. (1974) The Solid Gold Copy Editor. Chicago: Aldine.
RIVERS, W. (1970) The Adversaries. Boston: Beacon.
ROBBINS, H. (1981) Goodbye Janette. New York: Simon & Schuster.
SCHWARTZ, T. (1974) The Responsive Chord. Garden City, NY: Doubleday.
SCOTT, M. B. and S. LYMAN (1968) "Accounts." American Sociological Review 33, 1: 46-62.
SHEEHY, G. (1979) "Introducing the postponing generation." Esquire (October): 25-33.

SNOW, R. P. (1974) "How children interpret TV violence in play context." Journalism Quarterly 51 (Spring): 13-21.

——— and B. CUTHBERTSON (1979) "Learning and self-counseling through television entertainment: the prisoner." Teaching Sociology 7, 1: 65-78.

STEIN, B. (1981) "Love, rape, highway, diary." TV Guide (July 25): 34-35.

STEPHENSON, W. (1967) The Play Theory of Mass Communication. Chicago: University of Chicago Press.

STONE, G. P. (1962) "Appearance and the self," pp. 86-118 in Arnold Rose (ed.) Human Nature and Social Processes. Boston: Houghton MMifflin.

TALESE, G. (1971) Fame and Obscurity. New York: Bantam.

THOMPSON, A. and M. TUCHMAN (1981) "Exclusive interview: George Lucas." Republic Scene (December): 53-55, 76.

Time (1981) "Searching for hit teams." (December 21): 16-22.

———(1979) "The politics of the box populi." (July 11): 95.

TOWNLEY, R. (1982) "Wait till you read/see the book/show." TV Guide (May 1): 44-48.

TRILLING, L. (1950) The Liberal Imagination. New York: Viking.

TROMBLEY, W. (1982) "College text 'dumding' aids sales." Los Angeles Times (January 10): 1, 14-15.

WELLES, C. (1980) "The future of video." Esquire (June): 93.

———(1971) "Can mass magazines survive?" Columbeia Journalism Review (July/August). Also pp. 27-34 in Alan Wells (ed.) Mass Media and Society. Palo Alto, CA: National.

WHETMORE, E. J. (1979) Mediamerica. Belmont, CA: Wadsworth.

WOLFE, T. (1973) The New Journalism. New York: Harper & Row.

RECOMMENDED READING

ALTHEIDE, D. L. and R. SNOW (1979) Media Logic. Beverly Hills, CA: Sage.

BERGER, A. A. (1982) Media Analysis Techniques. Beverly Hills, CA: Sage.

BOORSTIN, D. J. (1961) The Image. New York. Harper & Row.

CANTOR, J. (1980) Prime-Time Television: Content and Control. Beverly Hills, CA: Sage.

CATER, D. and R. ADLER (1975) Television as a Social Force. New York: Praeger.

COLE, B. [ed.] (1981) Television Today: A Close-Up View. New York: Oxford University Press.

DAVIS, D. and S. BARAN (1981) Mass Communication and Everyday Life. Belmont, CA: Wadsworth.

FELL, J. L. (1974) Film and the Narrative Tradition. Norman: University of Oklahoma Press.

GUMPERT, G. and R. CATHCART [eds.] (1983) Inter/Media. New York: Oxford University Press.

HALL, J. (1979) The Sociology of Literature. London: Longman.

JOWETT, G. and J. LINTON (1980) Movies as Mass Communication. Beverly Hills, CA: Sage.

MANKIEWICZ, F. and J. SWERDLOW (1978) Remote Control, New York: New York Times Books.

NEWCOMB, H. [ed.] (1982) Television: The Critical View. New York: Oxford University Press.

PETERSON, T. (1956) Magazines in the Twentieth Century. Urbana: University of Chicago Press.

PHELAN, J. M. (1977) Media World. New York: Seabury.

SKLAR, R. (1980) Prime-time America. New York: Oxford University Press.

SOLOMON, S. J. (1976) Beyond Formula: American Film Genres. New York: Harcourt Brace Jovanovich.

TOFFLER, A. (1980) The Third Wave. New York: William Morrow/Bantam.

INDEX

ABOUT THE AUTHOR

ROBERT P. SNOW is currently Associate Professor at Arizona State University, where he teaches a variety of social psychology courses. His main research interests involve various aspects of electronic media, particularly the use of media in education. Aside from the usual academic interests and pursuits, he likes to fish, listen to jazz, and think that he still can go seven innings on the softball diamond (so much for vicarious behavior).